Perspectives on Mozart Performance includes essays by distinguished musicologists and performers, each exploring a different aspect of Mozart's music in performance. Several studies consider the eighteenth-century roots of Mozart's approach to performance and examine such issues as the role of ornamentation (Paul Badura-Skoda, Frederick Neumann), improvisation (Katalin Komlós), cadenzas (Eduard Melkus, Christoph Wolff), and Mozart's conception of tempos in a pre-metronomic age (Jean-Pierre Marty). Two studies examine Mozart's string writing (Jaap Schröder) and the influence of his father's remarkably popular *Violinschule* (Robin Stowell). An essay by Peter Williams treats Mozart's use of the chromatic fourth and performance styles associated with that *figura*. Finally, the later, nineteenth-century response to Mozart is explored through the study of Mendelssohn's performances of Mozart (R. Larry Todd).

Cambridge Studies in Performance Practice

Perspectives on Mozart Performance

Edited by
R. LARRY TODD AND PETER WILLIAMS

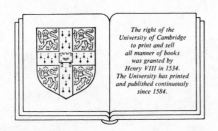

The right of the
University of Cambridge
to print and sell
all manner of books
was granted by
Henry VIII in 1534.
The University has printed
and published continuously
since 1584.

CAMBRIDGE UNIVERSITY PRESS

CAMBRIDGE
NEW YORK   PORT CHESTER
MELBOURNE   SYDNEY

Published by the Press Syndicate of the University of Cambridge
The Pitt Building, Trumpington Street, Cambridge CB2 1RP
40 West 20th Street, New York, NY 10011, USA
10 Stamford Road, Oakleigh, Melbourne 3166, Australia

© Cambridge University Press 1991

First published 1991

Printed in Great Britain at the University Press, Cambridge

British Library cataloguing in publication data
Perspectives on Mozart performance. – (Cambridge Studies in
Performance Practice; 1).
1. Austrian music. Mozart, Wolfgang Amadeus, 1756–1791
I. Todd, R. Larry. II. Williams, Peter,
780.92

Library of Congress cataloguing in publication data
Perspectives on Mozart performance/edited by R. Larry Todd and Peter
Williams.
　　p.　　cm. – (Cambridge Studies in Performance Practice; 1)
Includes indexes.
ISBN 0 521 40072 4
1. Mozart, Wolfgang Amadeus, 1756–1791 – Criticism and
interpretation. 2. Performance practice (Music) – 18th century.
I. Todd, R. Larry. II. Williams, Peter. III. Series.
ML410.M9P273　1991
780'.92 – dc20　90-37706　CIP

ISBN 0521 40072 4 hardback

ME

CONTENTS

viii   Contents

FIGURES

GENERAL PREFACE

No doubt the claim, heard frequently today, that 'authentic performance' is a chimera, and that even the idea of an 'authentic edition' cannot be sustained for (most) music before the last century or two, is itself the consequence of too sanguine an expectation raised by performers and scholars alike in the recent past. Both have been understandably concerned to establish that a certain composer 'intended so-and-so' or 'had such-and-such conditions of performance in mind' or 'meant it to sound in this way or that'. Scholars are inclined to rule on problems ('research confirms the following . . .'), performers to make the music a living experience ('artistry or musicianship suggests the following . . .'). Both are there in order to answer certain questions and establish an authority for what they do; both demonstrate and persuade by the rhetoric of their utterance, whether well-documented research on one hand or convincing artistic performance on the other; and the academic/commercial success of both depends on the effectiveness of that rhetoric. Some musicians even set out to convey authority in both scholarship and performance, recognising that music is conceptual *and* perceptual and thus not gainfully divisible into separate, competitive disciplines. In general, if not always, the scholar appears to aim at the firm, affirmative statement, often seeing questions as something to be answered confidently rather than searchingly re-defined or refined. In general, with some exceptions, performers have to aim at the confident statement, for their very livelihood hangs on an unhesitating decisiveness in front of audience or microphone. In the process, both sometimes have the effect, perhaps even the intention, of killing the dialectic – of thwarting the progress that comes with further questions and a constant 'yes, but' response to what is seen, in the light of changing definitions, as 'scholarly evidence' or 'convincing performance'.

In the belief that the immense activity in prose and sound over the last few decades is now being accompanied by an increasing awareness of the issues arising – a greater knowledge at last enabling the questions to be more closely defined – the Cambridge Studies in Performance Practice will attempt to make regular contributions to this area of study, on the basis of several assumptions.

Firstly, at its best, Performance Practice is so difficult a branch of study as to be an almost impossibly elusive ideal. It cannot be merely a practical way of 'combining performance and scholarship', for these two are fundamentally different activities, each able to inform the other only up to a certain point. Secondly, if Performance Practice has moved beyond the questions (now seen to be very dated) that exercised performance groups of the 1950s and 60s, it can widen itself to include any or all music written before the last few years. In this respect, such studies are a musician's equivalent to the cry of literary studies, 'Only contextualise!', and this can serve as a useful starting-point for the historically minded performer or the practically minded scholar. (The Derridaesque paradox that there is no context may have already affected some literary studies, but context is still clearly crucial across the broader field of music, the original Comparative Literature.) Cambridge Studies in Performance Practice will devote volumes to any period in which useful questions can be asked, ranging from at least Gregorian chant to at least Stravinsky.

Thirdly, Performance Practice is not merely about performing, neither 'this is how music was played' nor 'this is how you should play it in a concert or recording today'. (These two statements are as often as not irreconcilable.) In studying all that we can about the practical realisation of a piece of music we are studying not so much how it was played but how it was heard, both literally and on a deeper level. How it was conceived by the composer and how it was perceived by the period's listener are endless questions deserving constant study, for they bring one into intimate contact with the historical art of music as nothing else can. It is the *music* we fail to understand, not its performance as such, if we do not explore these endless questions. As we know, every basic musical element has had to be found, plucked out of thin air – the notes, their tuning, compass, volume, timbre, pace, timing, tone, combining – and they have constantly changed. In attempting to grasp or describe these elements as they belong to a certain piece of music, it could become clear that any modern re-realisation in (public) performance is a quite separate issue. Nevertheless, it is an issue of importance to the wider musical community, as can be seen from the popular success of performers and publications (records, journals, books) concerned with 'authenticity'. In recognising this practical importance, Cambridge Studies in Performance Practice will frequently call upon authoritative performers to join scholars in the common cause, each offering insights to the process of learning to ask and explore the right questions.

P. W.

PREFACE

'But admittedly a phenomenon like Mozart will always remain a miracle that cannot be explained further' ('Aber freilich eine Erscheinung wie Mozart bleibt immer ein Wunder, das nicht weiter zu erklären ist'). Goethe's awe-filled observation to Eckermann (14 February 1831), of course, did not deter nineteenth- and twentieth-century scholars from seeking to explore all aspects of Mozart's life and work. Now the arrival of the 1991 bicentenary has provided a fresh impetus to continuing attempts of explication. One particular area of Mozart research that has attracted increasing attention in recent years is performance practice, a vast arena in which scholars and performers have joined ranks to pose and elucidate questions about performing Mozart's music in a historically appropriate manner and context. In some instances, new insights into performance practice have forced us to rethink fundamentally our understanding of the music, and, indeed, to rehear the music as we struggle to grasp how Mozart conceived it and how it was perceived and received in his time.

During Mozart's lifetime, and in the decades immediately after his death, a host of legends and romantic accounts accrued to his biography, not the least of which concerned his stature as a performer and the vicissitudes of his career as a freelance Viennese musician. Inevitably, with the canonization of Mozart as a classical composer – a process that emerged fully during the 1830s and 1840s – ideas about 'proper' ways of performing his music gained currency. And composers seeking to pay homage to Mozart – composers, to cite a few examples, as divergent as Mozart's pupil Johann Nepomuk Hummel in the finale of his Sonata in F Op. 20 (1807), Ludwig Spohr in the second movement of his *Historical Symphony* Op. 116 (1839), Rimsky Korsakov in *Mozart and Salieri* (1898), and Richard Strauss in *Ariadne auf Naxos* (1912) – confirmed that the revival of a certain musical style – and, concomitantly, of certain performance practices associated with that style – could be viewed as Mozartean. (Others sought to invoke Mozart through a process of modernisation, e.g. Edvard Grieg in his second piano parts to Mozart's piano sonatas (1876–1877), or Max Reger in his Variations and Fugue on a Theme of Mozart Op. 132 (1914).) Our own contemporary notions about *Mozart-Praxis* have been influenced in innumerable ways by what was largely a nineteenth-century tradition of Mozart reception.

The present volume, the inaugural issue in the new Cambridge Studies in Performance Practice, seeks to explore only a few facets of Mozart's music in performance. Inevitably, the paths of several of the essays lead us back to the eighteenth century, to discover the roots of Mozart's approach to performance and to examine critically such issues as the role of ornamentation (Badura-Skoda, Neumann), improvisation (Komlós), cadenzas (Melkus, Wolff), and Mozart's conception and application of tempos in a pre-metronomic age (Marty). Two studies consider Mozart's approach to string writing, and the influence of his father's remarkably popular *Violinschule* (Schröder, Stowell). One (Williams) considers Mozart's use of the chromatic fourth and performance styles associated with that *figura*, a device that bore special significance too for composers such as Beethoven and Schubert who followed Mozart. And finally, the later Mozart *Rezeptionsgeschichte* is considered through an examination of Mendelssohn's considerable efforts as performer, a contribution that reinforced the canonisation of Mozart as a classical master (Todd).

It has been our aim throughout the volume to approach the topic from the competing, but complementary, viewpoints of performers and scholars, and if the results encourage a productive process of cross-fertilisation, then we believe performance practice studies, and, indeed, Mozart research, will have been furthered.

A number of individuals and institutions have assisted with the preparation of *Perspectives on Mozart Performance*, and the editors gratefully acknowledge them here. They include Kathryn Puffett at the Press, Isabelle Bélance, Tim Burris, J. Michael Cooper, Akira Ishii, Barbara Norton, and Janet K. Page. Illustrative material was provided by the Brotherton Collection of the University of Leeds; the New York Public Library; the Bodleian Library, Oxford; and Firestone Library, Princeton University. Finally, the editors are indebted to the Deutscher Verlag für Musik, Leipzig, for permission to include examples from Mendelssohn's *Die beiden Pädagogen* and *Sinfonia VIII*, on pp. 165 and 166.

R. L. T.
February 1990

MOZART'S TRILLS

PAUL BADURA-SKODA

Clearly there is widespread confusion regarding the proper execution of Mozart's trills. Some performers start them invariably with the upper note and others with the main note, while still others use a combination of ways. Widespread disagreement also exists about the length, the speed and the ending of Mozart's trills. Apparently this confusion is caused – at least in part – by ignorance or misinformation. The purpose of the present study is to clarify some of the open questions and to answer them in such a way that the demands of historical truth and good musicianship are satisfied.[1]

One of the main reasons for the prevailing confusion is that Mozart's ubiquitous trill sign takes on different meanings according to the context. Confusing indeed! Yet the notion that one ornamental symbol may assume different meanings, and, vice versa, that different symbols can mean the same thing, is an undeniable historical fact of eighteenth-century music.[2] Many modern performers are misled by the nineteenth-century tradition, still prevailing today, in which most ornaments were codified in an unambiguous way. Thus many may be surprised to learn that Mozart's trill sign (*tr*) can assume at least five different meanings:

(1) long trill with start on the upper note,
(2) long trill with start on the main note,

---

[1] Ever since the first publication in 1957 of our book (Eva and Paul Badura-Skoda, *Mozart-Interpretation* (Vienna, 1957), translated by Leo Black as *Interpreting Mozart on the Keyboard* (London, 1961; repr. New York, 1986)), I have upheld the axiom that good musicianship (based on a sense for melody, rhythm and harmony) and historical knowledge are not irreconcilable. After all, the great masters were known and loved for their outstanding musicianship, not their idiosyncrasies.

[2] I have dealt with this question in my article 'On ornamentation in Haydn', *Piano Quarterly* 135 (Fall, 1986), pp. 38–48.

(3) short trill (*Pralltriller* or *Schneller*) with start on the main note,[3]

(4) short upper appoggiatura,

(5) turn (*gruppetto*) starting invariably on the upper note.

Even more meanings than the five listed here may have been given the *tr* sign (e.g. inverted turn).

A convenient proof for the ambiguity of the trill symbol can be found in the unpublished piano tutor by Mozart's contemporary Johann Georg Albrechtsberger (1736–1809).[4] According to Albrechtsberger, the short shake (*der kurze Triller*) is 'always played without a closing turn' (*wird allezeit ohne Nachschlag gemacht*; see ex. 1). On the other hand, the long trill (*der lange [Triller]*, as in ex. 2),

Example 1 J. G. Albrechtsberger, *der kurze Triller*

Example 2 J. G. Albrechtsberger, *der lange Triller*

is 'always to be played with a closing turn, whether the two notes are written or not' (*wird alzeit mit dem Nachschlag [gemacht], die zwo Noten mögen hernach geschrieben seyn oder nicht*). The mordent (turn, *gruppetto*) starts on the main note (see ex. 3).[5] Albrechtsberger also mentions a fourth ornament (*der Tremolant*,

---

[3] Some readers might wonder why I forgot to mention the short trill (*Pralltriller*) beginning on the upper auxiliary. To my regret, however, I could find no evidence for it (see below) which might in any way apply to Mozart.

[4] Manuscript in the Archiv der Gesellschaft der Musikfreunde in Wien, Signatur VII 14372: *Fundamento per il Clavicembalo di Giorgio Albrechtsberger, Maestro di Capella in Wien*. It was probably written earlier than Albrechtsberger's *Anfangsgründe zur Klavierkunst* (1796) quoted on p. 110 of our book, *Interpreting Mozart*.

[5] In a later manuscript of 1796, however (Gesellschaft der Musikfreunde Signatur A 464, XIV 1952), Albrechtsberger makes a distinction between trills with closing turns and those without.

without a closing turn

with a closing turn

Example 3 J. G. Albrechtsberger, the mordent

 (a) written

 (b) performed

an anticipated main-note trill) with the same abbreviation, *tr* (this is not found in Mozart's works).

An example of Mozart's unwittingly demonstrating the identity of certain trills with turns occurs in the autograph of the first movement of the Sonata in B♭ major for violin and piano K 454 (see ex. 4). Obviously the trill sign here

Example 4 Sonata in B♭ for violin and piano K 454, first movement, bars 34–5

is a slip of the pen caused by old habits (in other, analogous, passages in this movement one finds only turn signs).

Of the many eighteenth-century treatises dealing with ornamentation, the most relevant for Mozart's ornaments is probably Clementi's *Pianoforte School* (London, 1801).[6] Born four years before Mozart, and an equally widely travelled cosmopolitan, Clementi can be regarded as a representative of their common Italianate musical culture. He met Mozart in Vienna on 24 December 1781, when both artists performed for the Emperor Joseph II and also improvised on two fortepianos.[7] Mozart's ill-humoured letter about Clementi did not prevent him from using the theme of the latter's Sonata in B♭ major Op. 24 No. 2, played by Clementi on this occasion, in the overture to *Die Zauberflöte* (a borrowing of which Clementi was very proud in later years). Clementi's *Table of Ornaments*, partly reproduced here in facsimile as fig. 1.1, therefore gives us valuable clues to Mozart's practice with trills.

As in most contemporary treatises published north of Italy, the common form of the long trill started with the upper auxiliary note. We may well assume that, like Clementi, Mozart began normal trills with a quick upper-note start. Still, there must have been a number of exceptions to this rule. We shall examine the different possibilities according to the list in fig. 1.

[6] Muzio Clementi, *Introduction to the Art of Playing the Pianoforte* (London, 1801); facsimile edition with an introduction by Sandra Rosenblum (New York, 1974).

[7] See Otto Erich Deutsch, *Mozart: die Dokumente seines Lebens, gesammelt und erläutert* (Kassel and Leipzig, 1961), p. 176.

N.B. The LOWEST note of EVERY sort of turn is MOSTLY a semitone:

The shake LEGATO with the preceding note, explained:

N.B. The GENERAL mark for the shake is this *ⵂ* and composers trust CHIEFLY to the taste and judgment of the performer, whether it shall be long, short, transient, or turned.

The BEAT

The LENGTH of the BEAT is determined, like that of the other graces, by the cir‑ ‑cumstances of the pafsage.

N.B. When the note preceding the beat is an interval of a SECOND, let the beat a‑ ‑dopt it, whether it be a semitone or a whole tone:

Ex:

But when the beat, is on the FIRST note of a pafsage; or, when it follows a note, whose interval is GREATER than a SECOND, it should be made with a semitone; as the following examples will show.

Clementi's Introd.

Figure 1.1 Ornament table from Muzio Clementi, *Introduction to the Art of Playing the Pianoforte* (London, 1801), p. 11

LONG TRILLS BEGINNING ON THE UPPER AUXILIARY

Ordinary cadential trills

Trills like the one in ex. 5a should be played with a number of repercussions *ad libitum* (ex. 5b), but not as in ex. 5c.

Example 5 Concerto in D minor for piano K 466, first movement, bars 354–5

(a)

(b) correct execution

(c) incorrect execution

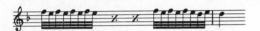

Trills preceded by the same note (but see also p. 16)

Example 6 Concerto in F for three pianos K 242, first movement, bars 112–13

(a)

(b) execution

Example 7 Concerto in E♭ for piano K 482, first movement, bars 83–4

Another authentic manner of executing such trills consists of playing the upper auxiliary note quickly and lightly before the beat (see ex. 8). This type of start,

Example 8 Frederick Neumann's 'grace-note trill'

which Frederick Neumann aptly calls the 'grace-note trill',[8] had been described by J. J. Quantz in his treatise on playing the flute.[9] Quantz recommended the light execution of ('the appoggiatura at the beginning of phrases after rests. Leopold Mozart made the same recommendation in his violin tutor.[10] In fact, violinists of today perform most trills in this way. (An expedient way for pianists to create a brilliant start is to play the first two notes simultaneously and then to continue with either note, thus dispensing with the problem of whether to begin on the upper or the main note.)

LONG TRILLS BEGINNING ON THE MAIN NOTE

Those shown in Clementi's table

A long trill should begin on the main note if the trill is preceded by the upper note in a legato context, as in ex. 9a. Probably only an unmusical person would play here a trill starting with the upper note (ex. 9b).

Example 9 Concerto in C for piano K 467, second movement, bars 33–4

(a)

(b) unmusical execution

etc.

---

[8] Frederick Neumann, *Ornamentation and Improvisation in Mozart* (Princeton, 1986), pp. 104, 110, 115–16, 118, 129–34.

[9] Joachim Quantz, *Versuch einer Anweisung die Flöte traversiere zu spielen* (Breslau, 1752, 1772, 1789); facsimile of the 3rd edn (Kassel, 1953), pp. 85–6.

[10] Leopold Mozart, *Versuch einer gründlichen Violinschule* (Augsburg, 1756), p. 223: 'If however a passage starts with a trill, the appoggiatura is hardly heard, and is nothing else than a strong emphasis of the start.' ('Wenn aber eine Passage mit einem Triller anfängt: so wird der Vorschlag kaum gehört, und er ist in solchem Falle nichts denn ein starker Anstoß des Trillers.')

Incredible as it may seem, many pianists start the trill in ex. 10 on the upper note, d″, thus ignoring one of the basic rules of ornamentation explained as early as *c.* 1720 by the French *clavecinistes* in connection with the *tremblement lié* and the *tremblement appuyé*. There is no slur before the first trill in ex. 11;

Example 10 Sonata in C for piano K 330 (300h), first movement, bar 65 (also third movement, bar 60)

Example 11 Sonata in A minor for piano K 310, second movement, bars 6–7

(a)

(b) execution

however, since in both cases the note preceding the trill is an accented dissonance, the old rule applies: the practice was to link (by slurring) the dissonance to its resolution. In fact, *all* grace notes in the eighteenth century should be slurred to their following notes. This is one of the few basic rules where absolutely no exception was allowed. In this context we should remember that in Mozart after about K 180 a single grace note before a trill always means a *long* accented appoggiatura. (Very short appoggiaturas were in any case taken for granted.) But why not before K 180?

Strangely enough, in the symphonies of 1772 Mozart wrote various appoggiaturas before trills in certain contexts which could only mean that these trills were to start, not with a long appoggiatura, but with a short upper auxiliary. These trills appear extensively, for example, in the second movement of the Symphony in C major K 128 (see ex. 12). There are further examples in the Symphonies in G major K 129 (first movement, bars 80–1), F major K 130 (first movement, bar 30) and E♭ major K 132 (first movement, bar 62). If we consider the examples from K 129 and K 130 (exx. 13 and 14), Mozart's notation makes clear not only that a very short start on the upper note was meant,

Example 12 Symphony in C major K 128, second movement, opening

Example 13 Symphony in G major K 129, first movement, bars 80–1

Example 14 Symphony in F major K 130, first movement, bar 30

but also that the following trills were to be played in the same fashion. Why did Mozart decide in 1772 to indicate the upper-note start of the trill according to the practice composers would later adopt in the middle of the nineteenth century? Most probably because otherwise some musicians in Salzburg may have begun those trills with the main note. Thus the start on the main note must have been more common in Mozart's time than is generally acknowledged today. These examples, however, represent only an exception to the general rule that a small note before a trill in Mozart (and Haydn) means a long accented appoggiatura (see ex. 15).

Example 15 Sonata in E minor for violin and piano K 304, second movement, bar 3

(a) written   (b) played

A special problem obtains in the appoggiatura shown in ex. 16. In order to

Example 16 Concerto in E♭ for piano K 271, second movement, bar 61

place the grace note f″ correctly, Mozart was obliged to alter the bass line from its shape in the preceding tutti: if he had retained the F in the bass in bar 61, forbidden parallel octaves between E♭ and F would have resulted, as shown in ex. 17.

Example 17

(trill may be played faster)

The main-note start of trills à la Clementi is certainly what Mozart intended when he wrote prefixes of three notes, either small or large (see exx. 18–20).

Example 18 Sonata in B♭ for piano K 333 (315c), third movement, bar 163

(a)   (b) execution

Example 19 Concerto in A for piano K 414 (368a), second movement, end of cadenza

Example 20 Concerto in B♭ for piano K 450, third movement, end of cadenza

These formulas are nothing but another notation of the baroque ⌒ and ⌒ . To begin the trills on the upper note, as unfortunately often happens, is a mistake. Another type of formula where a main-note start is advisable is seen in exx. 21 and 22.

Example 21 Sonata in C minor for piano K 457, first movement, bars 174–5

Example 22 Sonata in C for piano K 330 (300h), first movement, opening

Not only in piano music, but also in orchestral works, there are many instances where a main-note start of a trill is desirable for harmonic and melodic reasons. Two examples (exx. 23 and 24) should suffice. Alas, nowadays nearly all orchestral

Example 23 'Linz' Symphony in C major K 425, first movement, bar 25

Example 24 Symphony in G minor K 550, second movement, bar 3

players start these trills with the upper note, evidently because they are 'well instructed' that a Mozart trill *must* start from above.

Trills not mentioned in Clementi's table

It would be naive to assume that a table of less than one page could treat all questions regarding ornamentation. We shall examine some instances not mentioned by Clementi.

Written-out trills in ribattuta style

In the instance shown in ex. 25 Mozart easily could have written a trill 'according to the rule', in line with eighteenth-century theory, as in ex. 26. That he did not do so is a sign that an occasional main-note start was acceptable to him.

Example 25 Quartet in E♭ for piano and strings K 493, first movement, bars 58–61

Example 26

When the trilled note is a dissonance

Ex. 27 shows a typical example of this kind of situation. In such a context the

Example 27 Sonata in E♭ for piano K 282 (189g), first movement, bars 4–5

bass notes were usually played as crotchets (see ex. 28). The resulting parallel

Example 28

octaves may well not have been tolerated in Mozart's time, making such upper-note beginnings inadmissible. Thus a main-note start, as shown in ex. 29, was

Example 29

probably intended. Another alternative would be to start with a slight preceding grace note, *à la* Quantz and Frederick Neumann (see ex. 30). The latter is easily

Example 30

playable on a string instrument but rather difficult on a keyboard instrument. Similar examples occur in the second movement of the Concerto for three pianos K 242, bars 19 and 47; the Andante from the four-hand Piano Sonata in D major K 381 (123a), bars 1–2; the second movement of the Piano Concerto in C major K 246, bars 35–6; and in a few other works. In all these cases parallel octaves would result from the accented upper-note start of the trill.

Another typical application of a trill on a dissonant note is shown in ex. 31. If a

Example 31 Concerto in C for piano K 503, first movement, bar 151

(a)

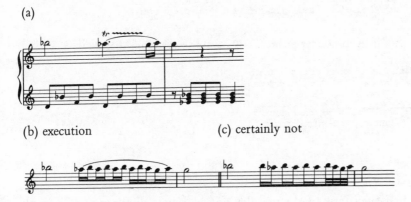

(b) execution   (c) certainly not

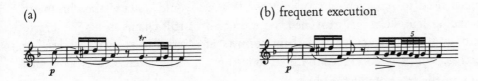

legato connection were indicated, this example would correspond to Clementi's explanation. But even without a slur the dominant seventh (A♭) should be emphasised, since B♭–A♭–G is the melodic line. Even a grace-note start would not be suitable here. On similar melodic grounds the typically encountered execution of the trill in ex. 32b is not recommended.

Example 32 Quintet in C for strings K 515, second movement, bars 11–12

(a)   (b) frequent execution

When the trilled note has a bass function

Here the fundamental line would be obscured by a start on the upper auxiliary (see exx. 33 and 34). In fact, an upper-note start of the second trill would be unplayable, as the tempo is a brisk allegro.

Example 33 Fugue in C minor for two pianos K 426, bars 69–70

Example 34 Sonata in A minor for piano K 310, second movement, bar 46

Trill chains

In ex. 35 the first two notes of the trill (bb′ and b′) create dissonances of a ninth

Example 35 Rondo in A minor for piano K 511, bars 134–5

which need to be accented. An upper-note start would obscure the chromatic ascending line. Hummel explained the execution of trill chains in his pianoforte tutor thus: 'The so-called trill chain consists of a series of stepwise or leaping pitches, which is continued without interruption. The after turn is appended only to the last note of the chain.'[11]

[11] J. N. Hummel, *Ausführliche theoretisch-practische Anweisung zum Piano-forte Spiel* (Vienna, 1828), p. 387.

Trills ex abrupto

A trill at the beginning of a piece should most likely begin on the main note or on a very short unaccented appoggiatura. In the case of the following example (36a), the return of the theme at the recapitulation (bars 69–70, ex. 36b) strongly

Example 36 Sonata in B♭ for piano K 281 (189f), first movement, opening

(a) opening

(b) bars 69–70

suggests that the trill start on the main note, B♭. Similarly, since the original cadenza to the first movement of the Concerto in E♭ major for two pianos K 365 must begin on the main note because of the preceding run, the opening entry of the two pianos should probably also begin with the main note, E♭ (see ex. 37).

Example 37 Concerto in E♭ for two pianos K 365

(a) cadenza

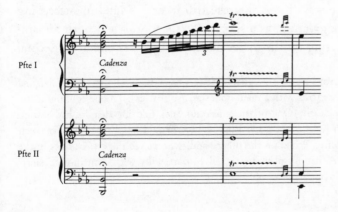

Ex. 37 (*cont.*)

(b) first movement, bar 54

Trills preceded by a short note of the same pitch

Mozart had a special liking for this type of motivic construction and used it in works such as the Serenade in C minor for wind instruments K 388 (384a), the Piano Concerto K 449 (first movement), the opening of the C minor Piano Sonata K 457, and the second-act finale of *Die Zauberflöte* (scene 30, 'Nur stille, stille. . .', ex. 38). Obviously the short semiquavers G and E♭ have to be played detached.[12]

Example 38 *Die Zauberflöte* (Act II, scene 30, 'Nur stille, stille. . .')

There are three possible ways to execute the trill in ex. 39 (and in succeeding passages): as a simple appoggiatura, as a short trill (snap, *Schneller*) with a main-note start, or as a trill starting on the upper note. Most players prefer the second

---

[12] In an excellent recent performance at the Vienna State Opera the violinists of the Vienna Philharmonic performed these trills with a main-note start, so that in bar 4 one could hear the chromatic step E♭–E quite clearly. One of the musicians later told me that he had started these trills with an ever so light grace note; this, however, could not be perceived as such by this listener! Professor Alfred Prinz, on the other hand, who played the first clarinet in the same orchestra, assured me that he plays nearly all Mozart trills with a main-note start. According to him, no conductor has ever objected.

Example 39 Sonata in C minor for piano K 457, opening

(a)

(b) executions

     (i)   (ii)   (iii)

method; yet i and iii are equally valid. The first solution is found in the cadenza to the first movement of the Piano Concerto K 449 (previously, in a parallel place, bar 64, the violins have had a trill; see ex. 40). I prefer the third method, which,

Example 40 Concerto in E♭ for piano K 449

(a) bar 64   (b) cadenza, bar 15

Vln. I

however, is the most difficult to play, especially on heavy modern piano actions.

Unclear though directions on ornaments in general may appear, a good 'rule of thumb' has been formulated by Frederick Neumann in his excellent book *Ornamentation and Improvisation in Mozart*:

The suggestion (rooted in musical logic) derives from the fact that 1) a trill starting with the upper note on the beat has the effect of a short appoggiatura; 2) a trill starting with a lengthened upper note has the effect of a long appoggiatura; 3) a trill starting with the upper note before the beat has the effect of a grace note. We find guidance by leaving out the trill and judging whether one of these ornaments would be a desirable addition to the bare melody; if so, the corresponding trill type is likely to be the proper or at least an acceptable choice. Where none of these ornaments seems to fit, the main-note trill is indicated. Where no clear-cut choice between one or more of the alternatives emerges, more than one trill design will be fitting. The test can also be extended to suggest compound trills whenever either a rising or a falling three-note prefix could be added to advantage.[13]

---

[13] Neumann, *Ornamentation*, pp. 113ff.

SPEED AND ENDING

Long trills should always be executed at a fast rate of speed (but not exaggerated like the bleating of a goat). Most important is the evenness of the execution. In early works Mozart rarely indicated closing turns at the end of (longer) trills because it was understood that they were required. Nearly all the treatises agree on this point. Still, in 1828 Hummel wrote in his pianoforte tutor:

Each true trill must have a closing turn even if it is not especially marked; if, however, the brevity of the trilled note or the following succession of notes does not permit the turn, it should not properly be called a trill but only a trilled note.[14]

(This rule is also valid for Beethoven and Brahms.)

Thus it is wrong to play a long Mozart trill without a suffix. Often Mozart wrote out the closing turn with large semiquavers or demisemiquavers. In such cases these notes can be performed in the speed of the preceding trill, i.e. faster than written. If these written-out closing notes ascend, the frequently heard mistake of adding two extra small notes should be avoided, e.g. as in ex. 41.

Example 41 Concerto in E♭ for piano K 482, second movement, bars 151–2

(a)   (b) correct execution   (c) incorrect execution

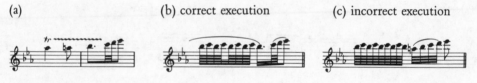

SHORT TRILLS AND SNAPS (*PRALLTRILLER* OR *SCHNELLER*)

Clementi and many other authors show these ornaments beginning on the main note. According to C. P. E. Bach, Türk and others, they are played with the utmost speed and a 'snap' of the finger on the penultimate note. Occasionally Mozart wrote out their execution in large notes, as in exx. 42 and 43. On the

Example 42 Concerto in E♭ for piano K 449, third movement, bars 302–3

---

[14] Hummel, *Ausführliche Anweisung*, p. 386.

Example 43 *Le nozze di Figaro*: Cherubino's canzona 'Voi che sapete', bars 14, 16, etc.

other hand, neither Mozart nor Haydn or Beethoven ever wrote out the formula, so dear to our harpsichordists, shown in ex. 44.[15]

Example 44

Mozart only rarely used the common *Pralltriller* sign. He did so sporadically in K 284, 449, 450, 452 and 456, and in some very early works. But it would be absurd to believe that elsewhere he deliberately ignored this common ornament. The occasional notation of ⌒ instead of *tr* in K 449–56 coincides with Mozart's first entries in the autograph catalogue of his works. Perhaps beginning in 1784 he intended to use a more precise notation of his ornaments, but old habits soon got the better of him? Incidentally, neither Mozart nor Haydn ever used the two small notes suggested by several theorists for the *Schneller*, a freely entering *Pralltriller* on detached notes.

Two of Mozart's rare notations of the *Pralltriller* sign are worthy of mention (see exx. 45 and 46). In other works the sign *tr* ought to be interpreted as *Pralltriller* (see exx. 47 and 48).

Example 45 Quintet in E♭ for piano and winds K 452, first movement, bars 65ff

[15] What appears to be a singular exception is in fact only a notational error. At the recapitulation of the first movement of the Piano Sonata in D major K 284 (205b), Mozart added an appoggiatura B before the first semiquaver A in bar 94 but forgot to cancel the 'tr' he had written earlier. The original edition (Vienna, 1784), revised by Mozart, has a trill sign on the first note in bars 23 and 94 but no trill sign over the following semiquaver. So far no editor has reported this fact.

Example 46 Concerto in B♭ for piano K 456, third movement, bars 5–6

Example 47 Sonata in C for piano K 330 (330h), first movement, bar 37

(a)   (b) correct execution   (c) incorrect execution

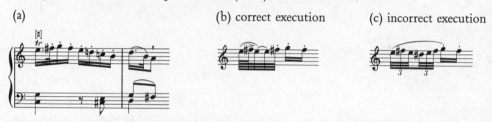

Example 48 Sonata in C for piano K 330 (300h), third movement, bars 39–41

(a)

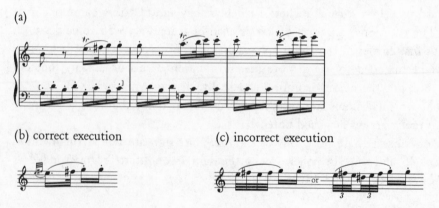

(b) correct execution   (c) incorrect execution

For the opening of the Piano Concerto in G major K 453 we opted for two solutions in our book *Interpreting Mozart on the Keyboard* and in the edition of the concerto for the *Neue Mozart Ausgabe* (see ex. 49). Today I see no reason to

Example 49 Concerto in G for piano K 453, first movement theme

(a)

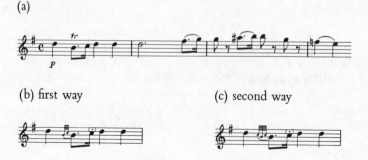

(b) first way   (c) second way

recommend the execution in ex. 49c, because it inevitably creates the wrong melodic effect (see ex. 50).

Example 50

In accordance with ex. 46 (Piano Concerto in Bb major K 456, third movement), *Schnellers* should also be played in the last movement of the Piano Sonata in D major K 311 (284c), bars 121 and 241 (ex. 51a and b), and at the beginning

Example 51 Sonata in D for piano K 311 (284c), third movement

(a) bars 121–3

(b) bars 241–2

of the second movement of the Piano Sonata in F major K 280 (189e) (ex. 52).

Example 52 Sonata in F for piano K 280 (189e), second movement, beginning

(a)

(b) correct execution   (c) incorrect execution

In ex. 52 the old rule (Quantz, p. 143) applies that in siciliano-type movements the ornaments must be as short as possible in order not to obscure the dotted rhythm. (Haydn placed a mordent sign in the otherwise identical opening of the Adagio in his Sonata in F major Hob. XVI No. 23.) On the other hand, if a dotted figure with a trill sign appears in a slow tempo in the middle of a phrase, a normal trill is preferred to a snap (see ex. 53). Naturally the *tr* sign

Example 53 Sonata in C for piano K 330 (300h), second movement, bars 14–15

(a)

(b) recommended execution

means *Pralltriller* in those passages where there is no time for a longer ornament, as in exx. 54, 55 and 56. It is not correct to change the basic rhythm into

Example 54 Sonata in A for piano K 331 (300i), first movement, Variation 2, bars 9–10

Example 55 Sonata in C for piano K 330 (300h), first movement, bar 129 [also 130, 135, 136]

(a)

(b) incorrect execution

Example 56 Concerto in E♭ for piano K 482, second movement, bar 43

triplets, as in ex 55b. In all these passages the ornament should not start prior to the harmony.

Execution of the *tr* sign as a short upper appoggiatura

There are many instances where even a *Pralltriller* cannot be played in time. In such cases an appoggiatura affords the best solution. Mozart himself furnished a fine example in his Serenade in C minor for wind instruments K 388 (384a). In the first movement (bars 14, 16) the first clarinet has a (*Prall-*) trill. In the development, however (from bar 112 onwards), the first oboe and the bassoons have appoggiaturas instead (see ex. 57). There can be only one plausible explana-

Example 57 Serenade in C minor for wind instruments K 388 (384a), first movement

(a) bars 13–16

(b) bars 112–15

tion: these instruments could not play fast enough to execute a trill. Even more telling is the fact that when Mozart arranged this work for string quintet (K 406/516b), he wrote trill signs for both the violin and the cello. In the Piano Concerto in E♭ major K 482 (third movement, bar 23) Mozart wrote a trill sign; however, in the otherwise unaltered recapitulation he wrote an appoggiatura instead (bar 376). In the Piano Sonata in A minor K 310 (second movement, bar 12) the last *tr*s are unplayable except as appoggiaturas. Incidentally, in the four-hand Piano Sonata in C major K 521 (second movement, bar 93) Mozart wrote appoggiaturas in a passage that is in all other respects identical to the one in K 310.

At the beginning of the Piano Sonata in F major K 280 (189e) even an appoggiatura is difficult to play because of the preceding c″ semiquaver (see ex. 58a). An excellent solution to this problem was offered in the *Vollständige Klavierschule* by Ignace Pleyel, who proposed to play the appoggiatura not before, but after the trilled note,[16] as shown in ex. 58b.

---

[16] Mollo (Vienna, 1804). I could not trace a copy of the earlier French original. In the Viennese edition this execution is shown on p. 6.

Example 58 Sonata in F for piano K 280 (189e), opening

(a)   (b) Pleyel's solution

Execution of the *tr* sign as a turn

This solution, mentioned above, had been proposed as early as 1753 by C. P. E. Bach in his *Versuch über die wahre Art das Clavier zu spielen* (p. 87). It is especially recommended where a phrase starts with a trill on a short upbeat note, as in ex. 59.

Example 59 Concerto in C for piano K 467, third movement, bar 120

(a)

(b) execution

In many earlier works Mozart placed trill signs in passages where only turns appear to be appropriate (see ex. 60). The same interpretation would be pos-

Example 60 Concerto in E♭ for piano K 271, first movement, bar 60

(a)   (b) execution

sible for the theme of the Variations on 'Ah vous dirai-je, maman' K 265 (300e), bars 7, 15 and 23. Variation 2 offers no fewer than three different meanings for the *tr* symbol (see ex. 61). For the third I prefer a trill with a start on the main note, since beginning from above would produce parallel octaves.

The evidence presented above demonstrates that only the context can determine which interpretation of the *tr* sign Mozart intended. The examples offered show

Example 61 Variations on 'Ah vous dirai-je, maman' K 265 (300e), Variation 2

only the most typical patterns; more space would be necessary to present a complete account. The interested reader may find other useful examples in Frederick Neumann's *Ornamentation and Improvisation in Mozart* as well as in our book *Interpreting Mozart on the Keyboard*. Clementi's statement that taste is needed to ensure the selection of the most suitable execution of ornaments (see fig. 1) would undoubtedly have met with Mozart's approval. 'The general mark for the shake is this tr and composers trust chiefly to the taste and judgment of the performer, whether it shall be long, short, transient or turned.'[17]

[17] Clementi, *Introduction to the Art*, p. 11.

2

'ICH PRAELUDIRTE UND SPIELTE VARIAZIONEN': MOZART THE FORTEPIANIST

KATALIN KOMLÓS

It is a fact well-known from numerous contemporary reports, letters, reminiscences, and other documents that Mozart was, from his early youth, an exceptional keyboard improviser. Extemporisation is a rather rare subject of musical investigation because of its elusive nature; yet, in Mozart's case, more may be deduced from his written words and musical jottings than one might think. Careful reading will show that improvisation was not a vague notion for him, but an art with clearly distinguished styles and manners. Nomenclature, the identification of keyboard instruments used (if known), and descriptions of the actual playing all assist in our understanding of Mozart's improvisational *styles*, even though we are unable to recapture those ephemeral moments.

Praeludiren, Phantasiren, Praeambuliren – well-known terms from earlier centuries – occur frequently in the letters of the Mozart family. 'Bimperl, please be so good as to send me soon a short *preambolum*. But write one this time from C into B[♭]*, so that I may gradually learn it by heart,*[1] writes Nannerl Mozart in September 1777 from Salzburg to her brother, then staying at Munich. Of course the sort of 'preambolum' she had in mind was not supposed to be written down, particularly by someone else, but Nannerl clearly had not the necessary gift or imagination for such improvisations herself. Her brother had to assist her on several occasions, with various concerto cadenzas and *Eingänge* as well. The request just cited raises a curious question: What was the purpose of the 'modulating prelude' she describes? Perhaps, instead of playing the more familiar introductory role, might such a prelude be used to make the necessary tonal transition between two pieces written in different keys? Wolfgang refers to the other function of *praeludia* in a later, Paris letter: 'I wanted to present my sister with a little Preambulum. The manner of playing it I leave to her own feeling. This is not the kind of Prelude which passes from one key into another, but

---

[1] *The Letters of Mozart and His Family*, ed. and trans. Emily Anderson, 3rd edn (London, 1985), p. 283.

only a sort of Capriccio, with which to test a clavier.'[2] None of this is new, of course. To test an unfamiliar instrument with improvised passages and various figures was established practice.

Three autograph pieces, presumably all from 1776–7, demonstrate the kind of preludes Wolfgang sketched for his sister.[3] None bears a title, and at least one is a fragment. Their identification and exact coordination with the information of the letters is not quite clear;[4] many similar fantasy-like jottings must have existed. They appear under the following titles:

Modulierendes Präludium (F–e)	K deest
Präludium in C	K 284a
Fragment eines Präludiums	K 624 (626a) Anh I (KV[6]: Anh C 15.11)

The manner is entirely that of the free fantasia: endless arpeggios and rambling passages follow each other in bizarre harmonic order, *senza misura*. (Only some parts of the sectional K 284a have regular barlines.) North German *stylus phantasticus*, the mother tongue of C. P. E. Bach, is unmistakable here. Since Mozart had to write down something essentially fluid and unfixed (a 'contradictio in objecto', as Schilling's *Lexicon* formulates it[5]), the notation and general layout of the C. P. E. Bach fantasias might have directly influenced him. The opening passage of the so-called *Modulierendes Präludium*, an elaboration of the harmonic gesture (augmented 6th → V chord as tension → resolution)[6] with both harmonic and non-harmonic tones, generates a representative type of momentum (see ex. 1).

Example 1 *Modulierendes Präludium* K deest

[2] Letter of 20 July 1778 (*Letters*, p. 573).

[3] Printed in *Neue Mozart Ausgabe* (*NMA*) IX/27/2, pp. 4–5, 5–9, 148–151.

[4] See Wolfgang Plath, Preface to *NMA* IX/27/2, xii–xv, xxiv.

[5] Gustav Schilling, *Encyclopädie der gesamten musikalischen Wissenschaft*, vol. 2 (Stuttgart, 1840), p. 654.

[6] Thus, the tonal framework is not really F–E, as marked in *NMA* IX/27/2, but rather A (minor)–E. The autograph is in the National Széchenyi Library, Budapest (Ms. mus. 6.341); facs. edn by Imre Sulyok (Budapest, 1977).

Ex. 1 (*cont.*)

A contradiction connected with Mozart's use of the term 'Capriccio' appears in K 284a, which is a compilation of apparently incongruous sections that Mozart may or may not have meant to belong together.[7] The first Capriccio, notated without barlines, contains a long series of broken chords, mainly diminished sevenths, a common device in free fantasias. The second, on the other hand, contains the most regular figuration in strict metre, a type of passage familiar in Mozart (see ex. 2). (An obvious parallel is Variation 2 from the series on

Example 2 Präludium in C major K 284a

'Ah vous dirai-je, maman' K 265.) Here, it seems, 'Capriccio' means merely something vigorous and virtuosic.

It is clear from various documents that the old distinction between the *gebundene* and *freie* arts of improvisation was still operating in the second half of the eighteenth century, at least in the German-speaking parts of Europe. In the letters and documents of the Mozart family strict style is marked as *org[e]lmässig*, *Kirchenstyl*, or *fugirte* playing. Wolfgang had a lifelong attraction to the organ, and several descriptions of his organ improvisations survive, dating from his childhood to his last years. His 'old-style' extemporisations, however, were not exclusively connected with that instrument. He writes about his *orglmässig* clavichord improvisation at the Holy Cross Monastery, near Augsburg, in October 1777.[8] Announcements, reviews, and letters describe his

---

[7] See *NMA* IX/27/2, Preface, pp. xiv–xv.
[8] *Mozart: Briefe und Aufzeichnungen*, ed. Wilhelm A. Bauer and Otto Erich Deutsch for the International Stiftung Mozarteum (Kassel, 1962–75), vol. 2, p. 82.

famous concert during this period in the Augsburg Fugger Hall, which, in addition to a performance of the Triple Piano Concerto K 242 on three new Stein fortepianos(!), contained a 'frey-fugirte Fantasie im Kirchenstyl'.[9] (In Mozart's own words, 'eine Fuge ex c minor, ganz orglmässig'.[10])

This unwritten tradition of extemporisation *in der gebundenen Spielart* must have gained a new dimension for Mozart through his direct acquaintance with baroque polyphonic music in Baron van Swieten's Sunday concerts during the early 1780s. His fascination and frustration with fugue writing can be studied in numerous fragments, in which his struggle with this nearly forgotten language is quite tangible. Mozart enclosed performance instructions in a letter of April 1782 that accompanied the one completed fugue from this period, written for Nannerl and preceded by a substantial *praeludio* (K 394). With regard to the tempo of the fugue, he wrote: 'I have purposely written above it *Andante maestoso*, as it must not be played too fast. For if a fugue is not played slowly, the ear cannot clearly distinguish the theme when it comes in and consequently the effect is entirely missed.'[11]

The new style of keyboard playing (primarily as it applied to fortepiano) was quite another matter. In Mozart's vocabulary, *galanterie* is the word for contemporary musical fashion and instrumental art. 'Go on practising and whilst scrambling through scores do not forget your galanterie performance,'[12] he warned his sister from Mannheim, when he found out that she and Leopold, on long winter evenings, played through the violin and basso continuo parts of all the music that was to be found in the cathedral library. (Leopold's account of this systematic project is a typical example of his purposeful and relentless pedagogy.[13]) In *galanterie* playing, the observance of fine nuances, articulation, precision, differentiation of light and shade, and *Geschmack und Empfindung* (Mozart's favourite expression) were the most important elements. Mozart requested these qualities from his pupils, as one observes in his work with Rosa Cannabich on the Sonata K 309, described in the Mannheim letters. Indeed, these were the qualities he missed most in the performances of his contemporaries (see more on this below). The clarity with which both professionals

[9] *Augsburgische Staats- und Gelehrte Zeitung*, 21 October 1777, quoted in Otto Erich Deutsch, *Mozart: die Dokumente seines Lebens, gesammelt und erläutert* (Kassel, 1961), p. 149.
[10] *Briefe*, vol. 2, p. 84.
[11] *Letters*, pp. 800–801.
[12] Letter of 7 March 1778 (*Letters*, p. 507).
[13] *Briefe*, vol. 2, p. 300.

and amateurs distinguished between the old and new styles is evident from a characteristic event connected with the Baroness Waldstädten, a close acquaintance of Mozart. The Baroness requested a music teacher for one of her trips, and Leopold suggested Ignaz Finck, court trumpeter in Salzburg. Wolfgang opposed the idea in his letter of January 1783:

I must tell you that Finck would not be at all suitable for her, as she wants to have someone for herself and not for her children. You see, therefore, that what is important is that he should play with taste, feeling and brilliance; and that a knowledge of thorough bass and extemporizing in the style of the organ [*orgelmässig praeludiren*] would be of no use to him whatever.[14]

The Viennese keyboard idiom of the last quarter of the eighteenth century, tailored for and inspired by the new fortepiano, evoked a new kind of virtuosity which naturally affected improvisation, the highest form of soloistic creativity. As the organ, the harpsichord, and the clavichord had in earlier times, the fortepiano created a specific language and aura of its own, with its unique means of expression and sound. The increasing vogue of public concerts in Vienna (a late development in comparison with the activities in some other European cities) promoted the status of the fortepiano virtuoso. It was chiefly Mozart who established that position, although some contemporary opinions attributed the role to Leopold Koželuch.[15] As far as we know, free extemporisations were offered at each concert. These included the Viennese *Akademien*; Mozart's appearances in Prague (1787), Leipzig (1789), and Frankfurt (1790); and his numerous performances in private circles. Playing 'aus dem Stegreife', as in previous centuries, represented the *non plus ultra* of instrumental art.

Mozart first used the term 'variations' to refer to his own improvised performance in June 1781. He wrote to his father about a *Hauskonzert* given by Archbishop Colloredo in Vienna: 'When the concert was over I went on playing variations (for which the Archbishop gave me the theme) for a whole hour and with such general applause that if the Archbishop had any vestige of humanity, he must have felt delighted.'[16] Five months later the Viennese visit of the Grand Duke of Russia prompted Mozart to remark, 'I have been looking about for Russian popular songs, so as to be able to play variations on them.'[17] The same

[14] *Letters*, p. 836.
[15] 'Ihm [Koželuch] verdankt das Fortepiano sein Aufkommen'. See *Jahrbuch der Tonkunst von Wien und Prag* (1796); facs. edn by Otto Biba (Munich and Salzburg, 1976), p. 34.
[16] *Letters*, p. 742.
[17] Ibid. p. 780.

event occasioned the famous fortepiano competition between Mozart and Clementi on Christmas Eve 1781;[18] the statement quoted in the title of this essay is taken from Mozart's well-known account of this meeting.[19]

There is nothing new, of course, in the notion of improvisation on a given melody. This was a common practice both before and after Mozart's time. Vogler's definition of *Fantasieren* as 'Ausführung eines gegebenes Themas'[20] suggests that for some south German and Austrian musicians of the classical period, this was the usual form of extemporisation, different from the rambling manner of the north German free fantasia. (It is not yet a lost art. Occasionally in contemporary organ recitals, one hears an organist improvise on a theme given by the audience.) Needless to say, the Voglerian definition implies no particular technique. 'Ausführung' might proceed in either a contrapuntal or a galant style, or both. Mozart's gifted pupil Johann Nepomuk Hummel recalled that in his youth he practised the art of improvisation 'bald im galanten, bald im gebundenen und fugierten Styl'.[21] The Mozart letters and documents and, perhaps more importantly, the improvisatory nature of some of the mature variation works, suggest that Mozart's famous fortepiano extemporisations were in fact sets of free variations on popular songs or operatic tunes of the day. Conversely, his surviving works in variation form may indeed reflect this highly praised art of improvisation.

It is curious that of the fourteen authentic completed sets of variations, only one survives in a complete autograph (K 455), and two further in autograph fragments (K 265 and 353). Some of these compositions circulated in various manuscript or even printed versions during Mozart's lifetime and after his death.[22] We shall see that he occasionally made changes himself. Therefore a *Fassung letzter Hand* generally does not exist; this gives the pieces an amorphous character that reinforces Mozart's free conception of the genre.[23]

Keyboard variations were highly popular and marketable in late eighteenth-century Vienna, and some of the Mozart sets clearly responded to this demand.

---

[18] See Katalin Komlós, 'Mozart and Clementi: A Piano Competition and its Interpretation', *Historical Performance*, Spring 1989, pp. 3–9.

[19] *Letters*, p. 793.

[20] Georg Joseph Vogler, *Betrachtungen der Mannheimer Tonschule* (Mannheim, 1778), p. 98.

[21] Johann Nepomuk Hummel, *Ausführliche theoretisch-practische Anweisung zum Piano-forte Spiel* (Vienna, 1828), vol. 3, p. 444.

[22] See Kurt von Fischer, 'Mozarts Klaviervariationen', in *Hans Albrecht in Memoriam*, ed. Wilfried Brennecke and Hans Haase (Kassel, 1962), pp. 168–73.

[23] Ibid. p. 173; also, the same author, Preface to *NMA* IX/26, pp. vii–viii.

Of the moderately difficult pieces K 265 ('Ah, vous dirai-je Maman'), K 352 ('Dieu d'amour', supposedly written for Mozart's first Viennese pupil, the Countess Rumbeck), K 353 ('La belle Françoise'), K 500 (written for Hoffmeister's printed series) – all published in the 1780s in Vienna – must have pleased the *Liebhaber* of fashionable keyboard music. On the other hand, some of the other Viennese sets (K 398, 455, 613), and the two Paris compositions (K 354 and 264) are in many ways quite different. They are freer in construction and more difficult from a technical point of view, and most are longer. Here it is Mozart the instrumental artist who speaks, and in these improvisatory moments we may catch a glimpse of his famous gift. In some cases the compositional circumstances support this assumption. According to Wolfgang's letter to his father, in his highly successful *Akademie* in the *Burgtheater* on 23 March 1783, he played, among other things, variations on the aria 'Salve tu, Domine' from Paisiello's *I filosofi immaginarii*, and on 'Unser dummer Pöbel meint' from Gluck's *Die Pilgrime von Mekka* [=*La rencontre imprévue*].[24] The later written versions (K 398 and 455) might not be exact copies of these improvisations (although Mozart was capable of keeping entire pieces in his head when there was no time to write them down);[25] but the fantasia-like nature of K 398 in particular speaks for itself. The date of composition of Mozart's last piece for the fortepiano, the variations on 'Ein Weib ist das herrlichste Ding' K 613, a song from Schikaneder's comedy *Der dumme Gärtner*, suggests that it was perhaps prepared for the last public concert appearance of his life, in March 1791. Again the increasingly complex, spontaneous development of the melody, with the splendid concluding section, is nothing like the more modest, conventional examples of the genre.

During the unfortunate Paris sojourn of 1778 Mozart wrote two grand variation works, whose standard, like that of the *Jeunehomme* concerto of the previous year, he never really surpassed. Written on popular French tunes of the time (on the romance 'Je suis Lindor' from *Le Barbier de Séville* of Beaumarchais, and the ariette 'Lison dormait' from the opéra comique *Julie* of N. Dezède), these extensive and highly virtuosic pieces, interspersed with cadenzas and other free

---

[24] *Briefe*, vol. 3, p. 262.
[25] He wrote to his father from Vienna on 8 April 1781:

> Today . . . we had a concert, where three of my compositions were performed – new ones, of course; a rondo for a concerto for Brunetti; a sonata with violin accompaniment for myself, which I composed last night between eleven and twelve (but in order to be able to finish it, I only wrote out the accompaniment for Brunetti and retained my own part in my head) . . . *Letters*, p. 722.

passages, must have originated in the young composer's extemporisations. His (or rather Leopold's) final ambition was to conquer the French capital. As a keyboard virtuoso, he could hardly have offered more resplendent productions than the elaborate paraphrases on fashionable tunes; Franz Liszt would do the same a good half century later, but with incomparably more success. Mozart played the 'Je suis Lindor' variations as late as 1789 at his Leipzig concert in the old Gewandhaus.[26] The 'Lison dormait' variations were performed just two months earlier, in March 1789 in Dresden, by Mozart's eleven-year-old pupil, J. N. Hummel.[27]

Unfortunately, the number of written-down variations, *alias* improvisations, is relatively small when compared with the many more Mozartian performances of this kind that remained only in the memory of his contemporaries. In some cases we even know the theme of these extemporisations. The most popular tune from *Figaro*, 'Non più andrai', was featured more than once. Alas, none of the variations survives. Caroline Pichler relates the following story in her memoirs:

One day when I was sitting at the pianoforte playing the 'Non più andrai' from *Figaro*, Mozart, who was paying a visit to us, came up behind me; I must have been playing it to his satisfaction, for he hummed the melody as I played and beat the time on my shoulders; but then he suddenly moved a chair up, sat down, told me to carry on playing the bass, and began to improvise such wonderfully beautiful variations that everyone listened to the tones of the German Orpheus with bated breath.[28]

In one of the most successful concerts of his life, in January 1787 in Prague, Mozart played variations on Figaro's aria again.

At the end of the concert Mozart improvised [*phantasirte*] a good half hour on the pianoforte, and with this, he inspired the enthusiasm of the overwhelmed Bohemians to the highest degree. The stormy success that followed his playing prompted him to sit down at the piano once more. The flight of this fantasia captivated the audience even more strongly: they stormed him for the third time . . . He started once more in an elevated spirit; he produced something that was never heard by anyone. Suddenly, in the dead silence a voice arose from the audience: 'From the Figaro!' Mozart introduced

---

[26] See *Allgemeine musikalische Zeitung* vol. 1, no. 1 (1798), 114.

[27] Deutsch, *Dokumente*, p. 303.

[28] *Allgemeine Theaterzeitung* (Vienna, 15 July 1843), p. 750; quoted in Otto Erich Deutsch, *Dokumente*; translated by Eric Blom *et al.* as *Mozart: a Documentary Biography* (London, 1965), pp. 556–7.

the melody of the favorite aria 'Non più andrai', and improvised a dozen of the most interesting and most artful variations. Roaring ovation closed this memorable concert.[29]

Another tune that inspired Mozart's fantasy was one composed by the Irish tenor Michael Kelly. Again, the piece seems never to have been notated. We read in Kelly's *Reminiscences*:

I had composed a little melody to Metastasio's canzonetta, 'Grazie agl' inganni tuoi', which was a great favourite wherever I sang it. It was very simple, but had the good fortune to please Mozart. He took it and composed variations upon it, which were truly beautiful; and had the further kindness and condescension to play them wherever he had an opportunity.[30]

Surely these are just a few cases of many similar instances.

In attempting to identify the improvisatory elements in the surviving compositions, one should first define the basic design of the Mozart variation. As with any formal categorisation, such a design serves as an abstract but useful framework.

Table 1. *The structural model of Mozart's mature keyboard variations*

Theme	Variations 1–x	Penultimate var. Adagio	Last var. →CADENZA→ change of tempo and metre	Original theme

The Adagio tempo of the penultimate variation, the changed metre of the closing one (in many cases a *Proporz*-like ending in fast triple metre), and the subsequent return of the original theme are fundamental to the dramatic effect of the form. In the course of the variations, conventional techniques (gradual diminution of the rhythmic values, crossing of hands, accompaniment of the theme with trills, use of the minor mode for one variation) are mixed with individual features and ideas.

The first and most obvious sign of improvisation is the presence of free passages and interpolated diversions. As in other classical instrumental genres (especially concertos), cadenzas and *Eingänge* function to highlight certain points of the structure and to enhance the virtuosic character of the music. In the

[29] Recollection of Jan Nepomuk Štepánek, quoted in Georg Nikolaus von Nissen, *Biographie W. A. Mozarts* (Leipzig, 1828), p. 517; trans. in Komlós, 'Mozart and Clementi'.
[30] Michael Kelly, *Reminiscences* (London, 1826), p. 222; quoted in Deutsch, *Dokumente*, p. 455.

variation genre, Mozart usually places a cadenza before the final return of the original theme at the end of the piece. Herald-like, this announces the return in the same manner as in rondo finales in the concertos, where such written or improvised *Eingänge* prepare the returning theme. We can be sure that Mozart, in his own performances, did not adhere to the written versions of these passages. ('Whenever I play this concerto, I always play whatever occurs to me at the moment',[31] he wrote to his father concerning the *Eingänge* in K 382.) The surviving sources include short decorations on the V^7 fermata chord (K 500, 573) as well as longer, more elaborate cadenzas that follow a properly emphasised fermata on I_4^6 (K 264, 398, 455, 613). Of the latter, the 'Cadenza' of K 455 (designated as such in the score) stands apart, for, in addition to free passage work, it contains extensive motivic material based on the main rhythmic figure of the closing variation. Through a developmental treatment this cadenza assumes the nature of a coda, as well; on the other hand, the use of thematic material brings it close to some of the concerto cadenzas (see ex. 3).

Example 3 Variations on 'Unser dummer Pöbel meint' K455

The last set of variations (K 613), Beethovenian in many respects,[32] arranges these techniques differently. The coda-like extension of the final variation leads the main motive through a surprising modulation to the key of the flattened submediant (D♭, the most Beethoven-like moment of the piece), and the sustained

[31] Letter of 22 January 1783 (*Letters*, p. 837).

[32] The same observation is made in Rudolf Flotzinger, 'Die Klaviervariationen W. A. Mozarts in der Tradition des 18. Jahrhunderts', *Mitteilungen der ISM* 23 (1975), vol. 3/4, pp. 22–7.

I_4^6 chord of the main key is reached only after this. The following short cadenza ends with a fermata over a rest; that is, further improvised passages are encouraged before the return of the original theme. The longer the delay, the more effective the arrival.

In contrast to the metric organisation of the above examples, the final cadenzas of the variations on 'Lison dormait' and 'Salve tu, Domine' are entirely free and fantasia-like, devoid of barlines. (The former is marked 'Cadenza', the latter 'Cadenz – Capriccio' in the score.) The wonderful spontaneity and virtuosity of the 'Lison dormait' cadenza displays no less than a glissando in sixths, and a long chain of thirds (see ex. 4); the creation and intensification of the state

Example 4 Variations on 'Lison dormait' K 264

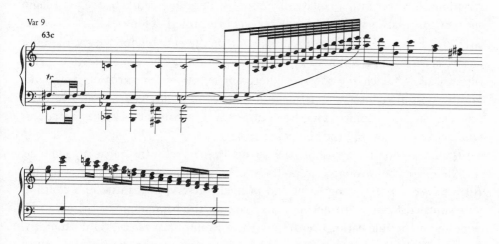

of suspense and expectation at the end of the 'Salve tu, Domine' cadenza may be cited as an arch-example of the powerful psychological effect of such passages (see ex. 5).

Example 5 Variations on 'Salve tu, Domine' K 398

Ex. 5 (*cont.*)

It is, however, not the single final cadenza that suggests the improvisatory character of these pieces, but the free treatment of the structure: the multiple passages in which the end of a variation rambles off, and the strict sequence of variations dissolves into a fantasia-like process. In K 455 and 500, the pre-adagio and adagio variations follow each other *attacca*, through a long cadenza (particularly grandiose in K 455); in the middle of the 'Je suis Lindor' set, Variation 8 (*Tempo di Menuetto*) is followed by an unexpected stormy passage marked 'Caprice' (Presto), after which the sober counterpoint of the *minore* variation brings the greatest possible contrast. A fermata in the theme itself (K 264, 353, 398, 613) provides an opportunity for short improvised ornaments in the variations, whether written out by the composer or not.

Of all the Mozart variations, the set on Paisiello's theme 'Salve tu, Domine' K 398 gives the strongest impression of a single fantasia or improvisation. All pre-1798 sources, manuscript and printed, preserve the music in a continuously notated form, with no numbers marking the beginnings of the six variations and no double barlines separating them from one another.[33] Unfortunately, modern Urtext editions are not faithful to such important details; as a result, the genuine fantasia character is less apparent to the Mozart student of today. Indeed, the second half of the piece is entirely through-composed and seems to recall that famous concert improvisation of March 1783. In variations 4–6, only the first part of the theme is treated, and from the middle of the *minore* variation the music takes on a free manner, breaking into long cadenzas between reappearances of the original melody. It is more than likely that the 1785 advertisement of Torricella (one year before the Artaria publication of the piece), announcing the 'Neueste Fantasie-Variationen vom Hrn. Kappelmeister A. W. Mozart', refers to K 398.[34]

[33] See *Kritischer Bericht*, NMA IX/26, ed. Kurt von Fischer (Kassel, 1962), p. 97.
[34] Ibid. p. 95.

The variations on 'Ein Weib ist das herrlichste Ding' K 613 present a similar case. In some old manuscript copies[35] the last three variations are written out continuously, without numberings or double barlines – with quite sound reasoning. The free handling of this extensive closing section is even more complex and elaborate than that of K 398. Variation 6 combines *maggiore* and *minore*; Variation 7 starts in the original tempo, then turns into a reflective adagio; Variation 8 transforms the second half of the theme into an allegro tune in 2/4 metre, then concludes with the coda-*cum*-cadenza described above.

If we compare the cadenzas of the variations with those of the piano concertos – an obvious parallel, surely – we find that they resemble the early concertos rather than the surviving cadenzas of the later Viennese concertos. The free spontaneity characteristic of the numerous Mozart cadenzas of the pre-1782 concertos (written mainly for performers other than himself) remains the chief feature of the variation cadenzas throughout, whereas the cadenzas of the mature concertos become more organised, considerably longer, and usually contain thematic material from the main movement. Christoph Wolff points out that with K 414, Mozart leaves the 'pure virtuosic improvisation-cadenza' behind, to turn towards a new model that is an integral, organic part of the composition.[36] Most of the later cadenzas follow a more or less designed structural pattern,[37] which is foreign to the flamboyant free passages of the variations. (Some of them, however, as mentioned earlier, are close to the *Eingänge* familiar from the rondo finales of the concertos.)

Improvisatory character is strikingly manifest in many of the adagio variations. The longest of these approach the size and weight of the slow movements in cyclic works, but their style and rhetoric are quite different. (To be sure, adagio slow movements are scarce in Mozart's works.) The infinitely elaborate notation and rich rhythmic vocabulary of the adagios of the Paris sets (and, to a somewhat lesser extent, those of K 455, 573, and 613) have no parallel in Mozart's keyboard music. Mozart takes great care to convey the rubato and the rhythmic freedom of the performance through this careful notation. The exceptionally florid ornamentation, especially in the written-out repeats of the adagio of the 'Lison dormait' variations, reflects Mozart's decorative art at its highest. These

[35] The MS copy examined for this essay is in the International Stiftung Mozarteum, Salzburg [Rara 613/2]. I am grateful to Geneviève Geffray, librarian, for her kind assistance and correspondence.

[36] See his preface in *NMA* V/15, vol. 3, pp. xiii–xiv.

[37] See Eva and Paul Badura-Skoda, *Interpreting Mozart on the Keyboard* (London, 1961), pp. 214–41.

pages are a treasure house for those who wish to borrow ideas for the occasional ornamentation of the more sparsely notated sonata or concerto slow movements.

Instrumental virtuosity, essential to the variation genre, appears in different technical levels in Mozart's keyboard variations. As players know, there is a considerable difference between glittery but moderately difficult passage work and a texture that is truly demanding to play. In Mozart's keyboard compositions we find quite a clear distinction between the two, depending on the purpose and genre of the piece. Mozart wrote much of his piano music – the majority of the sonatas (solo or accompanied), some of the variations, and other single pieces – for his pupils. Consequently, their level of sheer technical difficulty is not too high. (The generalisation allows for exceptions, of course.) In the works that he wrote for himself, his imagination produced a different keyboard style – none too easy for any performer, past or present. In addition to the mature concertos, it is in some of the variation pieces that we glean an idea of his exceptional performance abilities. (Perhaps it is no coincidence that one rarely hears these sets in public; the only one which appears periodically in concert programmes, 'Ah vous dirai-je, maman', for all its loveliness, lacks the real representative qualities of this emphatically personal genre of Mozart's.)

As discussed earlier, K 398 and 455 certainly, and K 264, 354, and 613 probably originated in improvisatory performances. To these we might add the D major variations on Duport's *Menuett* K 573, composed in April 1789 during Mozart's stay in Potsdam. (Jean-Pierre Duport was a cellist and distinguished chamber musician of the Prussian court. It is quite plausible that Mozart might have played variations on a theme from one of his cello sonatas as a gesture to Duport.) The general level of technical difficulty of these pieces is surprisingly high. In addition to the conventional devices of broken octaves, trills, crossing of hands, etc., they include textures rarely used elsewhere by Mozart. I know of no Mozart passage besides Variation 2 of K ·398 which anticipates the nineteenth-century virtuosity of Liszt and his contemporaries (see ex. 6). No less virtuosity is required of the left hand for Variation 6 of the 'Je suis Lindor' set (ex. 7), or for

Example 6 Variations on 'Salve tu, Domine' K 398

Example 7 Variations on 'Je suis Lindor' K 354

the repeated thirds and sixths in Variation 4 of K 573 (ex. 8). Passages such
as these show the instrumental standard and personal style of Mozart's own
playing – far beyond the ordinary general level of musical invention and imagination.

Example 8 Variations on a minuet by J. P. Duport K 573

Further investigation concerning Mozart's fortepiano performance must deal
with the mature concertos written for his own *Akademien*. Their technical
demands vary; Mozart was the first to comment on this. For the first subscription series, he intended pieces which were 'a happy medium between what is
too easy and difficult; . . . very brilliant, pleasing to the ear, and natural,
without being vapid'[38] (K 413, 414, 415). As a musician just embarking on a
performance career, he naturally wanted to please the audience. Shortly after
this, nevertheless, he wrote what were probably the two most difficult concertos of his *œuvre* (from a purely keyboard-technical point of view): K 450 and
451. 'I regard them both as concertos which are bound to make the performer
perspire. From the point of view of difficulty the Bb Concerto beats the one
in D,' he wrote in May 1784.[39] Quite true. The Bb Concerto (again, one of
those seldom performed works) is the portrait of a fortepiano virtuoso of the
first order: a composition *für Kenner*, as it were. It is very doubtful whether his

[38] Letter of 28 December 1782 (*Letters*, p. 833).
[39] Ibid. p. 877.

sister or any of his lady students could have played the solo parts of the outer movements properly. (See a sample from the middle episode of the rondo finale in ex. 9.) The last eight masterpieces of the genre, beginning with K 466, resist such examination; their individuality and completeness is beyond technical detail.

Example 9 Concerto in Bb major for piano K 450, third movement

To return to the variations: the existence of the many surviving versions of the compositions, mentioned earlier, is partly the result of their technical difficulty. The C major variations on J. C. Fischer's *Menuett* (K 179), a piece Mozart played frequently during the pre-Vienna years, is known in several simplified versions. In a Modena copy, the closing variation is made easier; a Berlin manuscript source omits Variation 10 with its rather difficult octave passages and leaps in both hands; a Venice manuscript version comprises only six variations – half of the piece.[40] Mozart himself, as usual, was aware that his music might be above the capacity of the average performer, even in such a cultivated milieu as the electoral court in Mannheim. When trying to offer his services to the Elector Carl Theodor, he sent a sample of his music: 'I decided to take my six easiest variations on Fischer's minuet, which I had copied out here expressly for this purpose', he wrote to Salzburg in November 1777.[41] There is an abridged and simplified version of the 'Lison dormait' variations in Dresden (*c.* 1800) and an early nineteenth-century Amsterdam print of the Duport set that includes three variations only, 'approprié pour l'usage des élèves'.[42] K 573, incidentally, is titled in Mozart's own *Verzeichnüss* as '6 Variazionen auf das Clavier'. The piece was advertised in this way by the Viennese music shop of Lausch (selling manuscript copies) in 1791.[43] The posthumous first edition (Artaria, 1792) contains the nine variations known today. Which six variations formed the original conception, and when Mozart added the three further variations, we do not know.

---

[40] These data are taken from Kurt von Fischer, 'Mozarts Klaviervariationen', pp. 169–71.
[41] *Letters*, p. 397.
[42] Kurt von Fischer, 'Mozarts Klaviervariationen', pp. 169–71.
[43] See *Kritischer Bericht*, NMA IX/26, p. 122.

Apparently, the eight variations on 'Dieu d'amour' from Grétry's opera *Les Mariages samnites* (K 352) went through the same compositional process. Several manuscript copies, probably from the dealer Lausch, preserve the piece in a 'Theme and 5 Variations' form; the Artaria first edition of 1786 shows the expanded final version.[44] In this case, however, a comparison can be made on the basis of the surviving copies.[45] The shorter piece includes Variations 1–4 and Variation 6 of the later print; for the publication, Mozart added a *minore* (Variation 5), an adagio (Variation 7), and a closing allegro in 3/8. Thus the supplementary variations are those that constitute the characteristic points in Mozart's structure of the genre. We may presume that when he prepared the Duport variations for publication, the same considerations directed his choices.

It is worth mentioning that the cyclic model of the Mozart variations drafted in Table 1 was used not only by Mozart, but by his Viennese contemporaries as well. Two pieces might serve as examples; both of them appeared under Mozart's name in Volume 6 of the Breitkopf & Härtel *Œuvres complettes* (1799). The ten variations in A major on an Allegretto from Sarti's *I finti eredi* (K Anh 289) were composed by E. Aloys Förster, the twelve variations in D major on 'Freundin sanfter Herzensstriebe' from Dittersdorf's *Der Gutsherr* (K Anh 287) by Anton Eberl.[46] Both compositions have the characteristic concluding adagio closing variation in changed metre and return of the original theme; the similarity even includes the free cadenza before the final reappearance of the theme. But the musical material of the neatly lined up variations largely consists of empty *clichés* of an unpretentious order. As for the free cadenza at the end, let the Förster excerpt demonstrate the sad lack of invention of a passage that should be born out of creativity and imagination (see ex. 10).

Example 10 E. Aloys Förster, Variations in A major on an Allegretto from Sarti's *I finti eredi* K Anh 289

[44] Ibid. pp. 87–8.

[45] A manuscript copy of the five-variation version preserved in the Cathedral Library in Györ, Hungary, is not included among the sources in the *Kritischer Bericht* [AMC TK, C.1.32]. See Kornél Bárdos, *Sopron zenéje a 16–18. században* (Budapest, 1984); thematic catalogue by Veronika Vavrinecz. Ms Vavrinecz kindly helped me to locate and to see the manuscript.

[46] *Kritischer Bericht*, NMA IX/26, pp. 159–60.

Ex. 10 (*cont.*)

Conversely, the fact that the eight variations on Giuseppe Sarti's 'Come un' agnello' deviate from the usual structural model does not prove that the set is not from Mozart.[47] After all, it is exactly the individual quality and the freedom from stereotypes that distinguish the genius. Nevertheless, Kurt von Fischer is probably right when he proposes that K 460, missing entirely from Mozart's *Verzeichnüss* (printed only in 1803), is the clever transcription of a genuine Mozart improvisation.[48] If so, it is highly instructive, for such imitations, in their effort to seem authentic, usually amplify the characteristic features of the original. To counterfeit great performers was not unusual at the time, as we learn from the young Beethoven. Explaining the deliberate difficulty of a passage in the variations on 'Se vuol ballare' for Violin and Piano (WoO 40), he wrote to Eleanore von Breuning in June 1794:

I should never have written down this kind of piece, had I not already noticed fairly often how some people in Vienna after hearing me extemporize of an evening would note down on the following day several peculiarities of my style and palm them off with pride as their own . . .[49]

---

[47] On the question of the authenticity of the piece, see the *Mozart-Jahrbuch*: Kurt von Fischer, 'Sind die Klaviervariationen über Sartis "Come un'agnello" von Mozart?' (1958), pp. 18–29; Paul and Eva Badura-Skoda, 'Zur Echtheit von Mozarts Sarti-Variationen KV 460' (1959), pp. 127–39; and Fischer's reply, 'Sind die Klaviervariationen KV 460 von Mozart?' (1959), pp. 140–5; and 'Come un'agnello – Aria del Sig.r Sarti con Variazioni' (1978/79), pp. 112–21.

[48] *Kritischer Bericht*, NMA IX/26, p. 152; also Fischer, 'Come un'agnello', *Mozart-Jahrbuch 1978/79*.

[49] *The Letters of Beethoven*, ed. and trans. Emily Anderson (London, 1961), pp. 14–15.

The authenticity of the variations on Sarti's theme, known as K 460, has never been proved.[50] The striking difficulty of the piece itself shows that if not by Mozart, it was composed by someone who knew Mozart's virtuosic style of improvisation very well. But the extremely uncomfortable figures in Variation 3, as Kurt von Fischer also points out,[51] are foreign to the always idiomatic (however demanding) keyboard textures of Mozart (see ex. 11). The final section seems to

Example 11 Variations on Sarti's 'Come un'agnello' K 460

be a conglomeration of the through-composed conclusions of K 398 and 613. Both the largely expanded Allegro (Variation 7) and the closing Adagio (Variation 8) incorporate shorter *minore* sections, and the fantasia-like *Fortspinnung* of the penultimate variation leads to a cadenza that is nearly an exact imitation of the 'Capriccio' of K 398 (quoted partially in ex. 5). Curiously, the Adagio (less ornate than usual) is last, and instead of the return of the theme, only an abrupt fast closure (a Variation 9, in fact) rounds off the piece. Indeed, even if pseudo-Mozart, K 460 tells a lot about Mozart's extempore playing.

'Und dann immer Phantasien', wrote Mozart about his solo performances in Munich during the fall of 1777.[52] The word *phantasiren* marks improvisations of any kind, and documents rarely specify the style. Mozart often talks about 'playing variations', but several descriptions mention 'fantasias' even if the result was definitely a series of variations on a given theme. An intriguing reminiscence suggests that some contemporary ears differentiated between 'variations' and

[50] Therefore it is surprising that in the Henle Urtext edition (*Variationen für Klavier*, ed. Ewald Zimmermann [Munich, 1978]) K 460 is printed with the subtitle 'Komponiert in Wien 1784'. We know that Mozart improvised on a Sarti theme in June 1784, but the autograph fragment, the theme and two variations on 'Come un'agnello', is totally different from K 460. See details in the literature cited in note 47 above.

[51] 'Sind die Klaviervariationen . . . ?', pp. 24–5.

[52] *Briefe*, vol. 2, p. 47.

'fantasias'. The church composer Ambros Rieder wrote in his *Autobiography*: 'I was fortunate enough to hear the immortal, mighty W. A. Mozart not only perform variations [*variieren*] on the pianoforte, but also fantasias [*fantasiren*], before a numerous and eminent gathering.'[53] For all that, any pedantic classification of the techniques would be meaningless, and contradictory to the very nature of improvisation. Mozart's extempore performances, especially the longer ones, must have included a large variety of styles. Another detailed description is worth citing here, this one from the *Autobiography* of Maximilian Stadler:

In the art of free improvisation [*freye Fantasie Kunst*] Mozart had no equal. His improvisations were as well-ordered as if he had had them lying written out before him. This led several to think that, when he performed an improvisation [*mit einer Fantasie auftratt*] in public, he must have thought everything out, and practised it, beforehand. Albrechtsberger thought so too. But one evening they met at a musical soirée; Mozart was in a good mood and demanded a theme of Albrechtsberger. The latter played him an old German popular song. Mozart sat down and improvised on this theme [*führte dieses Thema durch*] for an hour in such a way as to excite general admiration and shew by means of variations and fugues (in which he never departed from the theme) that he was master of every aspect of the musician's art.[54]

We know that Mozart even had a large fortepiano pedal made, to be used for special effects in his improvisations.[55]

Interestingly enough, if we take into account the keyboard compositions Mozart actually titled 'Fantasia', we find only one complete work (K 475) and one short fragment (K Anh 32). Two further pieces (both of them fragments), subsequently called 'fantasias', are problematic: K 396, originally a sonata movement with violin accompaniment from 1782, completed by Maximilian Stadler and published as a solo piece in 1802; and K 397, first printed in 1804, whose genesis is entirely unknown. (Note that all four compositions are in minor keys.) The surviving autograph fragment of the C minor 'Fantasia' (K 396) seems to contain a strictly organized exposition of highly rhetorical music; however, it is the wonderful dramatic sweep of the following 'development section' that is fantasia-like, whether entirely Stadler's invention or not.[56] Still more curious is the history

---

[53] *Neue Wiener Musik-Zeitung*, 29 May 1856, p. 97; quoted in Deutsch, *Biography*, p. 566.

[54] Quoted in Deutsch, *Biography*, p. 543.

[55] See Leopold Mozart's letter of 12 March 1785, in *Briefe*, vol. 3, p. 379; also Deutsch, *Dokumente*, pp. 211–12, 285, 286.

[56] See Hans Eppstein, 'Mozarts "Fantasie" KV 396', *Die Musikforschung* 21 (1968), pp. 205–11; Hans Christian Müller, 'Quellenkritische Bemerkungen zu Mozarts Fantasie KV 385f', 24 (1971), pp. 295–7, and Eppstein's reply in vol. 25 (1972), p. 73.

of the Fantasia in D minor K 397: an unfinished piece printed in the posthumous first edition as a torso (if that is indeed the case) is really rare.[57] What we have is a strange mixture of a preludial beginning, a recurring melody of melancholy mood, interrupted with stormy free cadenzas, and a rather incongruous, discontinued Allegretto in D major.

K 475, 'Eine Phantasie für das Klavier allein', introduced into the composer's *Verzeichnüss* with this title on 20 May 1785, is the only completed Mozart piece in the genre. Is it a 'free' fantasia? Is it the notated version of a true Mozartian extemporization? C. P. E. Bach said he was urged to write fantasias 'so that after my death one could see what a *Fantast* I was';[58] does the same apply to Mozart? Mozart was certainly the possessor of a well-ordered mind; does the overall structure of K 475 mean that his improvisation was also basically an organised process? According to the communication of O. E. Deutsch, the 'Fantasie auf dem Pianoforte' on the programme of Mozart's Leipzig concert on 12 May 1789 was K 475;[59] however, this statement, taken from Nissen's *Biography*, lacks foundation.[60]

'Freie Fantasie' is a frequent topic in German theoretical literature of the seventeenth and eighteenth centuries. The sources of Mozart's time, repeating in part the descriptions of earlier authors, establish that true examples of this peculiar genre have no main theme as such; they follow a free metric course, partially or entirely without barlines; they have an unusual and expanded harmonic language; finally, their abrupt changes of mood, tempo, or *Affekt* create a wholly free chain of events, with no definite form.[61] As is well known, north German musical style and aesthetics had little influence on Mozart; still, no classical keyboard fantasia can be properly studied without the C. P. E. Bach model in mind. K 475

[57] See Paul Hirsch, 'A Mozart Problem', *Music & Letters* 25 (1944), pp. 209–12; Rudolf Steglich, 'Über das melodische Motiv in der Musik Mozarts: Eine Analyse der d-moll-Phantasie für Klavier', *Mozart-Jahrbuch 1953*, pp. 128–42; Wolfgang Plath, 'Zur Echtheitsfrage bei Mozart', *Mozart-Jahrbuch 1971/72*, p. 31.

[58] Letter of 15 October 1782 to Breitkopf, quoted in Pamela Fox, 'The Stylistic Anomalies of C. P. E. Bach's Nonconstancy', in *C. P. E. Bach Studies*, ed. Stephen L. Clark (Oxford, 1988), p. 113.

[59] Deutsch, *Dokumente*, p. 300.

[60] The ultimate source of information, a report in the *AmZ* (see note 26 above), says about this solo number in the concert, 'Er begann einfach, frey und feyerlich in C moll.' The description fits K 475 partially, although the starting melodic line is not exactly 'simple'.

[61] See, among other sources, Johann Joseph Klein, *Versuch eines Lehrbuches der practischen Musik* (Gera, 1783), p. 61; Daniel Gottlob Türk, *Clavierschule* (Halle, 1789), p. 395; Georg Friedrich Wolf, *Kurzgefaßtes musikalisches Lexikon* (Halle, 1792), p. 63.

is a free fantasia in many respects. The wide range of emotions and characters, the boldness of the harmonies and modulations, and the presence of free improvisatory passages certainly support this notion, even if the structure is not so incoherently rhapsodic as it sometimes is in its German counterpart. The dramatic course of the subsequent sections brings no recurrences except the final return of the initial part in C minor. Textual and tonal recapitulation, however, is characteristic of many C. P. E. Bach fantasias, too.

The composer's intention concerning the relationship between K 475 and the Sonata in C minor K 457 is puzzling. The sonata was composed for Mozart's pupil Therese von Trattner seven months before the fantasia, and only the first printed edition paired them together ('Fantaisie et sonate pour le fortepiano', Artaria 1785), surely with Mozart's consent. A fantasia and sonata in the same key, in which the former stands as a kind of introduction to the main piece, would have been not at all without precedent at the time. In north German repertory such pairs appeared in G. S. Löhlein's 'Sei Sonate con variate repetizioni, Op. 2' (1768) and in the '6 Sonaten mit einer vorgesetzten Fantasie' (1776) and elsewhere in the music of J. W. Hässler.[62] We also find such combinations in Kittel and Neefe. Mozart probably knew about these works, although the sequence of composition contradicts the idea that it was his original intention to write a 'Fantasia and Sonata'. In addition, only the sonata bears a dedication to Madame de Trattner, although this later appears on the joint edition of the Artaria print.[63] For whom, then, was the fantasia composed? We must keep in mind that K 475 is the only complete piece Mozart himself titled 'Phantasie'. Therefore, it must reflect what the composer understood by that indefinable genre. With its fearsome moments of *schwarze Melancholie*,[64] K 475 remains one of the most individual, personal masterpieces of Mozart.

The unfinished autograph of an Adagio in F minor (K Anh 32, presumably from 1789),[65] titled 'Fantasia' by Mozart, represents the counterpart to the instrumental brilliance of the variations: if the latter demonstrate the virtuosic side of improvisation, this expressive writing imparts its subjective sentiments. The key itself, rarely used by Mozart, suggests something special, as in the Adagio in B minor K 540, another infrequent tonality in Mozart's output. In fact, the two pieces are related through a *lamento* mood of profoundly felt grief. This

[62] The information is taken from Peter Schleuning, *Die freie Fantasie: Ein Betrag zur Erforschung der klassischen Klaviermusik* (Göppingen, 1973), pp. 291, 303.

[63] See *NMA* IX/25/2, Preface, pp. xiii–xiv.

[64] Expression of Johann David Heinichen, for peculiar enharmonic effects; see *Der Generalbass in der Composition* (Dresden, 1728), p. 76.

[65] Printed in *NMA* IX/27/2, p. 152.

emotional character is also typical of the *Tombeau*, which is considered to be one of the instrumental predecessors of the free fantasia.[66] The intensely expressive harmonic language, achieved through chromatic and enharmonic means, defines K 540 in particular, some of whose moments seem to anticipate the *Todesverkündigung* of Wagner's *Die Walküre* (see ex. 12). The harmonic leitmotiv of K 540 has its parallel in the F minor fragment (ex. 13), and the choice of form

Example 12

(a) Adagio in B minor K 540

(b) Wagner, *Die Walküre*, Act II, scene 4

Example 13

(a) Adagio in B minor K 540

(b) Adagio in F minor K Anh 32

[66] See Schleuning, *Die freie Fantasie*, pp. 55–78.

is also similar, so far as is ascertainable from the remnant. (The surviving 14 bars strongly indicate a sonata-form exposition not unlike that in K 396.)

A curious feature connects these two pieces to K 475 and 397. In all four compositions, there appears a persistently pulsating, repetitive figure that gives a sombre, almost sinister feeling. The repetition accompanies chromatically descending harmonies of the baroque chaconne type[67] in K 475 and 397. It shows up briefly as a dominant organ point in the F minor fragment and becomes a prevailing rhythmic pattern in K 540 (see Example 14). Invariably marked 'adagio'

Example 14

(a) Fantasia in D minor K 397

(b) Fantasia in C minor K 475

(c) Adagio in F minor K Anh 32

(d) Adagio in B minor K 540

[67] 'The Chromatic Fourth', as Peter Williams calls it; see his essay in this volume.

and in a minor key, this rhythmic symbol plays a prominent role in the general *Affekt* of these pieces.

In 1792, Maria Anna von Berchtold zu Sonnenburg, née Mozart, related some of the early musical activities of her deceased brother at the request of Breitkopf in Leipzig. She wrote:

From his childhood on he liked playing the best at night. When he sat down to the *Klavier* at 9 in the evening, one could not take him away before midnight, and even then only by force, or he would have improvised [*phantasiert*] the whole night . . . I have no knowledge of his practising [*exerciren*] the *Klavier* after he was seven years of age, for he always had to improvise [*phantasiren*], to play at sight, and to play concerts in front of people, and that was his whole *exercicium*.[68]

This document is critically important, even if we keep in mind that practising, in the form of scales, etudes, and various exercises, was not customary before the time of Czerny. But Nannerl's note also says, indirectly, that Wolfgang *did* have instrumental training in his early childhood, until he was seven – that is, until the first big European tour of Paris and London. We can be sure that Leopold submitted both of his children to a strict keyboard regimen. There is meagre evidence of the material and the methods used; only the 'Fünf technische Übungen' in the *Notenbuch für Maria Anna Mozart* (1759),[69] written in Leopold's hand, give any idea about this training. (The collection, which gradually expanded from 1759 on, was surely used to teach Wolfgang, too.) Exercises for both hands, passages in thirds, and polyphonic playing are included in the short *Übungen*.

Later, during the extensive concert travels of the Mozart family, Wolfgang had the opportunity to play all kinds of keyboard instruments of the time: organ, harpsichord, clavichord, and fortepiano. This most certainly broadened his musical experience and his knowledge of styles. His special affinity for the new fortepiano, however, determined his performing career. 'Everyone thinks the world of Wolfgang, but indeed he plays quite differently from what he used to in Salzburg – for there are pianofortes here, on which he plays so extraordinarily well that people say they have never heard the like,'[70] his mother wrote in December 1777 from Mannheim.

---

[68] *Briefe*, vol. 4, p. 203. Translation by the author.
[69] Printed in *NMA* IX/27/1, p. 86.
[70] *Letters*, p. 436.

In trying to reconstruct the manner and the characteristics of the fortepiano playing of Mozart the performer, we have access to both indirect and direct evidence. The former is found in those letters in which Mozart formulated his opinion about the playing of others, the latter in descriptions and recollections of his own playing written by contemporary witnesses.

In his letters, Mozart wrote in detail about the playing of seven rather different persons: three amateurs (Fräulein Hamm, Nanette Stein, and Rosa Cannabich) and four professionals (J. F. X. Sterkel, Vogler, Clementi, and G. F. Richter). From his usually sharp criticism, we learn the principles he considered most important in keyboard performance: natural posture,[71] light hand,[72] precision,[73] a thoroughly trained left hand,[74] general abstention from rushed tempos,[75] keeping strict time,[76] and, most of all, taste and expression (*Geschmack und Empfindung*), as contrasted with insensitive playing. Mozart expressed the strongest contempt for Clementi as a musician and a performer, denouncing him as a '*blosser Mechanicus*'.[77] He considered Clementi's famous virtuosity entirely worthless (a certain amount of jealousy must have coloured this extreme judgment), and he criticized Richter's playing for its lack of *Geschmack und Empfindung*.[78] (Incidentally, both Clementi and Richter complimented and even admired Mozart's playing.)

So far as contemporary reports or later memories of Mozart's performances are concerned, those who simply sang panegyrics to Mozart without specifying the character of his playing are of little use to us. The descriptions with concrete content emphasise both the technical perfection and the supreme musical sensitivity of Mozart's instrumental art, qualities which are inseparable in the performance of any great artist. Judging from some of the documents, he must have possessed phenomenal manual abilities. Norbert Ignaz Loehmann's account of Mozart's improvisation on the organ of the Strahov Monastery in Prague in 1787 includes especially important details. (Although the alleged transcription

---

[71] See the humorous description of the playing of Fräulein Hamm and Nanette Stein, in letters of 16 October and 23–5 October 1777, respectively, in *Briefe*, vol. 2, pp. 62, 83.

[72] 'She [Nanette Stein] will never acquire great rapidity, since she definitely does all she can to make her hands heavy' (*Letters*, p. 340).

[73] See the criticism of the too fast and consequently inaccurate performances of Sterkel and Vogler, in letters of 26 November 1777 and of 17 January 1778 (*Briefe*, vol. 2, pp. 146–7, 228).

[74] See comments on the playing of Rosa Cannabich in letter of 14 November 1777 (*Briefe*, vol. 2, p. 124).

[75] See note 73.

[76] See the important and detailed discussion of this question in letter of 23–5 October 1777 (*Briefe*, vol. 2, p. 83).

[77] Letter of 16 January 1782 (*Briefe*, vol. 3, p. 192).

[78] Letter of 28 April 1784 (*Briefe*, vol. 3, p. 312).

of this extemporisation is highly suspect,[79] the following observations could hardly be Loehmann's fabrication.)

He . . . began a four-part fugue theme, which was the harder to perform in that it and its countersubject consisted largely of mordents, which are exceptionally hard to perform on an organ with such a heavy action. But the fourth and fifth fingers of the right hand as well as of the left hand were as strong as the first [the thumb], second and third fingers, at which every one was much amazed.[80]

Michael Kelly, Mozart's first Basilio, had the good fortune to hear the composer play several times. He remembers the first such occasion in his *Reminiscences*:

I went one evening to a concert of the celebrated Koželuch's, a great composer for the pianoforte, as well as a fine performer on that instrument. I saw there the composers Vanhall and Baron Dittersdorf; and . . . Mozart. He favoured the company by performing fantasias and capriccios on the pianoforte. His feeling, the rapidity of his fingers, the great execution and strength of his left hand particularly, and the apparent inspiration of his modulations, astounded me.[81]

Ease and elegance, essential qualities of Mozart's artistic personality, were the intrinsic hallmarks of his performance as well. Mozart himself humorously tells us of keyboard player Richter's reaction to his playing:

When I played to him [Richter] he stared all the time at my fingers and kept on saying, 'Good God! How hard I work and sweat – and yet win no applause – and to you, my friend, it is all child's 'play'. 'Yes,' I replied, 'I too had to work hard, so as not to have to work hard any longer.'[82]

Twenty-five years after their famous competition, Muzio Clementi remembered Mozart's playing with special reverence: 'Until then I had never heard anyone perform with such spirit and grace. I was particularly astonished by an Adagio and some of his extemporized variations.'[83]

Finally, a beautiful performing portrait from an authentic source, Franz Xaver Niemetschek, a close acquaintance and admirer of Mozart:

It was his pianoforte playing that first won admirers and devotees; for although Vienna had many great masters of the instrument, the public's favourite, none of them could compare with our Mozart. A remarkable quickness, which particularly in consideration

---

[79] Printed in *NMA* IX/27/2, pp. 166–8.
[80] Quoted in Deutsch, *Biography*, p. 517.
[81] Michael Kelly, *Reminiscences* (London, 1826), p. 222; quoted in Deutsch, *Dokumente*, p. 454.
[82] See note 78.
[83] *Caecilia* 10 (Mainz, 1829), pp. 238–9; quoted in Leon Plantinga, *Clementi: His Life and Music* (New York, 1977), p. 65.

of his left hand or bass could be called unique, neatness and delicacy, the most beautiful, most eloquent expression, and a sensitivity that went straight to the heart – these were the qualities of his playing which, with the richness of his invention and his profound knowledge of composition technique, could not help captivating every hearer and raising Mozart to the greatest keyboard player of his age.[84]

The composer/performer has an intimate relationship with his instrument and naturally writes differently in that medium than composers without that special attachment. In the eighteenth century, in the period of the coexistence of different keyboard instruments, the very essence of those instruments was understood best by their own composer/performers. The organ of J. S. Bach, the harpsichord of Domenico Scarlatti, and the clavichord of C. P. E. Bach tell us not only about the spirit of their age, the musical world, and the character and imagination of their composers, but about the life and soul of those instruments as well. In the 1770s, during the early developmental stages of the fortepiano, it was Mozart who immediately understood both the nature and potential of this new instrument and made it the vehicle of his self-expression and performance fantasy. The Viennese *Hammerklavier* became a celebrated concert instrument, the voice of the mature classical language, and, through Mozart's artistry, an instrument of personal expression and brilliant virtuosity.

---

[84] *Leben des k. k. Kapellmeisters Wolfgang Gottlieb Mozart nach Originalquellen beschrieben*, 2nd edn (Prague, 1808), p. 31; quoted in Deutsch, *Biography*, p. 504.

3

MOZART'S TEMPO INDICATIONS AND THE PROBLEMS OF INTERPRETATION

JEAN-PIERRE MARTY

Among all the signs and instructions of traditional musical notation, there are very few that carry unequivocal messages. As a matter of fact, apart from the actual notes the composer prescribes – D (not C or F), or a particular B♭ (not the one at the higher or lower octave) – nearly every element of musical notation requires some kind of interpretation. Consider, for example, the well-known opening phrase of Schubert's Piano Sonata in B♭ major D 960 (ex. 1).

Example 1 Schubert, Sonata in B♭ for piano D 960

To the pianist beginning to learn this sonata only one thing will be certain: the keys that his fingers should depress. Schubert writes *pianissimo*, but this indication refers to the 'global' sound effect: all five parts of the polyphony cannot possibly be performed at exactly the same *pianissimo* level, and it is up to the performer to decide how best to carry out the instruction in the light of the particular musical text. As for the articulation, although Schubert asks for legato, some notes are grouped together under a slur while others are not, and this apparent contradiction will have to be resolved – that is, interpreted. The tempo indicated is Molto moderato: there is, of course, no way to evaluate objectively such an indication. 'Very moderate' is a vague expression which can mean something different to different persons. But, one could object, is there not also another element which the musical notation clearly indicates – namely, the rhythm? Although this would seem clear enough, it is, in fact, by no means unequivocally notated. What kind of artist would assign to the two opening chords exactly the same duration, even though they are identically noted down? Who, in bar 2, would see to it that the quavers are performed exactly twice as fast as the crotchets, as musical theory teaches? By playing them in this way, a pianist would equate Schubert's inner message with its notation. The faithful interpreter of that sonata is the one who most convincingly decrypts all the secret, subtle inflections of Schubert's creative emotions from the abstract script in which the limitations of musical notation guided his pen. Let us always be aware that, if this notational system has proven convenient over the centuries, it is nonetheless rigid and therefore approximate, since its different units are all linked together by two-to-one or three-to-one ratios (or combinations thereof). Human feelings and emotions know no such clear arithmetic, and to reassign to the musical flow the vital ratios and also the spontaneous, irrational elements that are at the root of musical creation, but which no notational system can possibly transcribe – this is the challenge to the interpreter and is, one could say, the very essence of his art.

Igor Stravinsky's definition of music as a poetic organisation of time[1] has won wide acceptance. If the relative importance of the words 'poetic' and 'organisation' varies according to historical periods, styles and individual composers, that the primal characteristic of the art of music is its temporal dimension is beyond question. In fact, one could say that, without an awareness of time as perceived through the aesthetics of music, there is no real music, but merely a succession of sounds (no matter how pleasant). The restitution by the performer of those very elements that musical notation cannot possibly convey appears as the indispensable condition for the particular perception of time through musical flow – a perception that music has a unique power to modulate, in both quantity and quality, in an infinite number of ways. This quantitative and qualitative perception through music has a name, the same in most languages – tempo ('the most difficult and most important, and the main thing in music', in Mozart's own words, written to his father on 24 October 1777). For Mozart, tempo was by no means the mere equivalent of time (in the sense of the German *Takt* or the French *mesure*). In the same sentence, he predicts that Nanette Stein, the young daughter of his friend, the piano manufacturer Johann-Andreas Stein, will never 'obtain' tempo for the reason that she does not play 'in time' (*auf dem Takt*), a problem that he discussed with Mr Stein – he tells his father – 'a good

---

[1] Stravinsky's most commonly quoted definition of music comes, I believe, from his *Poetics of Music* and concerns 'an order between man and time'. I remember Nadia Boulanger telling us of the more precise definition I quote.

two hours'.[2] The distinction made by Mozart between tempo and time, together
with the length of the discussion, encourages us to believe that the issue may
have dealt precisely with the non-equivalence between the abstract notation of
the musical flow by the composer and its 'poetic' rendition, in which the interpreter acts as a catalyst of that mysterious transmutation from time to tempo.
At the very least these important remarks serve to orient our reflections on
Mozart's tempo indications, which were certainly meant to express the tempo as
he saw it – a most difficult, important and central aspect of music – and not
as a pre-metronomic attempt to evaluate musical time in its abstract notation.

Symphonies No. 38 in D ('Prague') K 504 (ex. 2) and No. 39 in E♭ K 543
(ex. 3) both start with adagio introductions. In traditional interpretations, ♩ = 46

Example 2 'Prague' Symphony K 504

Example 3 Symphony No. 39 in E♭ K 543

has served as an average marking for the two introductions, though it is somewhat on the slow side for K 504 and nearly always on the fast side for K 543.
This cannot be right. Although both introductions are indeed marked Adagio,
the former is in 4 (C) and the latter in 2 (₵). C and ₵ were by no means interchangeable in Mozart's mind, as we know from his remarks in a letter to his
father dated 7 June 1783: 'Clementi is a charlatan, as are all Italians: he writes
over a sonata Presto and even Prestissimo and Alla breve and plays it Allegro 4/4.
I know it, as I have heard him.'[3] For Mozart and his contemporaries, metre was
an inseparable part of the tempo indication. Certainly, then, the two introductions should not be performed at similar speeds; the *alla breve* of K 543 should
be faster than the common time of K 504. But the difference goes beyond a

[2] *Mozart: Briefe und Aufzeichnungen*, ed. Wilhelm A. Bauer and Otto Erich Deutsch (Kassel,
   1962–75), vol. 2, p. 83.
[3] *Briefe* vol. 3, p. 272.

simple difference in speed. If only speed were concerned, Mozart might as well have used the **C** metre for K 543 with a tempo indication more suggestive of movement, Andante maestoso, for example. The *alla breve* sign has its own significance, independent from the tempo indication: it promotes the minim to the role of key agent of the tempo, that is to say, of the internal (qualitative) organisation of the musical flow, as well as its quantitative aspect (speed). This implies, in the first place, that each bar is basically grouped into two minim pulsations, though not two even ones, since the second is the less accentuated upbeat and their alternation roughly corresponding to the inhalation-exhalation phenomenon of the respiratory system. This is not to deny the crotchet any organic importance: its pulsation is also perceptible throughout the introduction of K 543 (indeed, the fourth crotchet of the first bar is present in the timpani part). Yet the role of the crotchet in no way obliterates that of the minim, to which it is always secondary. If the fourth crotchet of the first bar is marked, the second is not, and the *piano* in bar 2 starts precisely on the second beat. Consequently, the conductor must see to it that the crotchet pulsation never takes command of the metre. This leads to a particular interpretation of all values: the musical flow in classical music is so regular and so rationally organised that the different values are always perceived within the binary groupings they form with those immediately faster or slower. There are, for example, two ways

for crotchets to be perceived: with reference to either minims – ♩ ♩ ♩ ♩ | ♩ –

or quavers – ♩ ♪ ♩ ♪ ♩ ♪ ♩ ♪ | ♩ ♪ ; these two possibilities are in conflict. The faster

notes first capture our attention, since the ear perceives the faster pulsation more immediately than the slower one. Obviously, then, if in the introduction of K 543 the quavers were performed with specific reference to the crotchets, that is to say, as exactly half their value, they would automatically promote the crotchet pulsation, to the detriment of the fundamental pulse in two. As a result, the *alla breve* indication would be effectively disregarded. Thus, regardless of the speed adopted for the crotchet, the conductor must never emphasise the quaver. An accent on the first demisemiquaver of the descending scales, a strictly arithmetic observance

of the semiquaver rest in the ostinato rhythm ♪♪♪♪♪♪♪♪ | ♪ from bar 9

on, a perfunctory performance by the flute of the motive ♪ ♫ ♪ ♫ between

bars 10 and 14 – any of these would unduly promote the crotchet to the detriment of the minim. To sum up, going beyond the strict observance of the principles of musical notation, the quaver in an *alla breve* is never exactly half of the crotchet, and its actual rendition is determined directly in reference to the minim, over the head, so to speak, of the crotchet. The *alla breve* sign in Mozart's music, in addition to pointing to the fundamental pulsation in two, is also the key to a particular reading of the musical notation. Once the supremacy of the minim pulse is established in performance, clearly this affects the quantitative element of the tempo, namely speed. In the case of the Eb Symphony, a crotchet at 60 implies a minim at 30, that is, one every two seconds. This is indeed a very slow pulse, but its combination in the ear of the listener with the underlying pulse, twice as fast, of the crotchet, will contribute to the perception – adagio – of the musical flow as a whole. If the correct interpretation of all written values is observed in performance, these figures can be taken as bases for all *alla breve* adagios in Mozart's music: the concert aria 'Vorrei spiegarvi' K 418, the Masonic Funeral Music K 477, the 'Mask' trio in *Don Giovanni* and the *Ave Verum* K 618, among many others.

Quite different is the case of the introduction of the 'Prague' Symphony. Its metre is unequivocally 4/4 (**C**), which means that the reference unit in this case is the crotchet, not the minim: any emphasis laid by the conductor on the minim would therefore betray Mozart's intentions. What is the main characteristic of the 4/4 bar? Not so much the fact that it contains four crotchets (so does the **₵** bar); more crucial is the position of the upbeat – on the fourth crotchet, not on the third as in the **₵** bar. The only so-called weak beat in the 4/4 bar is the fourth, the second and third being but temporal extensions of the downbeat. Consequently, the 'breathing rhythm' in a 4/4 bar is quite different from that in **₵** . When we look closely at the beginning of the 'Prague' Symphony we realise that the first note, the unison D, is prolonged until the fourth crotchet, not the third, as is the opening chord of the Eb Symphony, and that the dotted-crotchet rest on that beat represents the first breathing space in the opening bar (in this case, 'breathing' is a word taken literally by the wind players). Most important is the accentuation of the D major arpeggio in bar 3: if the F♯ is performed less strongly than the A, a feeling of *alla breve* will settle in, all the more easily since the second crotchet is absent from the three following bars (motive ♩   ♪ ⁷). In bar 7 (ex. 4), one must resist the temp-

Example 4 'Prague' Symphony, bar 7

tation to perform the rhythmic motive in the second violins, violas, and basses as in *alla breve*: the second beat must be slightly 'marked'. The treatment of this beat has an immediate effect on the character of the phrase in the first violins, the first expressive element in the introduction: in **C** , it would be intensely melodic; in **₵** , merely ornamental, and this for a quite objective reason. We have seen in the *alla breve* of K 543 that the crotchet is identified by its relationship with the minim and that its degree of autonomy is consequently limited. In **C** , on the contrary, the crotchet is the main agent of the tempo and therefore its own master. In this metre the motive in the first violins can be given all its intense and effusive character, since the metre allows us to broaden the third crotchet ever so slightly. In *alla breve* such a liberty is not possible, as it would contradict the metre. The actual duration of the semiquavers would be much closer to the written notation; and the motive would sound like an ornamented suspension. Thus the interpretation of the notated text will differ greatly depending on whether or not the **C** metre is effectively realised. It is obvious that if a crotchet pulsation is firmly established, the crotchet will have to be significantly slower than it would be in *alla breve*, in which the very slow pulse of the minim remains the basic quantitative element of the tempo. M.M. ♩=46, a far cry from the ♩=60 of the *alla breve* adagio, will do greater musical justice to the introduction of the 'Prague' Symphony and to countless other examples of adagio **C** in Mozart's music, such as Konstanze's aria 'Ach, ich liebte', the trial by fire of Tamino and Pamina, and the opening Kyrie of the Requiem.

On the other hand, this marking would never do for many other cases of adagio **C** in Mozart's works: for instance, the second movement of the G major Violin Concerto K 216 (ex. 5). At ♩=46, there would be no way to ensure

Example 5 Concerto in G for violin K 216, second movement

an adagio tempo, for a practical reason. From the start, the crotchet finds itself in constant relationship with the quaver, whose role in the overall shaping of the musical line is in this case essential. As a matter of fact, the initial values of the theme are all quavers, and the quaver pulsation does not cease until the end of the movement. Even though crotchets are also conspicuously present in the musical structure (particularly, from the third bar on, in the harmonic progression), they do not (as in the 'Prague' Symphony) serve as the only reference to all other values; the melodic importance of the quavers in this case is simply too great, and, therefore, so is the listener's perception of their movement. Consequently, an adjustment in the speed of the crotchet is indispensable in achieving an adagio feeling akin to that created at ♩=46 in the 'Prague' Symphony. One can evaluate at about ♩=36 the speed of the crotchet in the Violin Concerto Adagio, the underlying secondary pulse of the quaver at 72 compensating for the slower pace of the main rhythmic value.

There are many examples in Mozart's music of adagio 𝄴 on the models of the second movement of the G major Violin Concerto – all those that do not fit the model of the 'Prague' Symphony. The Adagio in E for Violin and Orchestra K 261 is one; others are the opening of the C minor Piano Fantasy K 475 and Fiordiligi's second aria, 'Per pietà, ben mio, perdona'. Of course, we do not know that Mozart himself was aware of comparative discrepancies in speed among the several works bearing the same tempo indication: without the use of an instrument such as the metronome, he had no way of knowing for certain, and, had he known, he probably would have cared little.

Simply put, his tempo indications applied to the musical flow as a whole, as they resulted from the particular structure of the individual piece, and were not attached to one value in particular, not even the one ostensibly indicated by the metre. All depended on how the musical structure was engineered. This is very likely what Leopold Mozart had in mind when he wrote in his *Violinschule* of 1756 (chap. 1, sect. 2): 'Each melodic piece has at least one phrase, from which one may discern with certainty the sort of movement expressed by the piece. To be sure, it often moves powerfully into its natural movement; whereas, at other times, one must look into it with meticulous attention.'[4] Fiordiligi's second aria offers a good example of the latter. Its beginning (see ex. 6) could well

Example 6 *Così fan tutte*, 'Per pietà, ben mio, perdona'

---

[4] 'Jedes melodisches Stück hat wenigstens einen Satz, aus welchem man die Art der Bewegung, die das Stück erheischet, ganz sicher erkennen kann. Ja, oft treibt es mit Gewalt in seine natürliche Bewegung; wenn man anders mit genauer Achtsamkeit darauf siehet.'

suggest an Adagio of the 'Prague' Symphony type, with the crotchet around 46. Only in bar 8 does the entry of the flutes and horns (ex. 7) reveal without

Example 7 *Così fan tutte*, 'Per pietà, ben mio, perdona'

any doubt the organic role played by the quavers in the musical structure, so that ♩=36 (or thereabouts, with, of course, an intensely felt quaver at 72) proves to be the correct tempo. This type of adagio **C**, with two disparate units contributing jointly to the determination of the tempo, is similar (though the rhythmic values are longer) to the *alla breve* Adagio of the Symphony in E♭ K 543, where the ♩/♩ relationship is essential. This is what I have called a *composite tempo*, in contrast to the Adagio of the 'Prague' Symphony with its *simple tempo*, in which only one unit (in that case the crotchet) acts as a reference to all others.

The two kinds of adagio **C** share one crucial element: the position of the upbeat on the fourth crotchet. This is an extremely important point for performers to bear in mind, for disregarding it will *ipso facto* radically alter the tempo, even if a correct speed is maintained. In the Adagio of the Violin Concerto K 216, there is indeed, as a result of the length of the phrase, the risk that the listener will perceive each 4/4 bar as two 2/4 bars. This perception is unavoidable if the position of the upbeat on the fourth crotchet is not respected: one could hear either ex. 8 or ex. 9. In the first case (ex. 8), one would understand

Example 8 Concerto for violin K 216, Adagio

Example 9 Concerto for violin K 216, Adagio

a 2/4 composite tempo (♩/♪) akin to that of 'Dalla sua pace' in *Don Giovanni*, where the tempo indication is Andantino sostenuto (see ex. 10). In the second case (ex. 9), one would understand a *de facto* simple 4/8 tempo (Mozart and his contemporaries never used 4/8, instead 'disguising' it as 2/4), and, at ♪=72,

Example 10 *Don Giovanni*, 'Dalla sua pace'

it would be the same kind of Andante ma sostenuto as Ilia's aria 'Se il padre perdei' in *Idomeneo* (see ex. 11).

Example 11 *Idomeneo*, 'Se il padre perdei'

We can formulate some conclusions from our survey so far. The same metre and tempo indications used in different musical contexts can lead to radically different speeds; conversely, the same metronome marking can be applied to rather different tempo indications. Speed is clearly only one – and not necessarily the most important – of several elements that lead, in combination, to the establishment of tempo. The other elements include the actual metre (characterised by the position of the upbeat) and the rhythmic structure. All these have implications for the practical rendition of all notated values. Mozart's tempo indications and those of his contemporaries bear equally on all these elements; regrettably, the introduction of the metronome eventually led to the overemphasis of the quantitative element (speed) at the expense of the others. When Beethoven, for instance, indicated ♪=92 for the third movement of his Piano Sonata Op. 106, he certainly did not mean to imply that a quaver at 92 was all that was needed to achieve the tempo Adagio sostenuto 6/8, much less 'appassionato e con molto sentimento'. Adagio sostenuto 6/8 is not synonymous with ♪=92. For Beethoven, too, the tempo indication bore on the musical flow as a whole. In the case of the slow movement of the Op. 106, the tempo was centred on the relationship between quavers and dotted crotchets. He might as well have indicated ♩.=30 – in fact, it would have been less misleading – but such a marking was impossible in view of the limitations of Maelzel's invention (strangely enough, our modern electronic metronomes are still rigidly graduated between 40 and 208!). During the nineteenth century, that purely quantitative element, because it was the only one the metronome could convey and because it inevitably followed the tempo indication proper, obscured in the minds of performers (and even of some composers) the equal importance of the qualitative elements of tempo. In comparison, these elements were very much on Mozart's mind, when he referred to tempo as something both 'important' and 'difficult'.

For difficult it is indeed to differentiate tempos through internal articulation rather than through speed, and it is difficult to convey the same tempo feeling through different means. For example, the distinction between the Largo (𝄵) of the B♭ major Violin Sonata K 454 (ex. 12) and the Adagio (𝄵) of the

Example 12 Sonata in B♭ for violin and piano K 454, Largo

the Violin Concerto K 216 (ex. 13) lies only in the different ways of performing

Example 13 Concerto in G for violin K 216, Adagio

the crotchet-quaver couple, for the marking ♩ = 36 appears justified in both cases. If, in the sonata, the semiquaver of the rhythm ♪.♩♪ is played for the full duration written, the quaver begins to assert itself as a subsidiary agent of the tempo – all the more if, as is often the case, the anacrusis that closes the bar is played too expressively. Consequently, the following rhythmic pattern will

suggest to the listener an underlying quaver pulse,

which, combined with the basic crotchet pulsation, will create an adagio feeling akin to that in the concerto. The only way to avoid this – and thus to respect Mozart's tempo indication – is to concentrate on the majestic pace of the crotchet by interpreting all other values in relation to it. In practical terms – and everything is practical when it comes to the actual rendition of tempo – the first semiquaver must be shorter than written, the anacrusis light, and the rhythmic pattern of bar 2 fluid. In this way no secondary, faster pulse becomes established and the progress of the musical flow is not only slow (adagio), but broad (largo).

A somewhat different kind of challenge is offered by the tempo indication, Andante 𝄵, for the quartet 'Non ti fidar' in *Don Giovanni* (ex. 14)

Example 14 *Don Giovanni*, 'Non ti fidar'

and for Donna Anna's aria 'Or sai chi l'onore', which immediately follows it
(ex. 15). The two pieces could not possibly be performed at similar speeds. We

Example 15 *Don Giovanni*, 'Or sai chi l'onore'

have already seen in the case of the 'Prague' Symphony and the Violin Concerto
K 216 that the same tempo indication (adagio **C**) suggests signficantly different speeds for the same metrical unit, because of the different roles played
by the quaver. In the case of andante **¢** , the problem is different, since it is the
crotchet-minim relationship that is at the heart of the qualitative aspect of
the tempo. The difference lies inside that relationship – more precisely, in the
quantitative aspect of each unit. In the quartet, the crotchet is from the start
entrusted – as far as the speed is concerned – with the determination of the
andante tempo, without undermining the reality of the *alla breve* bar (in two,
with the upbeat on the third crotchet). In the aria, it is the minim that plays
this role, with the crotchet adding an extra element of motion. Therefore, the
speed of the concerned values cannot be the same in both cases, since in the one
it is a 'fast' value that first captures our attention, whereas in the second it is a
'slow' one. All of Mozart's **¢** andantes follow one of these two models. Similar
to the quartet, for example, we find the concert aria 'Per pietà, non ricercate';
Tamino's aria 'Wie stark ist nicht dein Zauberton'; and the Tuba mirum of
the Requiem; and like the aria, the theme-and-variations finale of the D major
Piano Sonata K 284; the concert aria 'Nehmt meinen Dank'; the opening duet
of *Figaro*, Act III, 'Crudel, perchè finora'; and the Overture to *Così fan tutte*.
But, of course, in the end all these examples depend on how the crotchet/minim
relationship is executed in performance. The respective weight of each unit is
necessarily different in each group: heavier in the first and lighter in the second,
without ever affecting the basic minim pulse with its characteristic upbeat on
the third crotchet. All this presents rather subtle problems of interpretation,

and explains why, of all Mozart's tempo indications, andante ¢ is probably the most misunderstood and misinterpreted.

Once again we are reminded that the interpretation of the notated values is the principal key to our understanding Mozart's tempo indications. How does a conductor, entrusted with a performance of *Le nozze di Figaro*, mark the differences between the tempos of the opening duet, 'Cinque, dieci' (Allegro C ; ex. 16); the opening duet of Act III, 'Crudel, perchè finora' (Andante ¢ ; ex. 17); and the Count's aria 'Vedrò mentr'io sospiro' (Allegro maestoso ¢ ; ex. 18)?

Example 16 *Le nozze di Figaro*, 'Cinque, dieci'

Example 17 *Le nozze di Figaro*, 'Crudel, perchè finora'

Example 18 *Le nozze di Figaro*, 'Vedrò mentr'io sospiro'

Certainly not through differences in speed. If differences exist, they are too small to justify three tempo indications, since all three pieces could be performed convincingly at *c.* ♩=126. In each case, a particular reading of the written values creates a specific tempo feeling, even if the overall speeds are practically identical. How, at the same ♩=126, can the tempo be Allegro C in the opening duet and Allegro maestoso ¢ in the Count's aria? In the duet, the second crotchet is noticeably asserted, while the fourth remains the lighter upbeat. The quavers are assigned a melodic importance from bar 8 on (ex. 19), and their actual dura-

Example 19 *Le nozze di Figaro*, 'Cinque, dieci'

tion tends to be longer than the written notation. In the aria, by contrast, their role is quite secondary and their duration on the shorter side; the second crotchet remains in the background so that, as a consequence, the minim emerges as a secondary pulse, which, at 63, will create the sense of maestoso. In the duet from Act III, the same minim at the same 63 becomes the dominant element of the tempo, while the underlying crotchet pulse of 126 provides the extra motion to justify the indication Andante. One could readily cite other examples in which similar values are differently interpreted according to differing tempo indications. Thus, the fugue (Andante maestoso $\mathbf{C}$) of the Piano Fantasy in C major K 394 (ex. 20) and the Adagio $\mathbf{\mathfrak{C}}$ of the Fantasy in D minor K 397 (ex. 21) should both be performed at c. $\mathbf{J}$ =60; but, while in the former the quaver

Example 20 Fantasy in C for piano K 394, fugue

Example 21 Fantasy in D minor for piano K 397, Adagio

is assigned an organic role, in the latter this role is undertaken by the minim. Monostatos's first entrance in *Die Zauberflöte* is marked Molto Allegro $\mathbf{C}$ (ex. 22); his return at the end of the act, only Allegro (ex. 23). But if the quaver is not

Example 22 *Die Zauberflöte*, 'Du feines Taübchen'

Example 23 *Die Zauberflöte*, 'Na stolzer Jüngling'

strongly enough asserted in the first case and is overemphasised in the second, the tempo indications will effectively be reversed, should the crotchet be taken at c.168 in both cases. The real significance of such indications as Andantino,

Larghetto and Allegretto – the subject of so many controversies – lies outside the pure domain of speed. Why is 'Dove sono' in *Le nozze di Figaro* marked Andantino 2/4 and the opening duet of the Act I finale of *Così fan tutte*, 'Ah che tutto in un momento', an Andante 2/4? Which should be the faster? A difficult question to answer and, in any event, totally beside the point. For in the former the Andantino is the consequence of a particular articulation of the quaver with the crotchet in a nostalgic sway, while in the latter the movement of the quaver alone establishes the Andante tempo. In the manuscript of Zarastro's second aria, 'In diesen heil'gen Hallen', the first tempo indication, Andantino sostenuto (2/4), is crossed out and replaced by Larghetto. No change in metronome marking could ever translate this into reality. Only through a change in the crotchet/quaver relationship can the modification be carried out, so that the somewhat 'going' (andantino) quaver gives way to a somewhat 'broad' (larghetto) crotchet. As for Allegretto, its main characteristic lies in the light rendition of the shorter value in relation to the longer one. Whether the main unit is the short or the long value will affect the speed, not the tempo: at ♩. = 50, Don Giovanni's serenade is as much an Allegretto as Despina's aria 'Di pasta simile' is at 72. Mozart's 6/8 Allegrettos are almost evenly split between these two models. But if the dotted crotchet/quaver relationship is not correctly interpreted, the Allegretto tempo is vitiated, regardless of the speed. Similarly, it is the particular relationship of the crotchet to the minim which, before any question of speed, insures that the *alla turca* of the Piano Sonata in A major K 330 and Guglielmo's aria 'Donne mie' are performed allegretto (2/4) and not allegro (more or less) moderato.

To sum up, it is only through an exhaustive examination of the entire musical texture in each case that the correct interpretation of the notated values in Mozart can be determined and thus the tempo indications faithfully followed. This is quite apart from questions of speed. Before anything else must come recognition of the essential characteristic of the metre: the position of the upbeat. We have seen how in the slow movement of the Violin Concerto K 216 the tempo is decisively altered by merely displacing the upbeat. We have also seen that this distinction determines the difference between 𝄴 and 𝄵. The same principle is, of course, equally valid in the case of ternary metres. For example, not observing the upbeat in 6/8 essentially converts each 6/8 bar into two 3/8 bars, thereby fundamentally affecting the tempo. The finales of the Piano Sonata in F major K 280 (ex. 24) and the B♭ Piano Concerto K 456 (ex. 25) suggest a dotted crotchet at *c.* 100, though the first is marked Presto and the second only Allegro vivace. The pulsation of the dotted crotchet is much more vividly perceived if each of them is evenly accentuated, as in 3/8, than it is if the accent falls on alternate ones, as in 6/8 – in short, the perception of tempo is not the same. But occasionally, the metrical indication

Example 24 Sonata in F for piano K 280, finale

Example 25 Concerto in B♭ for piano K 456, finale

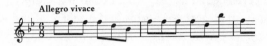

warrants further scrutiny. In the second movements of the 'Haffner' Symphony K 385 (Andante 2/4), the Symphony in E♭ K 543 (Andante con moto 2/4), and the 'Jupiter' Symphony K 551 (Andante cantabile 3/4), it is the quaver, not the crotchet (even as secondary pulse), that sets the tempo. It is very important to bear in mind that Mozart never used 4/8, and 6/8 always implies a ternary ratio: dotted crotchet to quaver. This is very important to bear in mind since 2/4 is never the equivalent of 2/2 (¢), nor is 4/8 the equivalent of 4/4, or 3/8 of 3/4, because each of the three values Mozart used as metrical units – the minim (¢, 3/2, 4/2), the crotchet (C, 3/4, 2/4) and the quaver (3/8, 6/8, disguised' 4/8 and 'binary' 6/8) – is endowed with a specific character or, more precisely, a specific weight, from the heaviest (minim) to the lightest (quaver). This explains why, when he rewrote in 2/4 the finale of the B♭ String Quartet K 458 (the 'Hunt'), which he had first sketched in C, he changed to a mere Allegro assai the original Prestissimo indication. No other value is ever used as a metrical unit (for instance, there is no 12/16, as in Bach), nor does any other value play a central role in determining the tempo, not even as a secondary pulse. To assign to the semiquaver in 3/8 or '4/8' the role played by the quaver in some 3/4 and 4/4 metres is a mistake. The determination of the principal tempo values is inseparable from our comprehension of the real metre: the actual rendition of the notated values is totally dependent on their role in the musical structure and on their relationship to the key unit(s) of the metre. The three examples quoted above from *Le nozze di Figaro* illustrate this point. Quite apart from the speed suggested by the tempo indication, quavers (for instance) should not be rendered the same way in C as in ¢.

We may now begin to understand Mozart's judgment of Miss Stein ('She will never obtain tempo') and his diagnosis ('because she did not play in time'). The understanding of tempo as Mozart saw it goes hand in hand with a particular rendition of the written text. Each tempo indication (inseparable from the metre, whether patent or disguised) suggests to the performer those slight deviations, those particular *interpretations* that restore to a lifeless script the vital realities of musical creation. But clearly no deviation can ever be perceived except in reference to an order. In the case of music, this order is 'time', namely, a coherent and constant ensemble of ratios that links all musical values together. To establish the foundation of such an order is the performer's first duty. 'Playing in time' is the indispensable groundwork without which the vital, but irrational, realities of tempo can neither be translated nor experienced. The dialectic of time and tempo, the paradox of a living order emerging from an abstract one, is at the centre of the art of the interpreter, entrusted, in Mozart's own words, with 'the most important thing in music'. Everyone knows that the harmonious rhythm of the Parthenon is the result of imperceptible deviations from the strict laws of symmetry. Translated into musical terms, this rhythm is called tempo, and it is a rhythm not in the hands of the creator, but in those of the interpreter. This immense responsibility enjoins us to reflect thoroughly on the link between creation and interpretation and involves, as well, considerations of a rather technical nature. More than likely, it must have been at the heart of the discussion between Mozart and Stein *père*, and, if such was the case, we may well understand how that conversation lasted 'a good two hours'.

Our discussions of Mozart's tempo indications led us to conclusions concerning a much broader field than Mozart's own œuvre. In the first place, these tempos were part of a common language, almost a code, which was shared by all eighteenth-century composers and, concomitantly, understood by all experienced performers. Thus, for example, the remarks made above about the special significance of the Allegretto indication (the relative lightness of the short value when articulated with the longer one) apply equally to the music of Mozart, Johann Christian Bach and Joseph Haydn (see exx. 26–8). In Haydn's *Pauken* Mass the difference between the Largo of the Kyrie (ex. 29) and the Adagio of the

Example 26 Sonata in D for piano K 576, finale

Example 27 J. C. Bach, Piano Concerto Op. 7 No. 3

Example 28 Joseph Haydn, 'Nelson' Mass, Benedictus

Example 29 Joseph Haydn, *Pauken* Mass, Kyrie

Sanctus (ex. 30) is of the same nature as the difference noted between K 454 and K 216. The two types of andante ¢ discussed earlier are present in Gluck, as well: see Orfeo's Act III aria (ex. 31) and the following trio (ex. 32). Both differ significantly from the Andante C of the Act II ballet (ex. 33). Of course, each com-

Example 30 Joseph Haydn, *Pauken* Mass, Sanctus

Example 31 C. W. Gluck, *Orfeo*, 'J'ai perdu mon Eurydice'

Example 32 C. W. Gluck, *Orfeo*, Act III trio

Example 33 C. W. Gluck, *Orfeo*, Act II ballet

poser used the common language according to his own personality. Some metrical indications are found in the works of one composer, but not in those of another. Largo ¢ and Lento ¢ , for instance, are found in Haydn, but not in Mozart (who, incidentally, never wrote anything in 9/8). But it is certain that they shared a common idea of tempo, an idea that transcended the mere question of speed. The invention of the metronome at the beginning of the nineteenth century represented a distinct setback for both the comprehension and the expression of tempo, which was now reduced to its purely quantitative element. This reduction had two major consequences: eighteenth-century tempo indications ceased to be understood; and metre lost its central role in the expression of tempo, so that composers were deprived of an essential element for conveying the expression of their musical message. For example, Schumann prescribed for the first movement of his Piano Concerto Allegro affetuoso C (♩ = 84); Allegro ¢ would be a more accurate indication. The tempo of the second movement, Andantino grazioso 2/4 (♪ =120), seems meaningless and certainly does not apply to the main theme. Andante 2/4 (♩ / ♪) is probably what Mozart would have indicated (as in 'Là ci darem la mano'); thus described, the movement becomes comprehensible. As for the finale, its bouncy and fleeting character would be better expressed by a simple Allegro 3/8 than by Allegro vivace 3/4 (♩· =72). In a similar way, the abandonment of ¢ for slow movements represented a great loss for the expression of tempo. César Franck used the rather obscure expression Molto moderato quasi lento for the beginning of his Piano Quintet (ex. 34), and Puccini designated Andantino C (♩ =56) for the entrance of Tosca in Act I (ex. 35). In both cases

Example 34 César Franck, Quintet for piano and strings

Example 35 Giacomo Puccini, *Tosca*, Act I

Adagio ¢ would have perfectly expressed the real tempo. Finally, had Schubert, in his great B♭ major Piano Sonata, used the same system of tempo indications as did Mozart, the inner message of the music would have come across unequivocally.

We cannot be really sure that Molto moderato **C** expresses precisely what Schubert had in mind. With Mozart, however, there would have been no doubt, for he would probably have indicated Allegro (or Allegretto) moderato **C** or Andante moderato **₵**; in either case the role of the musical values would have been clearly indicated, as would the relationships linking them together, relationships that lie, as we have seen, at the very heart of the problem of interpretation.

To understand Mozart's tempo indications leads us to reassess the relationship between creation and interpretation. The increased liberty taken by the performer in interpreting the written text in the course of the nineteenth century (and well into the twentieth) was very much linked to the decline of the true expression of tempo on the part of composers and the inadequacy of metronome markings as a substitute. At a time when a respect for the composer's intention (as evidenced by the search for the 'Urtext') has come to be the performer's first concern, a study of eighteenth-century tempo indications, so masterfully applied by Mozart, helps to restore to the noble word 'interpretation' some of its original scope and meaning.

4

ON THE PROBLEM OF CADENZAS IN MOZART'S VIOLIN CONCERTOS

EDUARD MELKUS
(translated by Tim Burris)

The cadenza in the eighteenth-century instrumental concerto was generally a product of improvisation. But the tendency to write out cadenzas appears to have been established rather early, in response to the increasing demands of virtuosity and the need for cadenzas to have definite contents. We may perceive a comparable development in the case of free ornamentation, which, originally improvised, was increasingly 'validated' from the beginning of the eighteenth century by means of specific notation.

A similar situation obtained in the case of the numerous cadenzas Mozart wrote for his own piano concertos. Evidently these cadenzas were designed primarily for pupils, that is, young amateurs; the master himself certainly improvised cadenzas when he performed his concertos. We can only regret deeply that none of Mozart's cadenzas for his solo violin and wind concertos survive. The only exceptions are the *Concertantes* for violin and viola (K 364) and for four winds (K 297b); here we shall pass over the debate concerning the authenticity of the latter.

In his excellent thesis 'Etude ou Caprice' (Munich, 1967), Dimitris Themelis has elucidated the development and the various forms of the classical cadenza. A primary source for this treatment is the comprehensive *Violinschule* by Pierre Baillot (Mainz, 1830). In this work three types of cadenzas are distinguished: (1) simple *fermate*, which involve chiefly free passagework introduced above a six-four chord; these correspond to old vocal cadenzas, which, at least in theory, were intended to last no longer than one breath; (2) the solo cadenza, which borrows thematic material from the movement; and (3) the accompanied cadenza, which is *de facto* integrated within the movement. (As an example of this third type Baillot cites the last movement of Viotti's Violin Concerto op. 22.)

In addition there is the capriccio, which comprised a longer, virtually self-contained whole that did not have to be inextricably joined to the thematic material of the movement. Often placed between movements, the capriccio functioned much like a fantasia. The cadenza (or final solo episode) in the first movement of J. S. Bach's Fifth Brandenburg Concerto and the 'Capriccii' in Locatelli's

Twelve Violin Concertos Op. 3 represent early examples of the large thematic type of cadenza which was expanded à *la capriccio*.

As a rule, Mozart's surviving cadenzas are far less prolix. Without exception they belong to the first or second category above. As an example of a non-thematic cadenza for two instruments, one could point to the cadenza in the third movement of the Violin Sonata in D major K 306.

Eva and Paul Badura-Skoda's book *Mozart-Interpretation* (Vienna, 1957; English trans. *Interpreting Mozart on the Keyboard*, London, 1961) provides an excellent summary, analysis, and guide to the process of creating stylistically fitting cadenzas (*Nachkomponieren*). Though their book was primarily designed for keyboard players, the authors provide many valuable suggestions which are most useful to the modern violinist and which essentially can be transferred to that instrument.

OPENING OF THE CADENZA

Thematic beginning

Preferably the main theme of the movement or the orchestral motive just preceding the fermata is employed. A theme from the middle of the movement is seldom used. In slow movement cadenzas, entirely new themes may sometimes appear. Almost without exception, the thematic beginnings give way to virtuoso passagework, in which a further reworking of material derived from the concerto movement occurs, though in new and different harmonic contexts.

Virtuoso beginning

For the most part this type is also drawn from the concerto movement; the material is seldom freely produced.

Considered as a group, cadenza openings represent the 'composing out' of the dominant harmony. Remarkably, the themes quoted in Mozart's cadenzas are always presented in the tonic. If the cadenza *begins* thematically, the quotation most often appears over a six-four chord on the tonic. If, however, the theme first enters in the middle section of the cadenza, it appears in its original form. First-movement themes are rarely quoted in their original version; most often they are reinstated in the six-four chord position, as a rule without the bass note for the first two bars, so that the harmony at first is only latently discernible.

MIDDLE SECTION OF THE CADENZA

When themes are quoted in the middle section of the cadenza, some sort of pattern usually obtains. Typically, a motivic fragment undergoes an unexpected sequential treatment and is often rhythmically condensed or subjected to diminution before the arrival of the cadence.

CLOSE OF THE CADENZA

In this section Mozart does not limit himself to a particular pattern. As a rule, he notates several virtuoso runs, partially with small note heads. Although the conclusions of the cadenzas for the Salzburg concertos are conspicuously short, Mozart's later cadenza endings are often extended and enriched with thematic material. Quotation of a new motive in the tonic is typically followed by moving again towards the six-four chord. The closing trill is usually very simple.

Those desiring to write stylistically correct cadenzas should acquaint themselves thoroughly with the harmonic and modulatory intricacies of the particular concerto. Mozart's diatonic passages are much easier to imitate than his sometimes highly involved chromatic runs and enharmonic transformations.

We have already established that in his cadenzas Mozart seldom moves far afield from the tonic. Even in cadenzas where there is considerable modulation, he always returns after a few bars to the tonic or a related key. This principle holds true even for his most daring harmonic turns involving major and minor triads, major and minor seventh chords (and all their inversions), chords of the dominant, and diminished triads.

Giuseppe Tartini's suggestions for the 'artful cadenza'[1] would seem to affirm the same principle; indeed, Tartini's most elaborate cadenza scheme consists only of I–V^7–V^7–I–IV–V–I.[2] Finally, in Daniel Gottlob Türk's *Clavierschule* (1789), we read the following about cadenzas:

2. Like any arbitrary ornament, the cadenza must not consist of so many intentionally introduced difficulties, but rather of passages that fit the principal character of the composition.
3. Cadenzas must not be too long, especially in pieces of a sad character. Unduly long cadenzas lasting several minutes [are] in no way excusable.
4. In no case should one explore tonal areas left untouched by the composer. This rule, it seems to me, is based upon the law preserving the unity of a work of art.
9. Moreover, every cadenza, including those already drafted, written out, or memorized, must be executed as if it were a *fantasia* that has just been invented during the actual performance.[3]

[1] *Traité des agrément[s] de la musique* (Paris, 1777), ed. Erwin Jacobi (Celle, 1961), p. 117.
[2] Themelis, 'Etude ou Caprice', p. 63.
[3] *Clavierschule, oder Anweisung zum Clavierspielen für Lehrer und Lernende* (Leipzig and Halle, 1789; repr. 1967), pp. 310–12:
2. Muss die Kadenz, so wie jede willkürliche Verzierung, nicht so wohl aus geflissentlich

What is the situation in the violin literature with regard to cadenzas? To begin with, let us consider their length. In filling out a distinct portion of the overall length of the movement, the cadenza performs a certain architectonic function. On this point Mozart demonstrates a remarkable consistency. Of the thirty-six cadenzas examined, nineteen (more than half) occupy from one eighth to one twelfth of the length of the movement, and eight from one sixth to one seventh, while only two are substantially longer (one fourth to one fifth of the movement's length); two are shorter (one thirteenth to one fifteenth) and two are very short (one twentieth to one twenty-third). In contrast, the length of the standard 'modern' cadenza for a violin concerto typically ranges from one third to one fifth of the length of the respective movement!

What is more, Mozart's preferred architectonic structure is often not followed by modern performers; all too frequently the thematic citations seem to chase one another about, creating the effect of a potpourri. (Mozart, on the other hand, quotes only short fragments and rarely employs more than three motives.) Sometimes the quotations are artificially worked out against countersubjects and/or are harmonically overburdened.

The narrow tonal confines of the Mozart models, where there really is no issue of a substantial modulation away from the tonic, are frequently ignored in today's performances. All of the familiar modern violin cadenzas modulate, and, indeed, most of them quite extensively. Most often now the themes are cited in rather distant keys, and the technical difficulty of the cadenza far surpasses that of the concerto movement itself. All of this reveals the neglect of another characteristic of classical models – namely, their uninterrupted progress, which actually achieves an end with few rhetorical pauses. Fermatas followed by metrically free passages are not often encountered in Mozart's cadenzas, though modern violinists employ them frequently, with the result that the accumulation of technical difficulties creates an unclassical congestion of conflicting tempi. There are exceptions, of course, such as the cadenzas by Paul Badura-Skoda for the concertos K 216, 218

angebrachten Schwierigkeiten, als vielmehr aus solchen Sätzen bestehen, welche [. . .] dem Hauptcharakter des Tonstückes, angemessen sind. 3. Die Kadenzen dürfen, besonders in Tonstücken, welche den Charakter der Traurigkeit u.s.w. haben, nicht zu lang seyn. Die ungeheuer langen Kadenzen, welche mehrere Minuten dauern [sind] keineswegs zu entschuldigen. 4. Auf keinen Fall sollte man in Töne ausweichen, worein der Komponist in dem Tonstück selbst nicht ausgewichen ist. Diese Regel gründet sich, wie mich dünkt, auf das Gesetz der Einheit eines Kunstwerkes. 9. Übrigens muss jede Kadenz, folglich auch eine bereits vorher entworfene und aufgeschriebene oder auswendig gelernte, so vorgetragen werden, als wäre es eine Fantasie, die nur erst während der Ausführung selbst erfunden würde.

and 219,[4] or those by Ernst Hess for K 219.[5] In these cases, all the appropriate stylistic criteria are ideally fulfilled with very few exceptions. But unfortunately from the standpoint of modern violin technique, these cadenzas are much less attractive than the older violin cadenzas of the romantics.

Let us consider three collections of didactic cadenzas from the classical period. The following examples from Ignaz Schweigl, Luigi Borghi, and Ferdinand Kauer have been selected on the basis of their keys, which are compatible with the keys of Mozart's violin concertos. They should not be viewed as ideal solutions for writing cadenzas; rather, they should be regarded as exercises that may encourage violinists to invent additional examples for their own use. First, let us consider two examples from Ignaz Schweigl's *Grundlage der Violine* (Vienna, 1786). *Fermata in G major* (ex. 1): this cadenza moves between the tonic and dominant, with a brief extension to the subdominant. (The first fermata seems to issue a formal invitation for us to insert a passage; here a thematic quotation can be introduced.)

Example 1 Ignaz Schweigl, Cadenza in G major

If this example were used as a cadenza to K 216, a passage such as that shown in ex. 2 could be added at the fermata in 'bar' 9.

Example 2 Insertion for Schweigl's Cadenza in G major (for use in Mozart's K 216)

⁴ Vienna, Doblinger, 1961.
⁵ Kassel, Bärenreiter.

Fermata in B♭ major (ex. 3): here the harmonic skeleton includes the tonic, secondary dominant, dominant, and tonic. The content of this cadenza is somewhat richer than that of the first example: 'bar' 1 reveals a thematic beginning, and the repetitions of motives in 'bars' 6–7 show similar points of thematic departure. In each passage, thematic quotations from the preceding movement can be inserted. Also, the fermata sign can be expanded by additional passagework, as in ex. 4.

Example 3 Ignaz Schweigl, Cadenza in B♭ major

Example 4 Insertion for Schweigl's Cadenza in B♭ major (for use in Mozart's K 208)

(a)

(b)

Next, we present four examples from Luigi Borghi, *Sixty Four Cadences or Solos* Op. 11 (London, *c.* 1790). On the whole, these cadenzas are somewhat more fully developed. Cadenza No. 5 (ex. 5) contains in 'bars' 6–7 a motive that could well be a quotation from a movement. After 'bar' 5 there is again room for expansion.

Example 5 Luigi Borghi, Cadenza No. 5 in D major

Examples 6 and 7 offer some cadenza insertions for K 218 or K 211. (By using several thematic quotations one may easily expand the insertion.)

Example 6 Insertions for Borghi's Cadenza in D major (for use in Mozart's K 218)

(a)

(b)

(c)

Example 7 Insertions for Borghi's Cadenza in D major (for use in Mozart's K 211)

(a)

(b)

Ex. 7 (*cont.*)

(c)

bar 6, *a* + bar 6, or *b* + bar 6 follows

As an example of a cadenza for a slow movement, let us consider Borghi's No. 13 in E major (ex. 8). 'Bars' 1–4 and 5 could suggest motivic allusions. Between 'bars' 4 and 5 an addition might be possible (see ex. 9). 'Bar' 6, by way of exception, is about one quarter too short.

Example 8 Luigi Borghi, Cadenza No. 13 in E major

Example 9 Insertion for Borghi's Cadenza in E major (for use in Mozart's K 261)

bar 5 follows,
doppio movimento

bar 5 follows

bar 5 or *a* follows

In Cadenza No. 32 in B♭ major (ex. 10) we find, aside from the tonic, only one modulation, to the supertonic. A motivic formation occurs at 'bars' 1–3 and 9, and a possibility for further expansion, after 'bar' 11 (see ex. 11).

Example 10 Luigi Borghi, Cadenza No. 32 in B♭ major

Example 11 Insertion for Borghi's Cadenza in B♭ major (for use in Mozart's K 208)

(a)

Ex. 11 (*cont.*)

(b)

(c)

(d)

Finally, exx. 12 and 13 present yet another cadenza in G major (No. 23) with suggested insertions for its use in K 216, first movement.

Example 12 Luigi Borghi, Cadenza No. 23 in G major

Example 13 Insertion for Borghi's Cadenza in G major (for use in Mozart's K 216)

Still lengthier cadenzas appear in Ferdinand Kauer's *Scuola prattica overa 40 Fantasia und 40 Fermaten* (Vienna, end of the eighteenth century). In No. 23, in G major, the actual cadenza begins at the fermata. From that point on there are no bar lines; nevertheless, most of the cadenza can be played quasi *a tempo*. As the suggested division in ex. 14 indicates, two 4/4 'bars' are followed by four 5/4 'bars'; after the demisemiquaver run and quaver ascent, a strict 4/4 metre is observed until the end. As in the earlier examples, here, too, we observe the simplest of harmonic progressions and discover opportunities for insertions.

Example 14 Ferdinand Kauer, Cadenza No. 23 in G major

The two G-major cadenzas by Schweigl and Borghi (exx. 1 and 12) can be inserted here at ⊕ or ✱.

Now let us compare these simple, didactic cadenzas with Mozart's own well-known piano cadenzas (see ex. 15). First we shall consider the early cadenzas, which are approximately contemporary with the violin concertos. Our first example is the cadenza for the Piano Concerto in D major K 175, of 1773 (K 624, No. 2, *Neue Mozart Ausgabe*). The overall plan of this cadenza remains harmonically simple; indeed, only in measures 6–8 is it enriched with passing harmonies and chromaticisms. Bars 15–18 contain the only thematic quotation (see further the transcription for solo violin in ex. 16). In the cadenza for the second movement of the same concerto (K 624, No. 2), the modulation to E♭ major at bars 3–4 is really only a deployment of the Neapolitan sixth. Nowhere does this key become stabilised; as a result, its subdominant function remains clearly recognisable. Two thematic quotations occur at bars 1–2 and 8–9 (readers are referred to the transcription for violin solo below in ex. 17).

In the third cadenza, for the first movement of the Piano Concerto in E♭ major K 271, we again encounter a harmonic expansion by means of the Neapolitan sixth. But despite the behaviour of the 'foreign' harmonies, a proper modulation is never confirmed; rather, Mozart returns to the tonic. In this cadenza we find two thematic citations (bars 1–9 and 17–20), both of which are in the tonic.

Now let us ponder some practical applications: How can we employ cadenzas from these examples in Mozart's violin concertos? Are the cadenzas from Mozart's piano concertos indeed suitable for adaptation in the violin concertos? In this connection, we may first summarise three general rules:

(1) *Avoid passages that are too pianistic* (including rapid and long chromatic passages, arpeggios that are too broad, and broken-octave passages that are too rapid for the violin).
(2) *Shorten or condense passages* (this results almost by default on account of the comparatively limited range of the violin; in addition, an excessive expansion of passages into the upper register should be avoided).
(3) *Simplify passagework* (piano passagework tends to be much more 'chatty' than its counterpart on the violin, a circumstance resulting from idiosyncrasies of the two instruments).

For some examples of simplification, see ex. 15.

Example 15 Passages from Mozart's piano cadenzas transcribed for violin

(a) from No. 3 (K 271)

(b) from No. 7 (K 414)

(c) from No. 23 (K 453)

Ex. 15 (*cont.*)

(d) from No. 7 (K 414)

(e) from No. 19 (K 450)

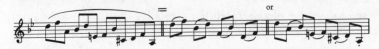

Keeping in mind these rules, one can transcribe the first cadenza from K 175 as in ex. 16, inserting thematic quotations from the Violin Concertos K 211 and 218, respectively.

Example 16 Mozart's piano cadenza for K 175, first movement, transcribed for violin

Ex. 16 (*cont.*)

The second cadenza for K 175 can be adapted to the slow movement of K 211, if we take into account the quicker movement of this Andante (see ex. 17).

Example 17 Mozart's piano cadenza for K 175, second movement, transcribed for use in K 211

Example 18 is a transcription for violin of one of the cadenzas from the Piano Concerto K 414 with thematic borrowings from the Violin Concerto K 219. This cadenza is roughly the same length as the models by Borghi and Kauer discussed above.

Example 18 Mozart's piano cadenza for K 414, first movement, transcribed for use in K 219

Ex. 18 (*cont.*)

Violinists should be encouraged to devise their own cadenzas accordingly, and in so doing give evidence of their own personality and understanding of style. Unfortunately, in practice this does not often happen. Neither the engaging virtuoso cadenzas of the great violinists, nor the stylistically correct cadenzas of many insightful contemporary performers are acceptable. In competitions and examinations, a certain repertory of cadenzas is expected, often even demanded, of students – for example, San Franko's cadenza for K 216 and Joachim's cadenza for K 219. The stylistic flaws of these cadenzas are manifest, despite all their musical and violinistic beauty; however, employing appropriate articulation and playing these passages in a proper Mozartean style could render a considerable improvement.

In the case of the San Franko and Joachim cadenzas, one may do well to produce a shortened version, as shown in exx. 19 and 20. The advantage of this solution is evident: the violinist cannot be accused of trying to evade completely the particular difficulties of these cadenzas by opting for a different cadenza. On the other hand, this solution is imperfect, for the very flaws occasioned by the demanding technical difficulties of the San Franko and Joachim cadenzas and the damage done to the concertos by their all-too-frequent quotation of thematic material remain.

Example 19 Joseph Joachim, cadenza to Mozart's K 219

Ex. 19 (*cont.*)

Example 20 Suggested revision of Joachim's cadenza

Finally, let us consider two more unusual cases. The first is Fritz Kreisler's cadenza to the rondo of the *Haffnerserenade* (K 250). Example 21 shows how much can be changed by articulating, shortening, and eliminating the chromaticism. The second concerns the problem of creating a cadenza for the third

Example 21 Fritz Kreisler, cadenza for the rondo of the *Haffnerserenade* K 250 and suggested revisions

(a) Kreisler   (b)   (c)

Ex. 21 (cont.)

movement of the Violin Concerto in D major K 218. In the autograph, Mozart gives d'''' as the goal of the solo violin. This close on the tonic is extremely unusual for Mozart, but it is found regularly in the concertos of Tartini and his school, where the cadenza makes a full close *before* the final tutti enters. Ex. 22 offers an attempt at a solution, based upon a passage – crossed out in Mozart's autograph – before the cadence.

Example 22 Suggested cadenza for Mozart's Violin Concerto in D major K 218, finale

Ex. 22 (*cont.*)

In conclusion, the observations of Pietro Tosi summarise the special challenge of designing and executing cadenzas:

Whoever carefully reflects upon what has been said will realize that it is not really possible to prescribe universal and good cadenzas; just as it is impossible for someone to commit witty ideas to memory. The one and the other are partly brought forth and determined by the circumstances and the occasion. Through diligent reading and observation of the witty ideas of others, however, one can awaken, sharpen and improve his own wit; in like fashion, instructed by reason, he can also come to control that wit.[6]

---

[6] Pietro F. Tosi, *Anleitung zur Singkunst*, ed. and trans. J. F. Agricola (Berlin, 1757), p. 205:

> Wer das bisher gesagte genau überlegt, wird einsehen, dass es nicht wohl möglich ist, allgemeine gute Cadenzen vorzuschreiben; so wenig als es möglich ist, jemanden witzige Einfälle vorher auswendig zu lehren. Denn eins und das andere wird durch die Umstände und die Gelegenheit theils hervor gebracht, theils bestimmt. Durch fleissiges Lesen und Beobachten der witzigen Einfälle anderer aber, kann einer seinen eigenen Witz erwecken, schärfen und verbessern; so wie er ihn durch die Vorschriften der Vernunft in Ordnung halten kann.

5

A NEW LOOK AT MOZART'S PROSODIC APPOGGIATURA

FREDERICK NEUMANN

Le appoggiature,
Se non son scritte,
Sono arbitrarie
E sol dipendono
Dal proprio gusto.

Antonio Salieri

In my book *Ornamentation and Improvisation in Mozart* (Princeton, 1986, hereafter *Ornamentation*) I have discussed the problem of the many instances where the addition, by the singer, of an unwritten vocal appoggiatura was probably intended, as well as instances where it probably was not (see chapters 12 and 13). In the vast majority of cases these additions occur in the recitative where a longstanding convention allowed the singer, on feminine endings that are written with note repetition ♩♩, to raise the first accented syllable through an added appoggiatura ♩♩, more rarely ♩♩. Such insertion was a licence, not an obligation.

This appoggiatura reflected the prosodic accent on the penultimate syllable of a feminine ending; hence it is occasionally referred to as a 'prosodic appoggiatura'. In the setting of a falling third ♩♩♩, the insertion was presumably very frequent because it produced a smoother line that often made good declamatory and musical sense. It was probably frequent too in a simple stepwise descent ♩♩♩, whereas after an upward leap the tendency to add an appoggiatura was lessened because the leap itself lent emphasis to the accented syllable and thereby could sufficiently reflect the prosodic accent. Yet many times, even for a descending third, the appoggiatura was out of place. Since the latter has a rounding, softening effect, such an appoggiatura was inappropriate where the meaning of the words called for force not gentleness, or for angularity not roundness.

To give a simple example, suppose that the words 'I love you' and 'I hate you' were notated in a recitative with note repetition after a falling third: ♩ ♩ ♩ I love you / I hate you . Certainly the appoggiatura is a requirement for the first sentence – ♩ ♩ ♩ I love you – with a musical declamation of maybe ♩ ♩ ♩ .

The second sentence will elicit an entirely different diction: as opposed to the caressing legato smoothness of 'I love you' there is harshness and a sharply accented angularity in 'I hate you' that is much more fittingly reflected by the drop of a third and note repetition – ♩ ♩ ♩ I hate you – with a likely musical declamation of ♪ ♩ ♪ ♪ .

The convention of the added appoggiatura spilled over into arias, and less frequently into other set pieces such as duets or larger ensembles. In these 'closed' numbers the appoggiatura assumed a different function as a result of the contrasting nature of aria and recitative. The recitative is purely rhetorical and in its pitch design follows closely the declamatory pattern of elevated prose in the *accompagnato*, or fast conversational exchanges in the *semplice* (or *secco*). In recitative, accordingly, the prosodic appoggiatura as a pure reflection of the prosodic accent, which in Italian and German normally involves raising and strengthening of the voice, had to be from above. 'Normally', because in fast informal speech the accent often disappears and with it the need for an appoggiatura. Since Mozart wrote out all downward *leaping* appoggiaturas either with symbols or in regular notes, the unwritten, inserted appoggiatura in recitative had to be a stepwise descending one.

The aria, by contrast, is purely lyrical, and is set to poetry. Its link to declamation is far looser and by and large limited to the need of having accented syllables fall on strong beats and having the melody respond to word meaning. But other than that the melodic impulse was sovereign; it did not have to follow the rise or fall of the spoken words and could take fancy flights extending over many bars on a single vowel, fully emancipating itself from any link with declamation. Thus the emphasis on accented syllables could be expressed in rising as well as falling appoggiaturas or in any kind of melisma of any length or design. The rising appoggiatura, being non-prosodic, has no place in recitative. In arias it can be very expressive, perhaps because it is a pure melodic inflection, not a declamatory one.

The need for additional appoggiaturas was far less frequent in arias of Mozart's mature operas, because he wrote out so many of them – both falling and rising – in regular notes, whereas only very occasionally did he write out appoggiaturas – and then only falling ones – in recitative.[1] Furthermore, there are in arias relatively more instances than in recitative where note repetition on feminine endings was meant to be sung as written.

Crutchfield's challenge

These ideas which I set forth in *Ornamentation* have been recently contested by Will Crutchfield in the *Journal of the American Musicological Society*.[2] It is my conviction that his essay arrives at wrong conclusions that, if adopted, would do great damage to many a Mozartean melody in arias and many a phrase in recitative. For this reason, I felt it necessary to take a close look at Crutchfield's theories, evidence and reasoning.

Briefly, Crutchfield's thesis is that any feminine line ending as well as most such endings in mid-line – all those that are followed by either a rest or a punctuation mark – *must* have an appoggiatura 'of some kind'. It can be falling, it can be rising, it can even be ornamented with florid inserts, but – and this is the crux – a note repetition on such endings is strictly prohibited. It was 'not considered an option' (p. 270). And furthermore, this strict law is to apply to arias as well as to recitative. Astonishingly, Crutchfield sees no difference between arias and recitative and criticises editors who assign them to different categories (pp. 236–7). He allows for a 'grey area' of ambivalence only for very brief 'rhythmic cells' in mid-line. Other than in that 'grey area', Mozart is denied freedom of musical thought, denied the right of desiring note repetition on feminine endings. This, I submit, is *prima facie* highly suspect, because the idea of such thought control contradicts every tenet of aestheticism, even if we did not have to do with a unique genius.[3]

---

[1] In one aria alone (Cherubino's 'Non sò più cosa son') there are no fewer than seventeen written-out appoggiaturas on feminine endings, whereas in all of *Don Giovanni* there may be no more than three or four such spelled-out appoggiaturas in recitative.

[2] 'The Prosodic Appoggiatura in the Music of Mozart and His Contemporaries', *JAMS* 42 (1989), 229–74. Unless otherwise stated, page references will be to this article.

[3] Four hundred years ago, Lodovico Zacconi, in his famous *Prattica di musica* (Venice, 1592), castigated a strikingly similar attempt at thought control on the part of unnamed theorists who had tried to outlaw binary/ternary conflicts. Zacconi writes (Bk. 3, chap. 73, fol. 183ᵛ): 'If we consider the great potentialities of music and the vast jurisdiction of the composers in arranging and using the musical materials ['la spaciosa iurisdittione che hanno i compositori nel disporre & adoperar le figure Musicali'] . . . everybody can judge for himself, if he is not out of his mind ['se non è privo di mente'] that . . . [binary/ternary conflicts] make no unpleasant effect, but a very satisfying one that gives great delight.' How amazingly these words fit our issue!

Surely there were at the time certain rules of counterpoint, such as the pro-
hibition of clearly audible parallel fifths or octaves. Composers generally abided
by the rule until past the mid-nineteenth century because they found parallels
ugly and offensive. This certainly is the only valid motive for an artistic pro-
hibition of any kind. But nobody has ever said that note repetition on feminine
endings is ugly. Crutchfield disallows it, not for aesthetic reasons, but because
he believes he has found convincing evidence that the appoggiatura was considered 'indispensable for feminine endings'. At the same time he admits that it
was considered 'low in purely musical importance, dispensable without a second
thought upon translation or transcription' (249). To put Mozart into a musical
straightjacket is incredible enough; to do so in a matter of low musical importance
borders on the fantastic.

The power of note repetition

Note repetition is an age-old means of reflecting insistence, determination, con-
stancy, solemnity, imperiousness, heroic resolve and similar states of mind. The
same suggestive power can invest note repetition on a feminine ending with dramatic force where an appoggiatura, so often connected with feelings of warmth
and tenderness ('appoggiatura sigh'), would emasculate the proper expression.
Often purely musical reasons will call for note repetition. Of numberless instances
I can offer here only a small sampling.

Consider in *Don Giovanni* the spine-chilling pronouncement of the Commendatore's statue with its severe note repetitions (ex. 1a); in the first finale of the same
opera (bars 516–18), Donna Anna's exclamation 'Traditore', which upon repetition is taken up in unison (and octaves) by Zerlina, Donna Elvira, Don Ottavio
and Masetto (ex. 1b). For practical reasons alone we cannot imagine that all
five singers would have spontaneously added the identical appoggiatura. For the
same singers see also bars 525–6, 'tutto, tutto'; bars 546–47, 'scellerato!'; bars
549–550, '. . . in mondo intero' (where the rising and falling scale passage has
to land on the principal note C); and bars 571–73, '. . . della vendetta', among
several others in this number alone.

For one more example of high drama from Mozart see the solemnity of the
oracle in *Idomeneo* (III, 28, 'Ha vinto amore') with no less than twelve note
repetitions on feminine endings. These and many similar cases are impervious
to the intrusion of appoggiaturas.

Example 1 *Don Giovanni*
(a) Act II, scene 1

Ex. 1 (*cont.*)

(b) Act I, finale

Yet Mozart's note repetitions are by no means limited to the expression of forcefulness and drama. Often he uses them with wonderful effect in humorous situations: in Bartolo's 'La vendetta' (e.g. 'coll' arguzia', 'col criterio', and the patter of 'si potrebbe, coll'astuzia', etc., all supported by the accompanying figurations); many times also in Leporello's 'Madamina', of which just one instance is shown in ex. 2a, where the marvellous surprise modulation to B♭ would be ruined by an appoggiatura; incontrovertibly in the case of the Terzetto of *Così fan tutte* (I, 2), where Don Alfonso jokingly compares women's fidelity to the myth of the Arabian phoenix. Here the numerous feminine note repetitions are confirmed by the unison violins, as shown in ex. 2b (just a few of the many instances in this number).

Example 2

(a) *Don Giovanni*, Act I, scene 4

(b) *Così fan tutte*, Act I, scene 2

There are of course countless passages in instrumental music that attest to the dramatic force of note repetition. Take for instance their impressive use in Beethoven's *Egmont* Overture, depicting the brutality of the Spanish oppressors (first in bars 82–3, later insistently repeated from bar 259 on). The point cannot be made that we have no words and no prosodic accents; the point is that if such passages demonstrate the power of note repetition on feminine endings, it makes no sense to deny such power to vocal composers.

Returning to vocal music, we find revealing illustrations for the power of note repetitions in Verdi and Puccini. Whereas Puccini was so fond of repetitions that he used them ubiquitously in all kinds of situations, Verdi tellingly exploited their dramatic potential. In *Rigoletto*, at a time when the appoggiatura convention was still alive, Verdi writes for the recitative of Rigoletto and Sparafucile 'Senza le solite appoggiature'. In this dialogue the professional killer and his client discuss how to dispose of the intended corpse. The grimness of the spooky scene is enhanced by the absence of softening appoggiaturas.

As Crutchfield acknowledged in correspondence with me, the later Verdi (at the latest from *Aida* on), wrote his feminine endings the way he wanted them sung. And here we have numerous eloquent illustrations. For example, *Otello* is filled with note repetitions next to written-out appoggiaturas. In a first-act recitative, Iago sings as given in ex. 3a. Of the three note repetitions in this brief passage the third is most interesting: after the fall of a third, the repetition on 'Moro' expresses his hatred of Otello much more graphically than would an inserted appoggiatura. Striking examples are in the duet at the end of Act II where Otello and Iago swear vengeance. Note repetition occurs in Otello's threefold wild outcry for blood: 'sangue' followed by the solemn pledge of vengeance with its threatening note repetition shown in ex. 3b and the phrase in ex. 3c with the powerful ending on 'tremendo'.

Example 3 Verdi, *Otello*

(a) Act I

M'a - scol - ta   ben - chè fin - ga d'a - mar - lo   O - dio quel Mo - ro

(b) Act II

Molto sostenuto

Sì, per ciel   mar - mo - reo giu - ro

(c) Act II

D'i - ra e d'im - - - pe - to   tre - men - do

Considering that Verdi used note repetitions to such music-dramatic advantage, are we seriously to believe that Mozart lacked the imagination to think of such design with its inherent power? Take, for example, Donna Anna's 'Or sai chi l'onore' (ex. 4a), which, as a call for vengeance, is related dramatically to Otello's outburst. I submit that the imperious tone of her summons is far more powerfully conveyed by note repetitions on 'onore' and 'traditore' than by the appoggiaturas that Crutchfield demands as a matter of course. Similarly, Donna Elvira's fury in her first aria (I, 3) is far more suggestively rendered by note repetition on 'l'empio' and 'scempio' (ex. 4b) than by appoggiaturas. In *Così fan tutte*, Fiordiligi's proclamation of 'rocklike' steadfastness would be weakened by appoggiaturas. (For more examples see *Ornamentation*, pp. 213–214.)

Example 4 *Don Giovanni*
(a) Act I, scene 10

(b) Act I, scene 3

Salieri's testimony

In chapters 12 and 13 of *Ornamentation* I made, I trust, a strong case for the selective insertion of the unwritten appoggiatura according to the meaning of the words. A hitherto overlooked piece of evidence to strengthen further the case is at hand in a statement by Salieri (from which the above motto is taken), the man to whom Beethoven, Schubert and a host of other eminent masters and famous singers turned for the study of the Italian vocal style. In default of an explanation by Mozart himself on the nature of the appoggiatura, there can be no more authoritative opinion than the one by his chief rival.

Salieri wrote in 1816 a *Scuola di Canto in versi/e i versi in musica a 4 voci/il tutto composto da me Ant. Salieri.*[4] He wrote it in order to introduce German youth

---

[4] MS in the library of the Gesellschaft der Musikfreunde in Vienna, shelfmark 915. Rudolph Angermüller had intended to publish an annotated version, which apparently has not come out so far. My quotes are from an article by Angermüller: 'Antonio Salieri und seine "Scuola di Canto"', in *Beethoven Studien: Festgabe der Oesterreichischen Akademie der Wissenschaften zum 200. Geburtstage von Ludwig van Beethoven* (Vienna, 1970), pp. 37–50.

('la gioventù tedesca') to the Italian singing style. The treatise is unique among theoretical writings in being in verse set to simple music. It was a pedagogical device to help with the learning and retaining of the rules. One of its several canons is devoted to the recitative. Here is the complete text:

Cio che si chiama Recitativo	(The so-called Recitative
Ha le sue Regole	has its own,
Ma un poco oscure.	if somewhat obscure, rules.
Quello che devesi	But what one
però sapere	needs to know
Si è che di raro	is that it is rarely
Si canta in tempo,	sung in tempo;
Che non la Nota,	that not the note[s],
Mà la parola,	but the word[s],
Dà il movimento.	set its pace.
Oltre di questo	Apart from that
Le appoggiature,	the appoggiaturas,
Se non son scritte,	when not written,
Sono arbitrarie	are arbitrary
E sol dipendono	and [their addition] is solely
Dal proprio gusto.	a matter of the proper taste.)

A substantial part of Crutchfield's article tries to invalidate evidence presented in my book, some of which is hardly less clear than Salieri's, and all of which points to variability in lieu of rigidity. I shall therefore first address Crutchfield's repeated efforts to negate contrary evidence.

Most of the theorists who explain the insertion of an appoggiatura for the accented syllable of a feminine ending make it clear that such insertion happens sometimes, or often, or mostly, but not always; such limitations alone contradict Crutchfield's law. Thus, for instance, Telemann says such a substitution is done 'from time to time' (*hin und wieder*); Johann Friedrich Agricola, speaking of an inserted appoggiatura between the notes of a falling third, has it done 'occasionally' (*zuweilen*); Johann Adam Hiller says an appoggiatura 'may' (*kann*) be used for falling thirds, as well as for the last of three or four ascending seconds; Johann Carl Friedrich Rellstab points out that in recitative the appoggiaturas are not written out but left to the judgment of the singers, then lists many instances where he prefers note repetition; Johann Baptist Lasser has the insert made 'most of the time' (*meistens*), and Johann Friedrich Schubert limits the appoggiatura to 'every so often' (*öfters*).[5]

---

[5] Telemann, *Der harmonische Gottesdienst* (Hamburg, 1725–6), Preface; Agricola, *Anleitung zur Singkunst* (Berlin, 1757), p. 154; Hiller, *Anweisung zum musikalisch-richtigen Gesange* (Leipzig, 1774), p. 202; Rellstab, *Versuch über die Vereinigung der musikalischen und oratorischen Declamation*

Crutchfield tries to deny the restrictive meaning of these various adverbs or adverbial expressions by referring to their 'putatively limiting force' (p. 255). Yet there is nothing putative about the limiting force of *may* (*kann*) as opposed to *must* (*muss*), of *sometimes* or *occasionally* or *from time to time*, or even *mostly*, as opposed to always (*immer*). There is no rational way of denying the categorical differences between the limited and the unlimited.

Agricola

Crutchfield does see a problem with Agricola when the latter writes, 'Occasionally (*zuweilen*) on the drop of a third onto a strong beat one inserts an appoggiatura from one step above . . .' (Agricola, p. 154). Crutchfield comments, 'It cannot be right to read *zuweilen* as a limiter here' (p. 257). Not only can it be right, but there is no other way to read it that does not do violence to the meaning of the word. Crutchfield's rendering of *zuweilen* as 'customary' (p. 256) is a mistranslation. Later in the same passage, Agricola again uses the word *zuweilen* in an interesting statement that also contradicts Crutchfield's principle. Agricola writes (p. 154), 'Occasionally on note repetition one may insert an actual mordent between the accented note and the following one' (the 'mordent' is in fact a miniature trill). He illustrates this statement with a passage containing four feminine line endings. This of course, is the *locus classicus* for Crutchfield's obligatory appoggiaturas, but Agricola shows instead the execution all four times with note repetition, with a miniature trill inserted at the end of the accented note (see ex. 5 for the last two of the four). No stretch of the imagination can mistake the miniature trill for an appoggiatura of any kind or fail to see and hear the note repetition.

Example 5 Agricola, *Anleitung zur Singkunst* (1757)

(Berlin, 1786 or 1787), pp. 47–8; Lasser, *Vollständige Anleitung zur Singkunst* (Munich, 1798), p. 160; Schubert, *Neue Singschule* (Leipzig, 1804), p. 145.

Rellstab

Rellstab, after saying that appoggiaturas in recitative are a matter of the singer's judgment, adds that 'in the theatre, a singer who knows what action means will add few if any appoggiaturas, and even in church or chamber . . . I prefer the even rendition (platte Ausführung).' He illustrates the latter – [♩ ♩ ♩ ♩] *Mit Freu - den* – as the one he often prefers to [♩ ♩ ♩ ♩] *Mit Freu - den* with the appoggiatura insert (his page 48).

Unable to deny this testimony, Crutchfield first tries to belittle it: quoting a dictionary, he writes that *platt* also means *dull, untutored, flat, low, vulgar,* and *North German* (p. 259).[6] This semantic excursion is pointless since Rellstab explained by his illustration that the meaning of his term was note repetition. He did not imply that the latter was untutored or vulgar.

Crutchfield then continues in the same vein with disingenuous reporting. Rellstab, he writes, 'uses the *Vorschlag* notation, which the singer "naturally" executes as . . . [♩ ♩♩ ♩ *Mit Freu - den*]. He then gives an example of a recitative by Graun; the appoggiaturas are not notated by the composer; by now we are not surprised to find that they have been added at every feminine line ending by Rellstab' (p. 259). This is a misrepresentation; Rellstab has not in the end turned witness for Crutchfield's law. After stating his frequent preference for note repetition, Rellstab discusses recent attempts by composers to specify any desired insertion of appoggiaturas. He prefers for this purpose the use of the little note, for which he shows the just-mentioned 'natural' execution. It is a 'natural' execution only when the appoggiatura is specified by the little note, *not* otherwise.

Moreover, Rellstab does *not* give an example of a recitative by Graun where appoggiaturas are added at every line ending. What he gives are five unconnected examples of cadences (four feminine, one masculine) taken, minus the words, from various unnamed Graun recitatives. Since they illustrate the use of the little note, each one of the examples of course has such a note. This demonstration, contrary to Crutchfield's implication ('by now we are not surprised'), neither weakens nor cancels Rellstab's stated preferences for note repetition.

---

6 The direct meaning of *platt* is *even, level, flat* (as in 'a flat surface'). Anyone who needs to consult a dictionary for a translation does well to consider first the direct meaning of a word before sampling the figurative, colloquial and slang meanings. In picking one of the latter because it better serves one's purpose, one risks absurd mistranslations.

Marpurg

In *Ornamentation* I quoted a lengthy serialised essay by Friedrich Wilhelm Marpurg on the recitative,[7] in which he criticises the notation of the feminine cadence with the falling fourth on the beat as ♩ 𝅘𝅥 𝅘𝅥 instead of ♩ 𝅘𝅥 𝅗𝅥 , as it is sung. He says: 'This notation is unquestionably reprehensible because one ought not naturally and without good cause write differently from the way one sings', since in doing so one confuses the singers. I added, and Crutchfield quotes me (p. 257), 'From this principle alone we can infer that when Marpurg writes repeated pitches, he means it, and his many examples contain numerous pitch repetitions. He is even more explicit on the matter when, in speaking of half-cadences (*schwebenden Absätzen*), he lists as one of their alternatives an execution with the repeated pitch' (*mit dem wiederholten Einklange* [n. 22]).

Crutchfield answers that 'it is a considerable leap to take a recommendation that the final cadence (falling fourth) be notated as sung. . . and to extrapolate from it an *unstated* recommendation about the falling second'. And regarding the note repetition in half cadences, he claims that the 'repeated pitch' refers to notation, not to execution.

Crutchfield is wrong on both points. The extrapolation involves no leap, only a logical step. Marpurg's statement, that one must write the way one wants it sung or else one confuses the singers, was made apropos the cadence with the falling fourth, but it was pronounced as a *general* principle that needed no restatement for the falling second. It makes little sense to interpret the passage to mean that while it is wrong to write ♩ 𝅘𝅥 𝅘𝅥 because it was meant to be sung differently, it is proper to write ♩ 𝅘𝅥 𝅘𝅥 though it too was meant to be sung differently. Had Marpurg wanted to exempt the falling second from his just stated principle he certainly would have had to say so, but he did not.

As to the half cadences, Marpurg refers *not* to notation but to execution: he writes that the half cadences 'may be done either with a single note [referring to a masculine ending] or with repeated pitch, or with the leap of a third, a fourth or a fifth' (*sowohl mit einer einzigen Note, oder dem wiederholten Einklange, als mit einem Terzen- Quarten- oder Quintensprunge geschehen können* [emphasis mine]). *Geschehen können* refers to a happening, a realisation, hence to execution.

On p. 358 Marpurg shows ten feminine cadences, all written with note repetition (the first of these is shown in ex. 6), whereupon he says, 'if one wishes to

---

[7] *Kritische Briefe über die Tonkunst* (Berlin, 1762), vol. 2, pt. 3.

change [these formulas] into masculine ones, one leaves out the last note of the voice' (*Wenn man sie männlich haben will, so wird die letzte Singnote weggelassen*). To do so is possible only when the penultimate note is repeated, not when it is an appoggiatura! With Marpurg, too, Crutchfield fails in his attempt to dispose of an undesirable body of contrary evidence.

Example 6 Marpurg, *Kritische Briefe über die Tonkunst* (1762)

Mancini

In *Ornamentation* I quoted a passage from Giambattista Mancini that rivals in importance Salieri's statement. Mancini, a castrato singer who became voice teacher for the Vienna imperial court and achieved international fame as a pedagogue, wrote at the threshold of the classical era the most important vocal treatise of that period.[8] In it he stresses the declamatory character of the recitative and emphasises the importance of the 'valuable appoggiatura' performed *one tone higher*. It was used primarily when two syllables of the same word are written on the same pitch (Mancini, pp. 237–9). For the issue at hand, the important statement refers to an aria where he says that exclamations of invective, great fervour of action, or the great passion invested in words like *tiranno*, *crudele*, or *spietato* would be weakened, indeed denatured, by an added appoggiatura. Inasmuch as arias are far more independent than recitative from declamatory intonation patterns, this statement has to apply *a fortiori* to recitative as well.

Other writers also refer to the softening effect of an appoggiatura, which should be avoided where such an effect is uncalled for. Among them is Daniel Gottlob Türk, who, speaking of instrumental music, lists defiant (*trotzige*) and sharply articulated passages among the contexts in which appoggiaturas do not fit well. In a footnote he adds, 'when an idea is to be rendered defiantly. . . appoggiaturas would be improper because they impart a certain smoothness to the melody that is unfitting for such occasions'.[9]

[8] *Pensieri e riflessioni prattiche sopra il canto figurato* (Vienna, 1774). The references here are to the revised and enlarged third edition, *Riflessioni prattiche sul canto figurato* (Milan, 1777).

[9] *Klavierschule*, 1789 edn, pp. 205–6.

The above-mentioned Lasser, one of Crutchfield's four chief theoretical witnesses, says, 'All those notes that according to the composer's intention should be rendered with seriousness and a certain rigidity, such as e.g. the word *Funeste*, do not suffer the addition of appoggiaturas'.[10]

Crutchfield gives short shrift to Mancini's important principle by arguing that the 'passage comes from a discussion of the role of ornamentation in arias . . . and perforce applies to ornamental appoggiaturas of the kind we see so abundantly in Mozart's and everyone else's ornamented arias. It is a plausible admonition but it has nothing to do with the present question' (p. 260). Mancini's principle, far from having 'nothing to do with the present question', strikes at its very heart. Words like *tiranno, crudele*, or *spietato* in violent exclamation have a prosodic accent whose power is intensified by the vehemence of utterance. They have feminine endings, and occur, if not at line endings, then certainly followed by 'a rest, a punctuation mark or obvious break' – Crutchfield's own words for a situation that, he argues, demands a prosodic appoggiatura. When Mancini says that one must *not* insert an appoggiatura in these circumstances, he squarely contradicts Crutchfield's theorem. Where that passage comes from, and what is or what is not discussed in the same paragraph is irrelevant: what matters is the meaning of the passage and that meaning could not be any clearer. It does not – let alone 'perforce' – apply to 'ornamental appoggiaturas' that 'abound' in Mozart's ornamented arias. It cannot possibly apply to them since 'ornamental appoggiaturas' in 'ornamented arias' can only 'abound' when they are either written out or marked by symbol, whereas Mancini's statement applies only to *unwritten* appoggiaturas that may or may not be added on note repetitions. Nobody would suggest that an appoggiatura specified by Mozart should be omitted!

That, as Crutchfield points out, Mozart, in his ornamented version of a childhood aria from *Lucio Silla* set the word *crudele* to an ornamented appoggiatura (260) is no proof against Mancini's principle: the word occurs not as defiant exclamation but in a sentimental vow of a proscribed senator to his fiancée that he will always be with her in spirit if 'cruel fate' ('il fato crudele') should deal him death. *This* surely 'has nothing to do' with the violent, or hateful, or belligerent outcries Mancini had in mind whose dramatic impact must not be 'denatured' by the softening effect of an appoggiatura.

As to Türk's passage, Crutchfield predictably tries to dispose of it by saying that it bears no resemblance to the feminine line endings of vocal music. That is

[10] *Singkunst*, p. 132. 'Alle jene Noten, welche nach dem Sinne des Componisten ernsthaft, und in gewissem Verstande steif vorgetragen werden sollen, leiden keine Vorschläge, z. B das Wort "Funeste".'

true but is not the point. The point is that *no* appoggiatura is appropriate for harsh, defiant, or violent dramatic situations, *wherever* they occur.

Crutchfield tries to parry any references to word meanings and dramatic context with the thesis that the prosodic appoggiatura has nothing to do with expression or drama. 'The idea that the prosodic appoggiatura is an expressive tool or an element of word painting . . . is clearly the result of a misunderstanding' (p. 270). It is, so it would appear, only a mechanical formula automatically inserted when Crutchfield's conditions are met. To sustain this extraordinary thesis Crutchfield erects an artificial wall between the 'prosodic appoggiatura' and the 'ornamental appoggiatura', each belonging to a separate category and having nothing in common with the other.

The wall is pure fiction, and Crutchfield admits that 'in sources specifying performance practices of the Classical period . . . no explicit distinction was drawn between the two [categories]'. He makes this distinction because he finds it 'useful for unraveling the appoggiatura question today' (p. 229). Yet this distinction is an arbitrary construct; its 'usefulness' consists in referring contrary evidence to the other side of the wall.

The prosodic appoggiatura is not a category of its own but a subspecies of the generic 'ornamental' appoggiatura when the latter is used as a musical reflection of the prosodic accent. Their relationship is that of a part to the whole, not that between two alien categories. When instruments reinforce a prosodic appoggiatura, it turns purely 'ornamental'; surely, there is no wall between the voice and the shadowing instruments. As a subspecies, the prosodic type shares all the characteristics of the generic appoggiatura, such as its enrichment of harmony and melody, its rounding, softening, expressive effect.

The idea that the prosodic appoggiatura has no link to expression is *prima facie* wrong. Since in the declamation of prose or poetry accent and word melody vary widely according to the underlying affect and emotion, the prosodic appoggiatura, as a reflection of the declamatory accent, must similarly heed affect and emotion and therewith become an 'expressive tool'.

As to the expressive potential of the prosodic appoggiatura, let us look at the Countess's cavatina in *Le nozze di Figaro*. When three times she sings 'o mi rendi il mio tesoro', the feminine ending written with note repetition (the last of which is given in ex. 7), an appoggiatura on 'te-SO-ro' is needed, not because that syllable is accented and should therefore be mechanically raised, but because the word is imbued with intense fervour that summons the expressive warmth of an appoggiatura; it would be rendered with a related nuance of rhythm, dynamics, and intonation in a poetic reading. And of course, at the very beginning there is the written-out prosodic appoggiatura on the masculine ending of 'Porgi a-MOR' with its similar intensity of feeling.

Example 7 *Le nozze di Figaro*, Act II, scene 1

Neumann

Crutchfield quotes my example from 'Popoli di Tessaglia' (K 300b [316]) shown in ex. 8a, and my comment that here 'in addition to the grimness of the word *funesto* the orthography of A♯ and A♮, following closely the high B♭, definitely precludes an appoggiatura. The latter would even theoretically be feasible only if Mozart had written a B♭ instead of A♯, since the solution given [in ex. 8b] is irrational' (p. 262). I reindorse this statement and am glad that in the meantime I have discovered, as mentioned, that Lasser, one of Crutchfield's four chief witnesses, happened to pick the very word *funeste* as one that does not suffer the addition of an appoggiatura. Lasser confirms Mancini's principle.

Crutchfield argues that on looking at the harmony, the correct reading is that shown in ex. 8c. Quite apart from the affect of the word, the very harmony supports the literal reading, not Crutchfield's 'correct' solution. The oboe and the violins move from a sustained A♯ to A♮ on the downbeat and with it strongly suggest the identical progression of the voice; the result is the poignant note repetition. Crutchfield's 'correct' solution not only denatures the effect but blurs the harmonic progression.

Crutchfield tries to justify his solution by referring to a passage in *Don Giovanni*, given in ex. 8d, with Don Ottavio singing 'Ti parla il caro amante'. He asserts that this passage is identical in voice leading and closely related in harmony to the one at issue. That simply is not so. The harmony is totally different, and, as to voice leading, just the last four notes would be similar *only* if we accept Crutchfield's 'correct' solution, which we must not do. Most importantly, the meaning of the words is diametrically opposed. Compare 'questo spettacolo funesto' with 'Ti parla il caro amante'. Could it be that Crutchfield considers word meaning to be irrelevant in Mozart's recitative? The very attempt to equate these two passages and to infer the appoggiatura on *funesto* from the spelled-out *amante* is incomprehensible, not to speak of the fact that Mozart's 'appoggiatura' is not an appoggiatura, as it falls on a consonance and 'resolves' to a dissonance. However we look at it, the comparison is fallacious.

Example 8
(a) 'Popoli di Tessaglia' K 316 (300b)   (b)

(d) *Don Giovanni*, Act II, scene 1, 'Porgi amor'

Gluck

Finally, a signally important case of ignored contrary evidence concerns Gluck. In *Ornamentation* I presented the two passages from *Orfeo* shown in ex. 9. They contain three cases of feminine endings written with note repetition where by a singular stroke of luck Gluck makes it clear beyond any possible doubt that he did not wish the insertion of appoggiaturas: they are followed in each case by an instrumental 'echo' that involves the whole violin section in addition to two chalumeaux.[11]

Example 9 Gluck, *Orfeo*, Act I, scene 1

---

[11] Crutchfield's statement that 'the editors of the new Gluck edition show an appoggiatura both for Orfeo and for the echoing instruments on both "Euridice" and "dove sei"' (bars 263–4) is misleading. The new edition *confirms the text* I had cited from the old one. The appoggiaturas are editorial suggestions that are incompatible with Gluck's text.

These examples are doubly important. First they prove, in what may be one of the few such indubitable pieces of evidence, that a great master of that era, certainly some of the time, and maybe most of the time, did not wish any appoggiaturas added that he did not spell out. Second, because they discredit the testimony of Corri, another of Crutchfield's four principal witnesses, for his theorem, since Corri, in illustrating other Gluck recitatives from *Orfeo*, shows appoggiaturas on every single case of note repetition. Crutchfield answers by writing, 'It is a slender indictment on which to dismiss so copious and specific a body of evidence, and even at that it is far from clear' (p. 263). Far from being slender and unclear, the evidence is massive, incontrovertible and crystal clear. That Corri's examples are 'copious and specific' does not guarantee their value: quantity is irrelevant when the quality is in question.

Crutchfield further tries to downgrade this evidence by referring to improvisation by orchestral players and wishfully invokes a scenario where the singer would make the appoggiatura and 'the players . . . could have listened to Orfeo and followed his execution' (p. 264). He finds that 'perfectly credible'. Though I find it perfectly incredible, inasmuch as the whole violin section is involved, it really does not matter. It is immaterial what one or the other player in the orchestra may have done; what matters is only what the composer had in mind. To bolster his case, Crutchfield refers the reader in footnote 28 to an article by Spitzer and Zaslaw[12] as if this article supported his idea. It fails to do so: while it chronicles the widespread use of orchestral improvisation in the eighteenth century, it also records the unanimous rejection of this practice by the leading composers. When Crutchfield critically quotes me as saying that 'improvisation . . . has no place in orchestral or choral performance', Spitzer and Zaslaw bear me out for the orchestra, and, as to a chorus, Salieri in paragraph 2 of his *Scuola di canto* writes, 'Whoever sings in a chorus must sing only what is written and has never the right to add ornaments'.[13]

Crutchfield's evidence

First, Crutchfield quotes four theorists 'who are close to Mozart chronologically': Johann Adam Hiller, Domenico Corri, Johann Baptist Lasser, and Gesualdo Lanza. Second, he refers to two of Mozart's youthful arias (one of them only incompletely preserved) and to one by J. C. Bach, to which Mozart spelled out ornamental additions. Third, he presents a number of transcriptions and

[12] John Spitzer and Neal Zaslaw, 'Improvised Ornamentation in Eighteenth-Century Orchestras', *JAMS* 39 (1988), 524–77.

[13] Angermüller, 'Antonio Salieri' (see note 4 above), p. 44.

arrangements of operas, mostly for piano, some for string quartet, etc., dating from the early part of the nineteenth century. In addition to these three main bodies of evidence there are scattered references to excerpts from other composers or theorists. But the core of his argument resides in the three listed groups.

He uses the inductive method of enumerating cases that agree with his ideas, then generalises them into an all-encompassing law. Four hundred years ago Francis Bacon articulated the danger of the inductive method: 'The induction which proceeds by simple enumeration is childish; its conclusions are precarious, and exposed to peril from one contradictory instance; and generally it decides on too small a number of facts, and on those only which are at hand.'[14] As we shall see, Crutchfield's induction suffers because the cases are ambiguous and the witnesses unreliable; more than one contradictory instance has already been detailed.

The four theorists

Hiller, the first of the four above-mentioned 'period theorists' is a dubious witness for Mozart. His sample recitative (presented by Crutchfield in his ex. 2) has far too many ornaments, among them several *Anschläge* ( ) that were foreign to Mozart's usage. We can gather from a letter Mozart wrote to his father on 12 November 1778 that he wanted the recitative rendered with an almost austere simplicity. After reporting on a melodrama he had just heard, he writes, 'one ought to treat most opera recitatives in such a manner [spoken as in melodrama] and sing them only from time to time, when the words can be well expressed in music' (*wenn die Wörter gut in der Musik auszudrücken sind*).) Hiller's lavish free ornamentation of arias is also at odds with Mozart's preference.[15]

But quite apart from his doubtful qualification, Hiller fails to confirm Crutchfield's thesis by writing that on descending thirds the skipped pitch 'may (*kann*) be linked to the following pitch as an appoggiatura' (Hiller, p. 202). He adds that an appoggiatura from above 'may be' employed for the last of three or four ascending seconds. Crutchfield misrepresents the statement by reporting the option as '*is*' instead of 'may be' employed (p. 234). The point is, Hiller says both times 'may be', not 'is to be', and certainly not 'must be'.

---

[14] *Novum Organum*, Bk. 1, Aphorism 105. Translation from Latin by L. Susan Stebbing, in *A Modern Introduction to Logic*, 7th edn. 1950 (repr. New York, 1961), chap. 14, p. 247.

[15] For documentation on Mozart's view by Ignaz Mosel and Franz Niemetschek, two musicians who knew him, see *Ornamentation*, p. 238.

Corri does show in his illustrations, some of which are from Gluck's *Orfeo*, appoggiaturas used consistently on note repetitions. As discussed above, Gluck himself disavowed such an interpretation; this casts a large shadow of doubt on the remaining examples and on the value of Corri's testimony in general.

Lasser speaks of appoggiatura inserts made 'mostly' (*meistens*) on falling thirds followed by a punctuation mark. He does not mention other intervals; as reported before, he, like Mancini, specifically excepts words that express hardness or severity (like his example of *funeste*) as being unreceptive of appoggiaturas. He too falls far short of supporting Crutchfield's thesis.

Lanza, an obscure London singing teacher of unknown authority, does use the word 'must' for replacing note repetition with an appoggiatura from above or below (this latter is not a prosodic type, as explained above). He precedes his rule with a statement (quoted by Crutchfield): 'When a word of two, or three syllables is found in the middle of a verse, or terminating a sentence, the music is always written with two, or three notes of the same sound . . .' As a glance at just about any Mozart recitative will confirm, the reference to three notes is wrong; this does little to enhance the credibility of this witness.

Regardless of qualification or credibility, Crutchfield's statement that his four witnesses are 'all unanimous . . . in showing an appoggiatura for every feminine line ending' is misleading. Their quoted examples – a typical case of incomplete induction – may show this feature, but at least two of the four writers implied verbally that there were exceptions. And such exceptions break the unanimity, and as Bacon observed, demolish the inference. That neither Marpurg, nor Agricola, Mancini, Rellstab, Gluck, or Salieri supported Crutchfield's thesis was shown before.

Mozart's embellished arias

In 1778, for the benefit of his beloved Aloysia Weber, Mozart wrote embellishments for an aria by J. C. Bach, 'Cara la dolce fiamma', and for two of his own, 'Ah se a morir mi chiama' from the youthful *Lucio Silla* K 135, and the concert aria 'Non sò d'onde viene' K 294. The essential parts of these latter two arias in both the original and the embellished versions are reproduced in *Ornamentation* (on pages 231–3 and 235–8 respectively). In these arias, note repetitions at line endings were changed to appoggiaturas of various melodic and rhythmic designs, some descending, some ascending, and a few original written-out appoggiaturas were further embellished. Crutchfield includes in his enumeration any other kind of ornamental alteration that he says 'leans' in one or the other direction, then feels entitled to say 'if we choose to sing a blunt ending as written, we will introduce a formulation that Mozart was at consistent pains to avoid'.

His conclusion is mistaken. All three arias have texts that are brimming with warm feelings; the sentimental one from *Lucio Silla* was referred to earlier. The concert aria is about tender feelings arising in the bosom and their mysterious origin, the Bach aria about the sweet flame in the soul and its everlasting emotions. All three deal with sweetness, love and tenderness – feelings that cry out for the caressing roundness of appoggiaturas. Mozart himself, while writing these embellishments, was brimming with tender feelings for his beloved Aloysia.[16] It is inadmissible to generalise from an emotional extreme upon the whole spectrum of feelings.

The evidence of transcribers

In the absence of direct evidence of Mozart's treatment of the appoggiatura convention in his mature operas, Crutchfield turns to contemporaries (the term rather flexibly applied) who 'in instrumental transcriptions and adapted or translated versions . . . *often* [my italics] specify the appoggiaturas. And copies made or annotated for use by singers *often* [my italics] do so as well' (pp. 242–3). He argues that the absence of appoggiaturas in those arrangements does not count, because the transcribers were not interested in performance practice. Only those count that do show appoggiaturas and only whenever they do so. When they show some appoggiaturas but not all, a failure to show is due to an 'oversight' or 'an assumption that even without the words as a guide, an instrumentalist would know how to interpret the figures as requiring an appoggiatura' (p. 248). 'Oversight' is too facile an explanation, and the would-be reliance on the instrumentalists' improvisation is too far-fetched to be credible: for instrumental music that knew no prosodic appoggiaturas to begin with, there was no semblance of a convention calling for their addition.

We have no right to assume that musicians, just because they were more or less contemporaries (all of Crutchfield's examples are from the early part of the nineteenth century) should (1) be privy to Mozart's intentions and (2) aim at rendering his music in *his* way rather than showing their own personal preferences.

Already during Mozart's lifetime, · his music was mistreated by true 'contemporaries'. A telling illustration is a performance on 23 September 1787 of *Le nozze di Figaro*, staged at the Court Theatre of the Prince of Fürstenberg in Donaueschingen as a German Singspiel. It was based on an adulterated Italian

---

[16] Except for the ending of 'Non sò d'onde viene', both Mozart arias were originally written with a kind of simple, semi-skeletal melodic line that is in need of animation – a type of melody that is not found in Mozart's later works. His attested violent aversion to singers' arbitrary diminutions of the written text applies to all of his mature operas beginning with *Idomeneo*.

copy of the original score. The translation was miserable and the parts have in a number of arias (e.g. in the Countess's 'Dove sono') embellishments of a lavishness that evince a callous disregard for Mozart's style and spirit.[17] Are we seriously to take all those garish distortions as proof of Mozart's intentions?

The Donaueschingen experience alone justifies profound skepticism regarding the value as evidence of all 'contemporary' documents, be they performances or arrangements. As to the arrangers, often publishers' hirelings who did piano scores, translations, or transcriptions for various instrumental groups, their opinions are of little interest and even lesser value as evidence. Besides, the arrangers do not agree with one another, as Crutchfield shows in his ex. 15. There various passages in Leporello's 'Madamina' are given in four different transcriptions that display vast differences. Which one is supposed to reveal Mozart's ideas?

Some of these transcriptions border on the grotesque, as, for instance, Mazzinghi's version of 'voi sapete quel che fà', (p. 253) shown here in ex. 10, in which Mozart's text is distorted beyond recognition. And when Bishop translates the same portion of 'voi sapete . . .' as 'ugly, pretty, short, and tall, He 'pon honor, lov'd them all', one has reason to wonder which is more mangled, the words or the music.

Example 10 *Don Giovanni*, Act I, scene 4

Another part of the aria – 'la piccia, la piccina. . .' (Crutchfield's ex. 15d) – receives a reasonably accurate rendition in only one of the four versions (viola) while the three others add appoggiaturas that are out of place because they destroy for this passage (bars 115–119) Mozart's perfect unison of voice, winds and basses.

Regarding an anonymous transcription published by Simrock in 1802 of *Don Giovanni* for string quartet, Crutchfield reports that in Donna Anna's recita-

---

[17] Worst of all is the part of the Count, which was sung by a tenor and leaps up and down in order to stay within the tenor range, with total disregard for the original melody and harmony. For details of this performance – one that was truly 'contemporary' but just as certainly un-Mozartean – see Ludwig Finscher, 'Verlorengegangene Selbstverständlichkeiten?', *Musica* 36 (1982), fasc. 1 (Jan./Feb.), pp. 19–23.

tive (I, 2) the arranger left 'agli occhi miei' (bars 7–8) with the 'blunt' ending
(p. 248, n. 15). He speculates that the arranger may have started out not marking
appoggiaturas, and commenced only [in mid-sentence!] at 'padre mio.' Yet, as
shown here in ex. 11 (Crutchfield's ex. 10), for 'padre mio' the arranger not only
added an appoggiatura, but recomposed the melodic sequence.[18] Then on the
next phrase, 'mio caro padre', he lets the 'blunt' ending on 'padre' stand. Later in
the recitative (bars 45–46) Don Ottavio's 'cercatemi' has an appoggiatura, but
the immediately following 'recatemi' is left 'blunt'. The same arranger recomposed the melody of 'Or sai chi l'onore', by substituting an A for the F♯ on
'L'O-[nore]', presumably better to prepare his added appoggiatura (see Crutchfield's ex. 11b). This arbitrary and erratic arranger is certainly not an effective
witness for Crutchfield's law. Or shall we explain all his 'blunt' endings and
recomposings as a series of 'oversights'?

Example 11 *Don Giovanni*, Act I, scene 2

The added appoggiaturas can be proved to be wrong in another example.
Crutchfield mentions Edward Holmes's arrangement of the Terzetto from *Le
nozze di Figaro* (I, 7) (p. 250), where the arranger kept the note repetitions in
Basilio's 'In mal punto . . .' (see ex. 12a) but added appoggiaturas on 'Ah! crude
stelle!' and 'Ah meglio ancora!' (see ex. 12b). As can be seen, the note repetitions
of 'in mal punto' are confirmed by the unison violins, but similarly confirmed
are those on 'Ah, crude stelle!' – (1) by the preceding figures of the violins, (2) by
being an inversion of 'In mal punto', and (3) by the simultaneous note repetitions of the violins and then the clarinets. Mozart could not have made his
intentions clearer.

The quoting of all these arrangements, to which Crutchfield devotes thirteen
pages, is in the end an exercise in futility. They only show how Mozart's music

---

[18] This is a passage where according to my 'proprio gusto' – and I am by no means alone – no
appoggiaturas should be added because they would weaken the dramatic impact of the outcry
(see *Ornamentation*, p. 199). That Mozart did not have appoggiaturas in mind becomes clear
four bars later when terror yields to compassion at the sight of the wound and he writes
out the appoggiaturas for the words 'quel sangue . . . quella piaga . . . quel volto'.

Example 12 *Le nozze di Figaro*, Act I, scene 7

(a)

(b)

fared at the hands of some musicians in the early nineteenth century and testify to the personal taste and judgment (or to the lack of it) on the part of the arrangers; they emphatically do not prove *quod erat demonstrandum* that Mozart never used, was not allowed to use, note repetitions on feminine line endings or in mid-line before punctuation marks. Like the first two groups of proofs proposed for Crutchfield's theorem, this third group fails to make its point.

The rising appoggiatura

According to Crutchfield's theorem, every feminine line ending had to be 'leaned upon in one way or another' (p. 270). This leaning could be accomplished, among other ways, by rising appoggiaturas. These latter were 'accepted and expected, but were used far less frequently than the falling ones; they were associated with high expressive coloration or the asking of questions'. Several comments are necessary.

First I would question the introduction of unwritten rising appoggiaturas in Mozart. They have no place in his recitatives since the prosodic accent never involves a lowering of the voice. In closed numbers, he wrote out countless rising appoggiaturas for reasons of their greater expressiveness; and in view of their number, we have reason to believe that in his mature operas and arias he wrote out all the rising appoggiaturas he wanted. To introduce an unwritten rising one would, in view of its much stronger flavour, constitute an intrusion into Mozart's lyricism. Eighteenth-century theorists from Scheibe and Agricola to Mancini, Hiller, Lasser, Corri, J. F. Schubert and Salieri agree that unwritten ones should be descending. Singers and editors are advised to limit their additions in Mozart to the stepwise descending type.

Second, Crutchfield's association of the (unwritten) rising appoggiatura with 'high expressive coloration' contradicts his repeated statements that the prosodic appoggiatura had nothing to do with expression; it was not 'an expressive tool or an element of word painting or a condiment to be applied ad libitum to vary the taste . . .' (p. 270).

This is not the only contradiction. Elsewhere in the essay, he extols the dramatic potential of the prosodic appoggiatura by listing among others 'Donna Anna's startled horror', her 'angry declaration', 'Leporello's droll commentary', the 'hotheaded threat of Ferrando and Guglielmo' (p. 245). Maybe the prosodic appoggiatura is a 'condiment' after all? Furthermore, it is not Mozart who 'proves' the fitness of the appoggiatura for these situations. It is the nineteenth-century arrangers and transcribers, the Crotches, the Bishops, the Mazzinghis, the anonymous scribes who distort and weaken the power of these passages by improper introduction of appoggiaturas. But why should Crutchfield worry about the dramatic potential of the prosodic appoggiaturas when, so he had told us, they had nothing to do with drama or expression?

The appoggiatura in questions

As to the insertion of appoggiaturas for questions, Crutchfield criticises me for writing that ascending appoggiaturas on questions should be avoided because they involve a misunderstanding of Italian and German diction (p. 267). While he apparently did not find in any Mozart recitative a rising motion on a question, he found one, written out with a rising fourth, in the Duettino of Susanna and the Countess (*Le nozze di Figaro* III, 20) on Susanna's 'sotto i pini?' which he says 'pointedly' confirms its 'rhetorical viability'. It fails to do so: the Duettino is perhaps the most lyrical piece in the whole of *Le nozze di Figaro*. At its start, the tender melody on 'Che soave zefiretto' with its encha…ing melismas could not be further removed from a declamatory pattern and is certainly rhetorically unviable. For rhetorical viability we have to look at recitatives.

Scanning the recitatives in *Le nozze di Figaro* I found that the overwhelming majority of questions are set to note repetitions, where in some cases prosodic appoggiaturas *from above* could be added; I found eighteen cases of downward leaps ranging from a fourth to a sixth, and *one* case only of an upward leap – obviously a rare exception.

In the recitatives of *Così fan tutte* most questions are again set with note repetition, there are thirteen downward leaps (of a fourth or a fifth), and in the whole opera there is not a single case of an upward move of any kind.

We also find a treasure trove of questioning designs in old Verdi and in Puccini, both of whom wrote after the demise of the appoggiatura convention. Looking through the first two acts of *Otello* I found in recitatives or recitative-like settings (the only ones that count for 'rhetorical viability') nineteen questions of which two have note repetition, sixteen step or leap *downward* and only one rises (Act II, Otello's 'Che parli?'). The statistics are again overwhelmingly weighed against the rise.

The picture is even more one-sided when we look at the first act of *Tosca*. There I found in recitative-like passages twenty-seven questions with feminine endings, of which twenty had note repetitions (sung here as written), seven moved downward and *not one* upward.

As to German diction, I found in the first act of *Tristan* in recitative-like settings only five questions with feminine endings. But since all five move downward, there is, I believe, some evidence value even in this small number.

I believe that my statement about Italian and German diction is in no need of revocation since the rising appoggiatura is so exceptional that it cannot serve as a model. The proper alternative is to sing as written or to add a stepwise appoggiatura from above.

Everything considered, I am confident that Crutchfield's monolithic law did not exist and that the insertion of appoggiaturas was a matter of music-dramatic judgement, not of legal obligation.

6

A PERFORMER'S THOUGHTS ON MOZART'S VIOLIN STYLE

JAAP SCHRÖDER

Recently I have been struck by the thought that my professional involvement with Mozart has covered exactly the time-span of his own life: in 1956, as a member of the Netherlands String Quartet, I recorded a number of quartets for the Phillips Jubilee series, and after playing the six quartets dedicated to Haydn for the Decca label in 1980 as leader of the Esterházy quartet (the first recording ever on classical instruments with gut strings) I am now repeating this same venture with my present group – the Smithson Quartet – in preparation for the Mozart year 1991, this time for Virgin Classics.

Studying the repertoire with the appropriate material (violin as well as bow), and recreating the sound and the playing style of each period, starting with the earliest violin literature, has convinced me that this approach clarifies many stylistic problems and, by penetrating the idiom of individual composers, helps better to realise their intentions. It is generally accepted by now that the violin music of the seventeenth century (Marini, Uccellini, and others) sounds much better played in the seventeenth-century way on instruments of the period than it does played on a modern violin with twentieth-century technique. The gradual development of the period-instrument movement and research into the performance practice of the eighteenth (and more recently the nineteenth) century have confirmed that our understanding of music of the classical period is refreshed by observing this same performance ideal. To recreate Mozart's spirit in performance means to rediscover the many stylistic points that have been obscured by later technical developments which have radically altered the sound.

Mozart's music brings to mind a certain number of qualities that set him apart from his contemporaries: the transparency of his writing, the impression of inevitability and efficient phrase construction embodied by a pure and clear sound. In his music, a high degree of logical thought is supported by an originality that provides a constant element of surprise, a surprise not upsetting but accepted immediately by the listener as soon as it reaches the ear. A simple example may serve to illustrate the difference between the more earthbound spirit of Haydn and the soaring inspiration of Mozart, starting from the same initial impetus (see ex. 1).

117

Example 1 (a) Joseph Haydn, Violin Sonata in G major Hob. XV:32

(b) Mozart, Violin Sonata in G major K 30

The apparent simplicity of Mozart's phrases requires an unpretentious inter-pretation that reflects his own violin technique, a technique that was based on that of the baroque masters. We know that Mozart had eagerly absorbed earlier compositional styles in his youth, and that later in life he conceived a renewed and enthusiastic interest in the polyphonic writing of the Bach era. His spiritual kinship to the compositions of W. F. Bach in particular is unmistakable, and we see how certain essential fugue subjects like the descending tetrachord and the diminished-seventh interval link him to the past throughout his life (see ex. 2).

Example 2 (a) W. F. Bach, organ fugue, transcribed by Mozart for string trio K 404[A]

(b) Mozart, String Quartet in D minor K 173

(c) W. F. Bach, Sinfonia in D minor

(d) Mozart, Fugue for strings K 546

(e) Mozart, Requiem, K 626, Kyrie

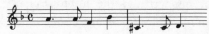

Clearly Mozart's style and technique were rooted in those of his predecessors. Faced with the difficult task of recreating his music in a way that he would have recognised, we must familiarise ourselves first of all with baroque technique and performance style, and discover in what ways Mozart's sound must have developed from there. Judging from the instrumental timbres of the classical period, a basic quality was still, as it had been throughout the baroque era, a clarity and brightness of tone that enabled players to produce a well-articulated sound, intense but not tense. If there is one word whose understanding is essential to our notion of the history of sound production up to our age, it is the word *tension*. Tension is the main ingredient in the musical notions of volume and speed, and throughout the history of musical performance it has assumed an increasing importance, to the point where modern playing technique is incompatible with the use of pre-twentieth-century instruments. The violin, although essentially the same instrument since its first appearance in the sixteenth century, has been able, together with its complement the bow, to adapt to the constant demand for more tension by making changes of a secondary nature. The invention of the steel string in the twentieth century (comparable to the introduction of the metal frame in piano construction in the nineteenth) multiplied the amount of inherent tension, as did the gradually rising pitch. The mounting tension had a direct influence on the volume and the character of the tone, making it darker and more sustained; in addition, it has led to a legato style of interpretation that is in absolute contrast to the ideals of the classical style. I would like to examine a number of ways in which contemporary violin technique has diverged from the classical manner of playing current in Mozart's time. I do not look at what has been gained, but rather at what has been lost. Only in this way is it possible to come close to the composer's intentions.

The String Quartet in A major K 464 contains a set of variations upon a theme, the beginning of which is shown in ex. 3.

Example 3 Mozart, String Quartet in A major K 464, Andante

This melody is unsophisticated and harmonious. The key of D major is very resonant on string instruments. Our first concern must be to preserve the simplicity of this theme and to avoid any disturbing tension. For the left hand of the violinist this implies that the player should stay in first position as much as possible and use many open strings. The longer the string, the more relaxed it will be, as will the hand itself. Besides, the clarity of the open string is a great virtue, and the brightness of its sound should be matched by the stopped notes. In the present case an embellishing vibrato can be applied to certain notes, but we have to bear in mind that vibrato belongs to the category of ornaments, and has to be used with discernment. It should relax and warm up the note in question, but not add more tension (as the modern vibrato usually does). The amplitude has to be very narrow and the speed gentle and unobtrusive. In any case the vibrating sound has to be compatible with the notes produced on open strings.

The intonation of the triads should be pure in order to convey the feeling of relaxed well-being. The sharpening of the major thirds (and, consequently, the narrowing of the minor ones) that became customary later is another sign of tension that, like the preference for higher positions and the omnipresent vibrato, has permeated the modern playing style. During Mozart's lifetime the trend towards longer melodic lines is clearly visible, and in that context a certain sharpening of the leading notes becomes an emotional necessity; but in the present example the player should give priority to the sense of harmonic warmth which demands a pure intonation of the thirds.

Tone quality and intonation are the basic ingredients contributed by the left hand and transformed into music by the action of the violinist's right arm. The classical bow, representing a transition between the baroque and the modern bow, than the earlier bow, but it was not yet glued to the string like the Tourte bow. The sound of a long stroke still showed a curved quality like that produced with the baroque bow (⌐‿‿‿⌐) and did not have the even 'horizontal' character of its modern counterpart (⌐———|———⌐——|). One could say that the sound of the pre-Tourte bow breathed and had an extreme flexibility; it articulated quite naturally and made a conscious (and intended) distinction between the weightier downbow (⌐) and the lighter upbow (∨). By comparison, the modern bow with its constant pressure is able to ignore any difference between the sound of up- and downstroke, and the natural articulation gap of the old bow has to be replaced, if necessary, by an interruption of the movement; the *martelé* stroke which can be visualised as ⌐——| ⌐——| ⌐——|.

Returning to the Mozart phrase, we may easily see how the classical bow achieves an ideal effect of flexibility by alternating down- and upbows (see ex. 4).

Example 4

An important factor of the bowing action is the bowing speed. I am convinced that the classical technique (as well as the baroque) was to use a slow bow. This has two distinct advantages:

a) The tone production is not tense but intense, and the proper weight of the bow can be put to maximum use by staying in the lower middle part as much as possible.

b) A slow bow allows more than one stroke in the same direction (⊓ + ⊓ or ∨ + ∨), a factor of importance when it comes to determining the weight of a given note. Thus the example should be bowed as in ex. 5 if we want the same weight on bars 2 and 4:

Example 5

Clearly it is the bow which brings the music to life; when the bow ignores the 'breathing' quality of the music as the result of constant pressure, players look for a different way to enliven the performance. During the nineteenth century this task fell to the newly invented *portamento*; our century has adopted the constant vibrato. But both these devices stand in the way of musical clarity: *portamento* covers up the openings in the articulation, while vibrato (when used as a device of tension) destroys the transparent quality of the sound. And a lack of clarity is damaging to the scores of Mozart, whose voice leading is eminently meant to be heard, the inner and lower voices as well as the principal voice.

Example 6 shows a typical example of this limpid sonority, taken from the String Quartet in E♭ K 428.

Example 6 Mozart, String Quartet in E♭ major K 428, Andante con moto

I mentioned earlier Mozart's ability to provide uncanny surprises that prove to be satisfying and logical; no better citation can be found than ex. 7, taken from the same movement:

Example 7 Mozart, Quartet K 428, Andante con moto

The clearer the presentation the better; we need an extremely well-balanced, pure sound here, a slow bow (to express the unhurried pace of the Andante) and no vibrato at all.

One aspect of Mozart interpretation that has been much influenced by the increasing inherent tension of post-classical instruments is the tempo. Playing the classical violin, with its gut strings and with the older, more flexible bow, helps to rediscover a sense of speed that is closely related to the human pulse and does not need extreme values at both ends of the scale. Slow movements retain an expressive fluency that avoids any heaviness and preserves a rhetorical quality, a sense of direction. Any excess of tension has the unfortunate effect of slowing down the natural pace and grace of such movements as that shown in ex. 8.

Example 8

(a) Mozart, String Quartet in Bb major K 458, Adagio

(b) Mozart, String Quartet in C major K 465, Andante cantabile

It is probably true that the metronome has had the effect of distancing the human pulse from the determination of musical tempo, not only in the slow but also in the fast movements. A certain excitement is lost when the tempo of an Allegro, such as that shown in ex. 9, is too fast to allow the bow to make refined articulations.

Example 9 Mozart, Quartet K 465, finale

Speed must always serve the purpose of the musical discourse if the music is not to degenerate into empty brilliance. No more than the spoken word, and for the same reasons, should music be hurried. In a slow tempo, such as that shown in ex. 10, we have to remember the speech-like character of the phrase and avoid the cultivation of beautiful tone as an end in itself.

Example 10 Mozart, String Quartet in D minor K 421, Andante

The importance of articulation in Mozart's music shows his links to the rhetorical principles of the baroque. The nineteenth century would cultivate the longer lines of legato playing: among the consequences of this new focus were a wider scale of dynamic nuances and a greater differentiation of tone quality. Mozart was still fairly limited in his dynamic vocabulary: his bow lacked the aggressiveness of the modern one and did not have the weight and tension necessary to realise the extensive crescendos that are part of the romantic language. The dangers for modern performers are twofold: on the one hand, they should avoid excessive dynamic contrasts that tend to distort the intention of Mozart's phrases; on the other, they have to bear in mind that in the classical period the basic bowstroke was still a downbow impulse followed by a lighter upbow reflex, much like the movement of the foot being put down and lifted afterwards. This basic unit can be expressed visually in the following way: − ∪. When, as in later times, the modern bow favours the longer legato line, the upbow movement gains in strength and develops a crescendo into the next downbow, with the

immediate loss of a strong rhythmic pulse: < —. This negation of the upbeat as a
light upward motion is particularly damaging to dance rhythms, and in the case of
Mozart's minuets (e.g. example 11) destroys the stimulating character of the
strong downbeats.

Example 11 Mozart, Quartet K 421, Menuetto

In general, upbeat crescendi have to be avoided, since they tend to flatten the
following strong beat and impart to the melodic line a horizontal feeling that
leads ultimately to the aesthetic concept of the endless legato (see ex. 12).

Example 12 Mozart, String Quartet in G major K 387, Andante cantabile

Mozart's music lives by constant impulses and relaxations, and the exact determination of the bowstrokes is very important; the wrong bow direction produces
the wrong effect. We should remember that Leopold Mozart's principles of
bowing, as laid down in his violin tutor, are valid throughout his son's life.

An important subject for consideration is, finally, the realisation of Mozart's
ornaments and embellishments. By nature they are light and unstressed, and
devoid of tension, like trills and turns themselves. In order to achieve weight-
lessness, however, the preceding appoggiatura (as the words *appoggiarsi/s'appuyer*
indicate) receives – *on* the beat – the stress necessary to propel the embellishment
up in the air. If the appoggiatura happens on a downbow, players must take care
to diminish the intensity of the initial impulse immediately after the appoggiatura, before the beginning of the trill or turn. If the ornament is marked on an
upbow, an upbeat crescendo should be avoided. A fast trill-action carries the risk
of tension in the left hand and results in a stiff, loud and uncontrolled movement.
Like vibrato, the trill has to produce an effect of relaxation after the stress of the
appoggiatura. It should resemble the manœuvres of a trapeze artist in the circus,
defying the law of gravity.

In the countless cases where the appoggiatura is followed only by the main note, Mozart's notation has to be realised by eliminating any weight on that main note, thus creating a difference between ♩♫♩ and ♪♩♫ . Most of the nineteenth-century editions of Mozart ignored this distinction, and unfortunately many of those have remained in print until the present day. (Similarly the baroque formula was routinely changed into in romantic editions, thereby creating an accent on the upbow trill.) Again, it is understandable, in light of the later development of bow technique, that longer sustained pressure was incompatible with the idea of lightly executed ornaments. Mozart is better served with a performance style that combines incisiveness and lightness: in other words, a high degree of flexibility that produces excitement and avoids dragging.

The common denominator in all of the points I have discussed is the notion that in Mozart performance, intensity can and must be achieved without the tension that became customary in the performance of nineteenth- and twentieth-century music. For modern musicians, going back to the older instruments of the classical period constitutes first of all a process of un-learning, of abandoning a technique that is based on a high degree of tension. Even if a sense of frustration is experienced in the beginning (our tradition of a muscular approach is useless and damaging to the instrument and to the music), this first reaction is most often followed by a refreshing sensation of freedom. Relaxation leads to elasticity; constant pressure is replaced by a multitude of differentiated impulses. And once these important principles have taken root in our way of interpreting the classical repertoire, it is certainly possible to achieve a workable compromise with modern instruments. In calligraphy the old quill pen is the ideal tool, but once we have mastered this art of beautiful writing and know how to differentiate the individual strokes, we will be able to produce artistic results even with a fountain pen.

7

LEOPOLD MOZART REVISED: ARTICULATION IN VIOLIN PLAYING DURING THE SECOND HALF OF THE EIGHTEENTH CENTURY

ROBIN STOWELL

Leopold Mozart's *Versuch einer gründlichen Violinschule* was probably the first major systematic treatise for the violin. In its extent, detail and comprehensiveness, it was, like the treatises of Quantz and C. P. E. Bach,[1] far more than merely a guide to instrumental mechanics, and it eclipsed all the other violin treatises of the early and mid eighteenth century, even that of Geminiani.[2] Drawing heavily on the Italian violin school of Tartini for inspiration, Leopold aimed primarily to lay 'the foundation of a good style',[3] solid technique and musicianship being prized more highly than virtuosity. His is professionally slanted instruction, written as much for the teacher as for the pupil and expressed with a strict, yet sympathetic, witty and personal pedagogical approach. As Marpurg put it: 'One has long desired a work of this kind but hardly dared to expect it. The sound and skilled virtuoso, the rational and methodical teacher, the learned musician; all of those qualities that make a man of worth are developed together here.'[4]

By 1800 Leopold Mozart's treatise had been through four German editions, including two in his lifetime (1756 and 1769/70), and he may have seen the

[1] C. P. E. Bach, *Versuch über die wahre Art das Clavier zu spielen*, vols. 1 and 2 (Berlin, 1753, 1762; repr. 1957), trans. W. J. Mitchell (New York, 1949); J. J. Quantz, *Versuch einer Anweisung die Flöte traversiere zu spielen* (Berlin, 1752; 3rd edn, 1789; repr. 1953), trans. E. R. Reilly (London and New York, 1966).

[2] F. Geminiani, *The Art of Playing on the Violin* (London, 1751); facsimile edn, D. Boyden (London, 1952).

[3] L. Mozart, *Versuch einer gründlichen Violinschule* (Augsburg, 1756), 'Vorbericht': 'Den Grund zur guten Spielart (überhaupts habe ich hier geleget).'

[4] F. W. Marpurg, *Historische-kritische Beiträge zur Tonkunst*, vol. 3 (Berlin, 1757), p. 160: 'Ein Werk von dieser Art hat man schon lange gewünschet, aber sich kaum getrauet zu erwarten. Der gründliche und geschickte Virtuose, der vernünftige und methodische Lehrmeister, der gelehrte Musikus, diese Eigenschaften, deren jede einzeln einen verdienten Mann macht, entwickeln sich allhier zusammen.'

publication of the third, enlarged edition of 1787, the year of his death.[5] Editions of his work also appeared in Dutch and French, and his principles were taken up by, amongst others, Cartier, Pirlinger, Woldemar and Schiedermayr in their violin publications, many of which incorporated his name in their titles, both as a sales ploy and as a stamp of authority.[6] Although much of Leopold Mozart's original instruction was thus perpetuated well into the nineteenth century, some of these revised editions incorporate notable emendations, many of which reflect changes in style, technique, aesthetics, instrument construction and bow making effected in the intervening years. For example, the preface to one such revision claims:

Although Mozart's *Violinschule* has kept its position throughout nearly fifty years . . . it is obvious that his book now displays the signs of age which make a large number of corrections necessary . . . A distinguished person[7] has taken over this difficult task with enthusiasm, and we hope that he has succeeded . . . Doubtful or incorrect passages have been omitted or corrected; what was missing has been completed, and, finally, the last chapter – that concerning good execution – has been added in a completely new version.[8]

---

[5] L. Mozart, *Versuch einer gründlichen Violinschule* (Augsburg, 1756; repr. 1976); facsimile edn, B. Paumgartner (Vienna, 1992); *Gründliche Violinschule*, 2nd and 3rd ends (Augsburg, 1769–70, 1787); facsimile, ed. H. J. Moser (Leipzig, 1956); 4th edn (Frankfurt, Leipzig and Vienna, 1791; [improved] Augsburg, 1800). Further editions of the work by anonymous revisers include: *Leopold Mozarts Violinschule oder Anweisung die Violin zu spielen. Neue umgearbeitete Ausgabe* (Leipzig, 1804); *Violin-Schule oder Anweisung die Violin zu spielen von Leopold Mozart. Neue umgearbeitete und vermehrte Ausgabe* (Vienna, 1806); *Leopold Mozarts Violinschule oder Anweisung die Violin zu spielen. Neue umgearbeitete Ausgabe* (Leipzig, 1817).

[6] *Grondig onderwys in het behandelen der viool, ontworpen door Leopold Mozart, Hoogvorstelyk-Saltzburgschen Kamer-Musicus. Met 4 Konst-Plaaten en een Tafel van de Regelen der Strykmanier enz. voorzien* (Haarlem, 1766; repr. 1965); V. Roeser, ed., *Méthode raisonnée pour apprendre à jouer du violon* (Paris, 1770; also [1783], [1788] and [1800]); M. Woldemar, ed., *Méthode de violon par L. Mozart rédigée par Wol demar, élève de Lolli. Nouvelle Edition enrichie des chefs d'oeuvres de Petiscus, Corelli, Tartini, Geminiani, Locatelli etc.* (Paris, 1801); J.-B. Cartier, *L'art du violon ou collection choisie dans les sonates des écoles italienne, françoise et allemande précédée d'un abrégé des principes pour cet instrument* (Paris, [1798]; 2nd edn, 1801; 3rd edn, 1803; repr. 1973); J. Pirlinger, ed., *Neue vollständige theoretische und praktische Violinschule für Lehrer und Lernende* (Vienna, 1799–1800); J. B. Schiedermayr, *Neue theoretische und practische Violinschule. Ein zweck-mässiger Auszug aus der grossen Violinschule von Mozart bearbeitet von Joh. Bapt. Schiedermayr* (Mainz, c. 1818); *Mozart's Violin School on the Art of Bowing* (London, [1812]).

[7] The identity of this reviser is unknown.

[8] Preface to the 1804 edition (Leipzig, Hoffmeister & Kühnel):
Obgleich Mozarts Violinschule sich durch einen Zeitraum von fast fünfzig Jahren im Credit erhalten . . . so lehrte doch der Augenschein, daß dies Buch die unvollkommene Gestalt seiner Zeit und viele Mängel habe, die gegenwärtig durchaus einer Verbesserung bedurften . . . Die verbesserte Gestalt hat ihm ein Mann zu geben versucht, der mit Eifer

A thorough examination of all the various revisions to Leopold Mozart's technical and interpretative principles included in the numerous treatises that bear his name would make, indeed, a fascinating survey. That is not, however, the object of this essay. The aim here is rather to investigate approaches to articulation and its interrelated matters of phrasing and accentuation in violin playing during Wolfgang Mozart's lifetime, using the editions of his father's *Versuch*, including the numerous 'revisions', as principal source materials. But to rely exclusively on the evidence of Leopold's treatise would be dangerous and misleading, even though the felicity of Wolfgang's string style is normally attributed to the solid technical basis established under his father's guidance.[9] Wolfgang was exposed from an early age to rich and varied musical experiences on countless foreign tours, and he gradually emancipated himself from paternal influence musically, if not personally, during his lifetime. Consequently, the writings of other contemporary theorists such as Türk, Milchmeyer, Clementi and Koch must be taken into account, acknowledging their bias towards other instruments, in order to gain a balanced understanding and substantially comprehensive overview of the string articulation practices of the period.[10]

'The principal, if not indeed the sole function of a perfect musical composition is the accurate expression of emotions and passions in all their varying and individual nuances . . . Every piece of music must have a definite character and evoke emotions of a specific kind.'[11] It was the performer's role to convey

die schwierige Arbeit übernahm; und wir hoffen, daß es ihm gelungen ist . . . das Zweifelhafte oder völlig Unrichtige ist weggelassen oder verbessert; das Fehlende ergänzt, und endlich die Lehre vom guten Vortrage (im letzten Hauptstück) ganz neu bearbeitet hinzugefügt worden.

The new version of the final chapter concentrates on three specific areas – accuracy and precision in performance (tempo, rhythm, intonation, etc.); elegant and agreeable playing (tone, intelligibility of phrasing, and tasteful variety in playing); and expression (tempo rubato, dynamics, accentuation, etc.).

[9] See, for example, E. S. J. van der Straeten, *The Romance of the Fiddle* (London, 1911), p. 235.

[10] D. G. Türk, *Clavierschule, oder Anweisung zum Clavierspielen für Lehrer und Lernende. . .nebst 12 Handstücken* (Leipzig and Halle, 1789; enlarged 2nd edn, 1802; repr. 1967; Eng. trans. [abridged], 1804; trans. R. H. Haggh, 1982); J. P. Milchmeyer, *Die wahre Art das Pianoforte zu spielen* (Dresden, 1797); M. Clementi, *Introduction to the Art of Playing on the Piano Forte* (London, 1801); H. C. Koch, *Musikalisches Lexikon* (Frankfurt am Main, 1802). N.B. Post-1791 methods are considered relevant to our study as published theory inevitably lags a whole generation behind actual practice.

[11] J. G. Sulzer, *Allgemeine Theorie der schönen Künste* (Leipzig, 1771), 'Ausdruck in der Musik': 'Der richtige Ausdruck der Empfindungen und Leidenschaften in allen ihren besondern Schattirungen ist das vornehmste, wo nicht gar das einzige Verdienst eines vollkommenen Tonstückes . . . Jedes Tonstück . . . muss einen bestimmten Charakter haben, und . . . Empfindungen von bestimmter Art erwecken.'

faithfully, yet personally, the composer's intentions according to the music's mood(s), character(s), tempo(s) and style(s). Character was determined to a great extent by melody, since 'the essence of melody, says Sulzer, consists in expression. It must always portray some passionate feeling or mood.'[12] Articulation is a vital factor in this expressive process. Türk equated it with punctuation of the written word and the radical change in meaning that may result from faulty placement of a comma – he compares 'He lost his life, not only his fortune' with 'He lost his life not, only his fortune.'[13] Incorrect musical punctuation can naturally lead to similar 'fatal' results when resources of articulation are treated incorrectly or handled without sound musical judgement and good taste. In violin playing such resources include tempo, rhythm, timbre, nuances, accentuation and prolongation, as well as specific technical considerations, most of which appertain to the art of bowing.

The so-called 'ordinary manner' of bowing in the mide eighteenth century involved a non-legato stroke, borne out by Leopold's description of the 'small, if barely audible, softness' at the beginning and end of each stroke.[14] The changing demands of musical taste were gradually prompting the development of a more expressive, vocal style, in which legato playing was assigned a new importance. 'To play well,' said Tartini, 'it is necessary to sing well',[15] and Leopold himself requires violinists to 'play with earnestness and manliness' and to aim, as in voice production, for an even and consistent, well-rounded and singing sound quality:[16]

Singing is at all times the aim of every instrumentalist, because one must always approximate to nature as closely as possible. Where the Cantilena of the piece demands no break, therefore, one should take pains not only to leave the bow on the violin when changing the stroke, in order to join one stroke with another, but also to play several notes in one stroke, and in such a way that those notes which belong together

[12] Koch, *Musikalisches Lexikon*, p. 941: 'Das Wesen der Melodie sagt Sulzer besteht in dem Ausdrucke. Sie muss allemal irgend eine leidenschaftliche Empfindung, oder eine Laune schildern.'

[13] Türk, *Clavierschule*, chap. 6, §19, p. 340: 'Er verlor das Leben, nicht nur sein Vermögen. Er verlor das Leben nicht, nur sein Vermögen.'

[14] L. Mozart, *Versuch* (1756), chap. 5, §3, p. 102: 'eine kleine obwohl kaum merkliche Schwäche'.

[15] In B. Campagnoli, *Metodo della mecanica progressiva per violino diviso in 5 parti distribuito in 132 lezioni progressivi per 2 Violini e 118 studi per violino solo Op. 21* (Milan, [1797]; repr. 1945); trans. J. Bishop (London, 1856), pt. 2, no. 115, p. 11.

[16] L. Mozart, *Versuch* (1756), chap. 5, §2, pp. 101–2 and chap. 5, §§12 and 13, pp. 106–7: 'Man bemühe sich allezeit mit Ernst und mannhaft zu spielen.' Leopold even discourages the practice of inclining the bow towards the fingerboard in the interests of producing a strong, virile and even tone from the full ribbon of hair (chap. 2, para. 6, p. 55). Such inclination of the bow is included in most of the revised editions of the early nineteenth century.

run into each other, and are only differentiated in some degree by means of *forte* and *piano*.[17]

His dictum, fully endorsed by Türk and others, involves the description of such a *cantabile* style as 'the greatest beauty in music'; and he goes so far as to call those who introduce improvised ornamentation into slow movements as 'note-murderers', who 'expose thereby their bad judgement, and tremble when they have to sustain a long note or play only a few notes in a singing style, without inserting their usual preposterous and laughable finery'.[18]

With the highly articulated style of the Baroque and early Classical periods gradually adopting a more legato character in late eighteenth-century performance, the so-called 'ordinary manner' of playing became a principal element of change. This is demonstrated by the differing opinions held by theorists of the period regarding the degrees of articulation appropriate for staccato, legato and the 'ordinary manner'. In their keyboard treatises, for example, C. P. E. Bach, Marpurg and Türk all require the finger to be lifted before the next note is played in ordinary touch, resulting in a silence between notes (for legato, the finger remains on the key for the full note-value).[19] C. P. E. Bach recommends that such notes should be held for half of their written value unless otherwise marked, but Türk, in keeping with the more *cantabile* trend, suggests a more literal interpretation, claiming that 'the finger should be lifted shortly before the written value of the note requires it. Consequently the notes in [ex. 1a] should

Example 1 Daniel Gottlob Türk, *Clavierschule* (1789)

(a) written   (b) played   (c) or

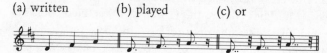

[17] Ibid. chap. 5, §14, pp. 107–8:

> [Und wer weis denn nicht, daß] die Singmusik allezeit das Augenwerk aller Instrumentisten seyn soll: weil man sich in allen Stücken dem Natürlichen, so viel es immer möglich ist, nähern muß? Man bemühe sich also, wo das Singbare des Stückes keinen Absatz erfordert, nicht nur bey der Abänderung des Striches den Bogen auf der Violin zu lassen und folglich einen Strich mit dem andern wohl zu verbinden; sondern auch viele Noten in einem Bogenstriche und zwar so vorzutragen: daß die zusammen gehörigen Noten wohl aneinander gehänget, und nur durch das *forte* und *piano* von einander in etwas unterschieden werden.

[18] Ibid. chap. 1, §3, p. 50: 'Solche Notenwürger legen dadurch ihre schlechte Beurtheilungskraft zu Tage, und zittern, wenn sie eine lange Note aushalten oder nur ein paar Noten singbar abspielen sollten, ohne ihr an gewöhntes, ungereimtes und lächerliches Fick Fack einzumischen.'

[19] C. P. E. Bach, *Versuch*, chap. 3, §22; F. W. Marpurg, *Anleitung zum Clavierspielen* (Berlin, 1755), p. 29; Türk, *Clavierschule*, chap. 6, §40, p. 356.

be rendered approximately as in [exx. 1b and 1c]. Where single notes are supposed to be held for their full value they should be marked *ten.* or *tenuto*.'[20]

The favoured legato style was gradually infiltrating the 'ordinary manner' during the second half of the eighteenth century and effectively became the norm well before 1800. The oft-quoted theory that legato was employed only when indicated (by an appropriate Italian term or slurs) was not necessarily practised. Türk, for example, distinguished between articulation and legato slurs and warned that the annotation of slurs in the opening bars of a movement implied a legato interpretation until otherwise indicated (by dashes or rests).[21] A conversation between Clementi and his pupil Ludwig Berger provides further light on this matter:

I asked Clementi whether in 1781 he had begun to treat the instrument in his present [1806] style. He answered 'no', and added that . . . 'he had subsequently achieved a more melodic and noble style of performance after listening attentively to famous singers, and also by means of the perfected mechanism of English pianos, the construction of which formerly stood in the way of a cantabile and legato style of playing.'[22]

Clementi expresses his legato preference even more clearly in his piano treatise: 'The best general rule is to keep down the keys of the instrument the full length of every note.' He further advises: 'N.B. When the composer leaves the staccato and legato to the performer's taste the best rule is to adhere chiefly to the legato, reserving the staccato to give spirit occasionally to certain passages, and to set off the higher beauty of the legato.'[23]

Acceptance of the legato style as the norm, however, was never as clear-cut as some scholars would have us believe. With taste the all-important arbiter, late eighteenth-century performers would never have contemplated adopting a highly articulated style for the sustained notes of a slow *cantabile* movement. Conversely, Czerny considered the nineteenth-century legato 'too dull and monotonous' for fast passagework, preferring a more bell-like touch;[24] and his vivid description of Wolfgang's piano playing should not be ignored, especially

[20] C. P. E Bach, *Versuch* (trans.), chap. 3, §22 (N.B. he earlier expresses some reservations about this), p. 157; Türk, *Clavierschule*, chap. 6, §40, p. 356: 'hebt man den Finger ein wenig früher, als es die Dauer der Note erfordert, von den Tasten. Folglich werden die Noten bey a) nach Umständen ungefähr wie bey b) oder c) gespielt. Sollen einzelne untermischte Töne völlig ausgehalten werden, so schreibt man *ten.* oder *tenuto* über die Noten.'

[21] Türk, *Clavierschule*, chap. 6, §38, p. 355.

[22] Grove V, vol. 2, pp. 345–6, 'Clementi'.

[23] Clementi, *Introduction*, p. 8.

[24] C. Czerny, *Complete Theoretical and Practical Pianoforte School, Op. 500* (London, 1839), vol. 3, §2b, p. 52.

with the *cantabile* ideals of the period in mind: 'a clear and already very brilliant style more inclined to staccato than to legato; a subtle and spirited rendering. The pedal hardly ever used and never necessary.'[25]

The change of emphasis in articulation practice effected during our period thus involved the clear, distinct mid eighteenth-century style of playing gradually giving way to a late eighteenth- and early nineteenth-century manner founded on a legato approach as a general rule. This legato style, in which the shortest notes were performed as distinctly as possible, applied not only in slow pieces, as in earlier traditions, but also in fast movements, as Clementi's notational procedures amply prove – long slurs, countless legato markings, and frequent use of the word 'tenuto' over those notes that otherwise might not have been held for their full value. However, general trends in performance should not be considered in isolation from the approaches of individuals and the particular instruments at their disposal, and Clementi, it must be remembered, specifically attributed his cultivation of a legato style to developments in instrument construction.[26] Clearly, too, the act of touch and management of the 'sustaining' pedal had as important a bearing on the development of a true pianistic legato in the nineteenth century as the type of bow (weight, curvature, shape, width of hair, etc.), the bow-grip and the fundamental principles of bowing and expression used by violinists in this remarkable period of transition.[27]

Bow-changes were to be made as imperceptibly as possible, and *messe di voce* were to be applied only sparingly, on appropriate long notes, in order to sustain the 'singing' style desired. Index-finger pressure was to be exerted between the second and third joints and the little finger rested on the stick for additional control, the hand apparently adopting a position nearer the frog than formerly.[28] Many of the revised editions of Leopold's treatise from 1787 onwards place increased emphasis on freedom of the bow arm and hand, the requirement of keeping the right arm near to the body, and the recommendation to tilt the violin slightly towards the E-string side (1787), confirming the need for greater wrist participation in the 'ordinary' bow-stroke for the cultivation of a singing style.[29] Furthermore, the adoption of the so-called 'Geminiani grip' for greater left-hand accuracy and facility overall (1769–70), especially in double stopping, and the more advanced left-hand position recommended to facilitate extensions

---

[25] Ibid. vol. 3, p. 72.

[26] See note 22.

[27] On the earliest pianos, stops (and later knee levers) were used to lift the dampers from the strings. See D. Rowland, 'Early Pianoforte Pedalling', *Early Music* 13 (1985), p. 5.

[28] L. Mozart, *Versuch* (1756), chap. 2, especially Fig. IV.

[29] See L. Mozart, *Versuch*, trans. E. Knocker (London, 1948; 2nd edn, 1951), pp. 57–8 and p. 60.

and avoid too many shifts (1787 and 1806), also assisted greatly towards a *cantabile* goal.[30]

Although articulation markings were notated inconsistently throughout the eighteenth century, they appear to have been added more regularly, if not totally reliably, from *c.* 1750. Ambiguities remain, however, in Wolfgang's autographs over dynamic markings, slurs, staccato dots and vertical dashes, which are not always carefully drawn or consistently applied. Slurs are sometimes begun too soon on the page and ended too late. Dots may resemble dashes, or vice versa, raising the question whether a distinction was intended between the two. Indeed, many scholars have argued for the creation of a wide range of staccato shadings to accommodate these inconsistencies of notation, particularly the various shapes and sizes of dashes employed, claiming, for instance, that dots denoted a lighter, shorter and less accentuated staccato interpretation than dashes and wedges.[31] Paul Mies recognised some consistency of policy in the staccato designations in Wolfgang's autographs, notably the prevalence of dashes for single notes and chords irrespective of context or function (or for small groups of closely-spaced consecutive staccato notes) and the predominance of more dot-like markings for extended series of staccato notes. But he attributed the numerous variations in notation to the 'writing factor' (*Schreibfaktor*), i.e. the actual mechanics of the act of writing.[32] Ewald Zimmerman, like Mies, has emphasised the importance of musical context in determining staccato degree and nuance, maintaining that the variety and inconsistency of Wolfgang's notation is such that he could scarcely have intended any specific differentiation between the shape of the staccato signs and their interpretation.[33]

The deeper one investigates the problem of interpreting staccato notation the more confusing the situation becomes. Evidence from the various instrumental treatises, for example, is itself conflicting. Few theorists suggest any differentiation between the interpretation of dots and dashes, and, as Koch points out, the views of those who do are in some cases diametrically opposed.[34] But the vast majority employ either a single staccato sign – in most cases the dash – or both the dot and dash, and consider these two signs interchangeable. Hiller,

[30] Ibid. pp. 57 and 73.

[31] H. Albrecht, ed., *Die Bedeutung der Zeichen Keil, Strich und Punkt bei Mozart. Fünf Lösungen einer Preisfrage* (Kassel, 1957).

[32] P. Mies, 'Die Artikulationszeichen Strich und Punkt bei Mozart', *Die Musikforschung* 11 (1958), pp. 428ff.

[33] E. Zimmerman, 'Das Mozart-Preisausschreiben der Gesellschaft für Musikforschung', in *Festschrift Joseph Schmidt-Görg zum 60. Geburtstag*, ed. Dagmar Weise (Bonn, 1957), pp. 400–8.

[34] Koch, *Musikalisches Lexikon*, 'Abstossen'.

like C. P. E. Bach, Marpurg, and Türk,[35] certainly suggests this synonymity in his consideration of bowing designations:

> Often if a whole piece is to be performed slurred, the word *legato* or *ligato* is found under the notes instead of a slur. Without this word, and without a slur over the notes, they may all be bowed separately; and if this is to be done throughout, sometimes the word *sciolto* is found underneath. If this bowing is to be performed in a faster and more separated style, dashes are placed over the notes, or the word staccato (which is generally expressed in German as *gestossen*) is placed under them. A different designation above the notes with dots . . . requires, if these dots are not supposed to imply strokes, a completely different execution.[36]

The ambiguity and lack of uniformity in eighteenth-century notational procedures invariably point to musical context, notably the character of the piece and the particular melodic function or harmonic significance of the notes in question, as the most satisfactory guide to staccato interpretation. Türk certainly subscribes to this and classes dynamic gradation, articulation, and the correct tempo as the chief factors in realising the character of a piece.[37] His recommendations concerning articulation are introduced with the concept of 'heavy' and 'light' execution discussed below,[38] and he claims that 'the more careful composers are accustomed to indicate the character of a composition as well as its tempo.'[39] In line with many of his contemporaries, he subdivides his consideration of character into broad categories of emotion and emphasises the significance of tempo 'qualifications' in determining whether the relevant feeling or passion 'is represented in a more vehement or more moderate manner', concluding that 'a *forte* in an Allegro furioso should therefore be a good deal louder than in an

---

[35] Interestingly, however, Türk does point out that some theorists require a shorter staccato of the dash than of the dot, while Riepel and Knecht, among others, claim that the dot demands a shorter staccato than the dash! (See note 47.)

[36] J. A. Hiller, *Anweisung zum Violinspielen, für Schulen und zum Selbstunterrichte* (Leipzig, 1792), pp. 40–2:

> Wenn ein ganzes Stück gebunden vorgetragen werden soll, wird oft, statt der Bogen das Wort *legato* oder *ligato* unter den Noten gefunden. Ohne dieses Wort, ohne Bogen über den Noten, können sie alle abgestrichen werden; und wenn das durchaus geschehen soll, wird bisweilen das Wort *sciolto* (gelöst) darunter gefunden. Soll dieses Abstreichen mit einem raschern, mehr getrennten Bogenstriche geschehen, so werden Striche über die Noten, oder das Wort *staccato* (das man insgemein durch gestossen verdeutscht) unter dieselben gesetzt. Eine andere Bezeichnung über den Noten mit Puncten . . . fordert, wenn nicht diese Puncte Striche bedeuten sollen, einen ganz andern Vortrag.

[37] Türk, *Clavierschule*, chap. 6, §28, p. 348.

[38] See p. 151.

[39] Türk, *Clavierschule*, chap. 1, §77, p. 115: 'so pflegen sorgfältigere Komponisten, außer der Bewegung, auch noch den Charakter anzuzeigen.'

Allegro in which only a moderate degree of joy prevails.'[40] Although Wolfgang
did not make extensive use of such tempo 'qualifications', his music certainly
expresses similar broad categories of emotion and incorporates inherent expressive qualities or 'character' that were required to be conveyed in performance.
His exploitation of variety and contrast was a significant characteristic of the
Classical style which is encompassed in Türk's insistence that certain parts of a
piece 'should be given light and others shade.'[41]

Despite the predominant *cantabile* trend, non-legato and even staccato appear
to have been the dominant types of touch in Mozart's (piano) playing.[42] Beethoven
described it as 'subtle but broken-up; no legato.'[43] Staccato was generally indi-
cated by a dash (|), a dot (•), or a wedge (▾) in the early eighteenth century –
wedges were used particularly in printed music, where they may be regarded
as stylised dashes. However, the dot later seems to have gained preference –
Wolfgang certainly appears to have employed dots more freely in his mature
years – so that the dash (or wedge) denoted either a normal staccato or an
accent, or a combination of the two, generally, but not exclusively, in *forte*
contexts. Further confirmation of this trend is provided by Nottebohm, who
verifies that Beethoven made a distinction between dots and dashes (probably
from *c.* 1800 but certainly from 1813 onwards), citing as evidence a letter from
Beethoven to Karl Holz (regarding Holz's copy of the String Quartet, Op. 132),
in which the composer states that dots and dashes (strokes) are not interchangeable, and Beethoven's own corrections of articulation in the manuscript
parts of his Seventh Symphony.[44] Mies has opposed Nottebohm's argument on
the grounds that Beethoven never notated articulation markings consistently
and systematically in his autographs;[45] furthermore, available autograph facsimiles
reveal that he normally used dashes (of varying sizes, possibly in relation to
expressive intention) to indicate staccato.[46] Nevertheless, although few eighteenth-
century instrumental treatises differentiate between staccato with dashes and

---

[40] Ibid. chap. 6, §30, p. 349: 'je nachdem die Empfindung oder Leidenschaft heftiger oder
gemäßigter dargestellt wird. Ein *forte* in einem *Allegro furioso* muß daher ungleich stärker seyn,
als in einem Allegro, worin nur ein gemäßigter Grad der Freude herrscht'.

[41] *Ibid.* chap. 6, §50, p. 364: 'gewisse Stellen müssen Licht, andere aber Schatten erhalten'.

[42] E. Anderson, *The Letters of Mozart and His Family*, 3rd edn (London 1985), p. 363.

[43] A. Thayer, *Ludwig van Beethovens Leben*, ed. and trans. H. Deiters, vol. 1, pp. 197ff, in Badura-
Skoda, *Interpreting Mozart on the Keyboard*, trans. L. Black (London, 1961), p. 66.

[44] G. Nottebohm, 'Punkte und Striche', in *Beethoveniana* (Leipzig, 1872), p. 109. Several important early nineteenth-century piano treatises encourage such a differentiation.

[45] P. Mies, *Textkritische Untersuchungen bei Beethoven* (Munich, 1957).

[46] Slurred tremolo was always notated with dots above/below the note heads and a slur
above/below the dots.

dots,[47] Friedrich Starke's *Wiener Pianoforte-Schule*, to which Beethoven was a contributor, provides early nineteenth-century evidence in support of Nottebohm. It describes three kinds of detached or staccato playing, including some interesting guidelines regarding note lengths:

(1) the short, sharp touch which is marked by dashes and in which each note receives a quarter of its value; (2) the semi-sharp [*halbscharfe*] touch, marked by dots, in which the notes receive half their value; (3) portamento [*appoggiato*][48] which is marked by dots below or above a slur in which each note receives three-quarters of its value.[49]

Interestingly, Reichardt's bowing rules provide a notable parallel with the three basic keyboard touches of the period. He remarks: 'all notes which have neither the dash (|) indicating staccato nor the slur (⌒) indicating legato, are to be played with a separate bow but are less sharply attacked than those marked with a dash'.[50] Thus, staccato bowing involved a greater attack and articulation than the 'ordinary' stroke. It was generally conveyed by lifting the bow from the string after each stroke, but the practicalities of this depended on tempo and, to some extent, convention. Koch explains:

In *Adagio*, *Largo*, *Lento* and similar pieces in slow tempo, all notes which are to be played staccato should be marked with one of the specific staccato signs, as the ordinary manner of performing such pieces requires the notes to be played with a long bow and smoothly connected with each other. In fast movements, however, there are numerous kinds of passages which musicians customarily play staccato without any special instructions to this effect.[51]

---

[47] Joseph Riepel, *Gründliche Erklärung der Tonordnung* (Frankfurt and Leipzig, 1757) and Justin Heinrich Knecht, *Kleine theoretische Klavierschule für die ersten Anfänger* (2 vols; Munich, 1800–2) are among the few exceptions.

[48] Groups of repeated notes – see p. 138.

[49] F. Starke, *Wiener Pianoforte-Schule* (Vienna, 1819–21), quoted in Nottebohm, 'Punkte und Striche', p. 110:

> 1) der kurze scharfe Stoss, welcher mit Strichen bezeichnet wird, und wo jede Note den vierten Theil ihrer Geltung erhalten soll; 2) der halbscharfe Stoss, wo die Noten mit Punkten bezeichnet werden und die Hälfte ihrer Geltung erhalten sollen; 3) der tragende Stoss (appoggiato), welcher mit Punkten unter oder über einem Bogen (⌣⃛) bezeichnet wird, und wo jede Note den dreivierten Theil ihrer Geltung erhält.

[50] J. F. Reichardt, *Über die Pflichten des Ripien-Violinisten* (Berlin and Leipzig, 1776), p. 81:

> alle Noten, die weder den Strich (|) zum Abstoßen, noch den Bogen (⌒) zum Schleifen haben, werden mit einzelnen Bogenstrichen gemacht, aber nicht so scharf gestossen, als jene mit einem Strich bezeichnete Noten.

[51] H. C. Koch, *Musikalisches Lexikon*, p. 43, 'Abstoßen oder absetzen':

> In dem *Adagio, Largo, Lento* und dergleichen Sätzen von langsamer Bewegung, müßen alle Noten, die abgestoßen werden sollen, mit einem von den genannten Zeichen bemarkt sein, weil die gewöhnliche Vortragsart solcher Sätze erfordert, daß die Töne in einander

In faster tempos the bow was inevitably kept on the string, the pre-Tourte bow generally producing an effect similar to modern *spiccato*.

With most pre-Tourte bows, a true legato was achieved only by slurring. With the physical characteristics of the bow and the techniques of bowing undergoing modification practically throughout the second half of the eighteenth century, there is tangible evidence that the inaudible bow-change was increasingly being encouraged. Tartini claims that 'in *cantabile* passages the transition from one note to the next must be made so perfectly that no interval of silence is perceptible between them'; and l'Abbé le fils was the first writer directly to acknowledge the importance of suppleness of the fingers in bowing, claiming that they should 'instinctively make imperceptible movements which will contribute considerably to the beauty of the sounds'.[52] Leopold Mozart himself added the following significant amendment (1787) in respect of bow control and the so-called divisions of the bow:

Now if a string be bowed again and again, and is therefore pushed each time from the old vibration into either similar or slower or quicker movement according to the strokes following each other, the stroke must necessarily be started gently with a certain moderation and, [without the bow being lifted, played with so smooth a connection that] even the strongest stroke brings the already vibrating string quite imperceptibly from one movement into another and different movement.[53]

By the time of Wolfgang's death, the Tourte-model bow was rapidly being acknowledged as the tool best equipped to meet the aesthetic ideals of the period. Its particular merits, among them a capacity for greater tonal volume and accentuation (especially in the upper part of the bow), a greater capability to sustain long phrases, a wider range of bow-strokes (including 'bounding' strokes), and a greater capability for smooth bow-changes, were fast being appreciated and exploited.

Before *c.* 1800, composers generally eschewed long slurs. Wolfgang employed slurs sparingly and inconsistently and such indications as were prescribed during

---

schmelzend und gezogen ausgeübt werden. In Sätzen von geschwinder Bewegung hingegen giebt es viele Arten von Passagen, bey welchen die Ausführer gewohnt sind, die Noten ohne besondere Anzeige von selbst abzustoßen.

[52] G. Tartini, *Treatise on Ornaments in Music*, ed. E. R. Jacobi and trans. C. Girdlestone (Celle, 1961), p. 55; l'Abbé le fils [J. B. Saint-Sevin], *Principes du violon* (Paris, 1761), p. 1: 'les doigts feront naturellement des mouvements imperceptibles qui contribueront beaucoup à la beauté des sons.'

[53] L. Mozart, *Gründliche Violinschule* (1787), chap. 5, §10, p. 106. The square-bracketed section originally read as follows in the first edition: 'mit solcher Art genommen werden' ('played in such a way that').

the period often required supplementation from the performer.[54] He annotated slurs either as articulation guidelines or as indications of legato, only very rarely including multi-bar slurs as phrasing marks; typically for the period, he usually indicated a continuous legato by slurring each bar separately, but with no break intended between.[55] Türk warns that slurs placed over the notes of the first bars only normally imply a legato interpretation until the contrary is indicated by dashes or rests.[56] An authentic verbal 'legato' marking in Wolfgang's music is rare.

The expressive quality of the slur was foremost in the minds of late eighteenth-century performers. Traditionally, the first note under a slur was gently stressed and 'marked with a vigour that inspires the whole performance', after which the others were played evenly and legato, becoming gradually softer.[57] In pairs of slurred semiquavers, the first note was held 'a little long', the second being played rather late, and more quietly, thus counteracting the natural tendency to hurry. So-called 'articulating' slurs were performed in such a way that each pattern could be heard, the first note of each slurred group being more strongly stressed than the following ones.[58] When notes of uneven length were slurred together, the longer notes were generally sustained for more than their prescribed duration; short–long note-pairings were normally slurred, 'in which case the short note is always played quickly, not hurried, but so slurred onto the longer note that the whole weight falls on the latter'.[59] The performer's good taste and sound judgement were the arbiters in the addition of slurs, but Leopold provides a useful guideline: 'Notes at close intervals should normally be slurred, but notes far apart should be played with separate strokes and in particular be arranged to give a pleasing variety.'[60] The convention of slurring appoggiaturas and other such dissonances to their 'resolutions' (except possibly when the resolution was delayed) was tacitly understood.

A hybrid articulation termed *portamento* (or *appoggiato*) was also notated by means of a slur (ex. 2). The accompanying dots (the use of dashes was exceptional in this context) above or below the note indicated that it was a combination

[54] See L. Mozart, *Versuch* (1756), chap. 12, §11, p. 259.

[55] This convention is still mentioned by Czerny as late as 1839.

[56] Türk, *Clavierschule*, chap. 6, §38; L. Mozart, *Versuch* (1756), chap. 1, sect. 3, §17n, p. 44, adds a similar footnote in respect of bow-strokes.

[57] See Türk, *Clavierschule*, chap. 6, §48, pp. 361–3; L. Mozart, *Versuch* (1756), chap. 7, sect. 1, §20, p. 135 and chap. 6, §8, p. 116.

[58] L. Mozart, *Versuch* (1756), chap. 7, sect. 1, §20, p. 135.

[59] Ibid. chap. 7, sect. 2, §7, p. 146: 'Wo die kurze Note allemal still genommen, nicht übereilet und so an die lange geschlissen wird: daß die ganze Stärke auf die lange Note fällt.'

[60] Ibid. chap. 4, §29, p. 83: '[Daß man] die nahe beysammen stehenden Noten mehrentheils schleifen, die von einander entfernten Noten aber meistentheils mit dem Bogenstriche abgesondert vortragen, und hauptsächlich auf eine angenehme Abwechselung sehen solle.'

Example 2 *portamento* or *appoggiato*

of legato and staccato, and it was described by Türk and Hummel, among others.[61] Its string equivalent, the slurred tremolo, was employed in passages of singing character, each of the notes under the slur being gently detached and given a certain degree of emphasis.[62] Starke's claim that notes so indicated should be held for three-quarters of their written value would appear to present a reasonable guide as to optimum note-length.[63]

Wolfgang employed dynamic markings somewhat sparingly in his early works, but prescribed them more freely in his mature years (see, for example, the Rondo K 511 of 1787). Only rarely were the extreme dynamics *pianissimo* and *fortissimo* and such gradations as *mezzo forte* or *mezzo piano* included, his basic markings (*forte* and *piano*) thus implying sudden, 'terraced' changes from dynamic extremes when a more graduated and expansive approach to dynamics was normally intended. Leopold confirms this,[64] but omits indication of crescendos (except the long crescendo with the accelerating trill)[65] and any degree other than *forte* or *piano*, even though definitions of many such gradations are included in his opening chapter!

Parallels between instrumental performance and the human voice (either in speech or vocal performance) were commonly cited by theorists when considering the shaping and colouring of phrases. As dynamic inflection was inherent in vocal performance, nuances were applied in string playing to give life and character to the individual bow-strokes. They were thus generally added (whether notated or not) to establish the 'peaks' and articulate the general contours of phrases, as well as their expressive content, and were also freely employed to highlight dissonances, cadences (especially interrupted cadences), ornaments, and chromatic notes. The so-called 'divisions' of the bow were four types of bowings categorised by Leopold (Division 1= $\mathrel{<}\mathrel{>}$; Division 2= $\mathrel{>}$; Division 3= $\mathrel{<}$; Division 4= $\mathrel{<}\mathrel{>}\mathrel{<}\mathrel{>}$) that provided the backbone of his expressive vocabulary, offering excellent scope for the cultivation

[61] Türk, *Clavierschule*, chap. 6, §37, p. 354; J. N. Hummel, *Ausführliche theoretisch-practische Anweisung zum Piano-Forte-Spiel* (Vienna, 1828; trans. London, 1829), §5, p. 66.
[62] L. Mozart, *Versuch* (1756), chap. 1, sect. 3, §17, p. 43.
[63] See note 49.
[64] L. Mozart, *Versuch* (1756), chap. 12, §8, p. 256.
[65] Ibid. chap. 1, sect. 3, §27, p. 48 and chap. 10, §7, pp. 220–1.

of tonal purity and complete mastery of the bow, as well as variety of nuance. Divisions 1 and 4 were only selectively employed on certain long notes,[66] but the cultivation of a perfectly even stroke was also considered 'highly necessary for the proper performance of a slow piece'[67] and proved a vital factor in promoting the favoured *cantabile* style. Leopold's divisions were retained in the early nineteenth-century revisions of his treatise, and Campagnoli, probably with the Tourte-model bow in mind, repeats Leopold's description of the four divisions almost *verbatim*. However, he omits reference to Leopold's 'small softness' at the beginning or end of the stroke, thus suggesting that the divisions were not uniquely associated with pre-Tourte bows or their characteristic articulation.[68] They were nuances which were considered indispensable in the cultivation of a good tone and expression, as well as in achieving mastery of the bow.

Frequent opportunities for subtle, small-scale nuances were presented by *fp* minims and crotchets in Wolfgang's music. In such cases, the bow remained on the string, the stroke continuing 'so that the sound continues, although gradually dying away, just as the sound of a bell, when struck sharply, by degrees dies away'.[69] Wolfgang's use of *sf*, *fp* and *mfp* as substitutes for > requires particularly careful differentiation in the strength of the initial accent, and a distinction was doubtless intended between *fp* and *for: pia*, this latter suggesting that the *forte* should be sustained at greater length. Where no dynamics were indicated, Leopold recommends that long notes surrounded by shorter ones might be played *fp*. The second (dotted) note in ex. 3 should not be accented but rather

Example 3 Leopold Mozart, *Versuch* (1756)

played 'warmly with a sustained yet gradually decreasing tone'.[70] Notes that were sharpened during the course of a phrase should be played rather more loudly; similarly, notes that were suddenly flattened were to be emphasised by a *forte*.[71]

[66] Ibid. chap. 5, §4, pp. 102–3.
[67] *Ibid.* chap. 5, §9, p. 105: '. . . welches zu vernünftiger Abspielung eines langsamen Stückes höchst nothwendig ist'.
[68] Campagnoli, *Metodo* (trans.), no. 41, p. 6.
[69] L. Mozart, *Versuch* (1756), chap. 12, §8, p. 256 and §12, p. 259; chap. 1, sect. 3 §18n: 'Solche Noten müssen stark angegriffen, und durch eine sich nach und nach verlierende Stille ohne Nachdruck ausgehalten werden. Wie der Klang einer Glocke, wenn sie scharf angeschlagen wird, sich nach und nach verlieret.'
[70] Ibid. chap. 7, sect. 2, §4, p. 145: 'sondern durch ein sich verlierendes gelindes Anhalten nahrhaft vorgetragen werden'.
[71] *Ibid.* chap. 12, §8, p. 256. See below, p. 210.

In contexts such as that in ex. 4, the first note should be played less loudly than

Example 4 Leopold Mozart, *Versuch* (1756)

down   up   down   up   down

the second.[72] Clearly, the Mozarts preferred such detailed, subtle nuances to broad dynamic contrasts; this is amply verified by Leopold's insistence on maintaining an even quality of tone throughout the entire range and avoiding where possible extremes of tonal dissimilarity as might be caused, for example, by the use of harmonics and open strings or any over-aggressive attack.[73]

Tasteful articulation and variety of expression were (and still are) vital agents in clarifying structure, particularly in respect of phrasing, which was generally considered analogous to punctuation in language or to breathing in singing. Phrasing entailed the division of a piece into its constituent sections (rounded off in most cases by cadences of varying strength), which were then articulated into subsections in order to give shape to the melodic line and delineate its structure.[74] Wolfgang's music tended to be articulated into a clearly intelligible series of events – motives (*Einschnitte*) and phrases (*Abschnitte*) on the smaller, and sections (*Periode*) on the larger level.[75] Interestingly, the 1806 revision of Leopold's treatise cites the opening bars of Wolfgang's String Quartet in G major K 387 (ex. 5), and illustrates how that initial phrase is made up from interconnected

Example 5 W. A. Mozart, Quartet in G for strings K 387, first movement

smaller sections. The melody may, for example, be divided into two groups of two bars, or even further into four groups of one bar; it is the performer's responsibility both to recognise this and to execute the music accordingly, 'for the comprehensibility of a performance depends principally on bringing together

[72] Ibid. chap. 7, sect. 2, §7, p. 146. See n. 59.
[73] Ibid. chap. 5, §13, pp. 106–7.
[74] See Sulzer, *Allgemeine Theorie*, p. 1250, 'Vortrag'.
[75] The reader is referred to J.-J. Momigny's *Cours complet d'harmonie et de composition* (Paris, 1806) for an early nineteenth-century French view of the various levels of phrase structure within the first movement of Mozart's String Quartet in D minor K 421. Momigny includes a 'programme' for the movement and supplements his poetic analysis with both an annotated score and an arrangement for soprano solo with piano accompaniment.

what belongs together and making apparent the ends of periods, phrases and their related smaller sub-phrases.'[76]

Although Wolfgang's balanced, complementary phrasing was rarely indicated (the slur was employed largely to designate a legato interpretation), it was occasionally implied in the notation, notably by breaking of the beams. Schulz and Türk were among the few late eighteenth-century composers to encourage the use of phrase markings. Schulz, for example, indicated the beginning and end of a phrase with a cross (+) and circle (○) respectively. Others employed a dash (|) on a single note or the breaking of the beams to prescribe such phrase separations,[77] but Türk, for one, warns of the danger of misinterpreting the dash as a staccato marking:

Just as it is necessary to lift the finger at the end of a phrase, it is equally mistaken to accompany this with violent accentuation, as in [ex. 6] (a). This incorrect playing is

Example 6 Türk, *Clavierschule* (1789)

(a) incorrect   (b) instead of   (c) staccato sign (d) *Einschnitt*

particularly common when the *Einschnitt* is indicated, as in (c), with the common staccato sign. For many players have the wrong idea that a staccato note – as it is technically described – should always be played with a certain degree of force. In order to prevent such faulty playing wherever possible, and at the same time to indicate the smaller, less obvious *Einschnitte*, I have used a new sign in my little sonatas. This sign, which I simply call the *Einschnitt*, is shown above (d).[78]

---

[76] Anon., *Violin-Schule* (1806), p. 71: 'Denn das Fassliche des Vortrags beruht hauptsächlich darauf, dass man das, was zusammen gehört, gehörig verbinde, und dass man das Ende der Perioden, die Abschnitte und kleinern Einschnitte gehörig bemerklich mache.'

[77] J. A. P. Schulz in Sulzer, *Allgemeine Theorie*, pp. 1250–1, 'Vortrag'; Türk, *Clavierschule*, chap. 6, §§24–5, pp. 345–6.

[78] Türk, *Clavierschule*, chap. 6, §22, pp. 342–3:

So nöthig das Abheben des Fingers bey dem Ende einer Periode ist, so fehlerhaft wird hingegen der Vortrag, wenn das erwähnte Abheben mit einem heftigen Stoße verbunden ist, wie in dem Beyspiele a). Besonders hört man diese fehlerhafte Ausführung sehr häufig, wenn der Einschnitt durch das gewöhnliche Zeichen des Abstoßens, wie bey c), angedeutet ist. Denn viele Spieler haben die unrichtige Idee, daß ein gestoßener Ton – wie man ihn in der Kunstsprache zu nennen pflegt – jedesmal mit einer gewissen Heftigkeit abgestoßen werden müsse. Um diesen fehlerhaften Vortrag, wo möglich, zu verhindern, und zugleich die kleinern, weniger fühlbaren, Einschnitte kenntlich zu machen, habe ich mich in meinen kleinen Sonaten eines neuen Zeichens bedient . . . Dieses Zeichen, welches ich schlechthin den *Einschnitt* nenne, ist das oben bey d).

Türk's suggestion, however, did not catch on, and composers (W. A. Mozart and Beethoven included) continued to indicate an *Einschnitt* by a single dash.

Phrasing was carefully articulated in performance. This normally involved pausing briefly on the last note of one phrase and starting anew on the first note of its successor, reducing slightly the tonal volume of the last note and re-establishing it with the first of the next phrase, or shortening the last note of one phrase when necessary to separate it from the first note of the next, which was commenced with rather more strength.[79] Subtle nuances (whether notated or not) were thus all-important in the articulation of phrases, providing them with colour and character.

Prolongation of important notes was also vital for comprehension of the performer's, and hence the composer's, intentions. As Türk points out: 'The more important notes should be prolonged and emphasised, and the less important ones played more quickly and with less emphasis, in the way that a sensitive singer would sing the notes or a fine orator would declaim the words.'[80] The 1806 edition of Leopold's treatise makes rather more of this analogy between music and speech, the various emphases effected by intensification of tone or prolongation of note-duration proving vital in giving life and character to a melody, especially when distinguished from the 'natural' accents of the bar.[81] Eighteenth-century musicians essentially observed the three categories of accent used in everyday speech – 'grammatic', 'rhetorical' and 'pathetic' – to give shape and meaning to their performances. 'Grammatic' accents were those that occurred regularly at the beats of a bar, while, according to Koch, 'rhetorical' (*oratorisch*) and 'pathetic' accents were 'distinguished from grammatic accents not only by the more pronounced manner in which they are made . . . but also by the fact that they are not restricted to any particular part of the bar, but are created by the composer's fantasy, which he conveys by notes, and they must be discovered by the sensibility of the performer'.[82]

---

[79] Ibid. chap. 6, §21, pp. 341–2.

[80] Ibid. chap. 6, §64, pp. 370–1. 'Die wichtigern Noten müssen daher langsam und stärker, die weniger wichtigen aber geschwind und schwächer gespielt werden, ungefähr so, wie ein gefühlvoller Sänger diese Noten singen, oder ein guter Redner die Worte dazu deklamiren würde.'

[81] Anon., *Violin-Schule* (1806), p. 74.

[82] Koch, *Musikalisches Lexikon*, p. 52, 'Accent':

Sie unterscheiden sich von den grammatischen Accenten nicht nur durch den oben beschriebenen mehr hervorstehenden Vortrag, sondern auch dadurch, daß sie auf keinen bestimmten Theil des Taktes eingeschränkt, sondern blos in dem Ideale des Tonsetzers, welches er durch Noten dargestellt hat, enthalten sind, in welchem sie der Geschmack des Ausführers entdecken muß.

'Grammatic accents' were not all given equal length and emphasis. The good notes (*Note buone/gute Noten*) received most stress, but in accordance with their position in the bar. Thus, the first beat of a 4/4 bar received the most emphasis, the second less, the third more than the second but less than the first, and the fourth less again. Metres such as 2/2 and 2/4 involved one major stress (on the first beat), while in triple metres, the first time-unit was the 'good' (*Note buone*) and the second and third were the 'bad' (*schlechte Noten*). In order to explain this aspect of expression more fully, Marpurg distinguishes in performance between the written note-value – the outer value (*äusserliche Wert*) – and the actual duration – the inner value (*innere Wert*).[83] Hiller endorses this distinction, claiming that it 'originates from the natural feelings of human beings and is present even in speech'.[84]

The system of accentuation based on good and bad notes persisted throughout the Viennese Classical period.[85] It was accommodated in string playing by the traditional rule of downbow, a long-standing principle which is still a guiding force in bowing nowadays. If the composer indicated no other expression, the rule required the accented beat(s) of the bar to be played with the stronger downbow and the unaccented beats with the weaker up stroke. The greater strength of the downbow was due to a combination of the downward force of gravity, the weight exerted on the bowstick by holding it from above with the hand in a palm-down position, and the natural weight of the arm.[86] Geminiani was one of the few theorists of the time to despise the 'wretched rule of downbow' and he warns against 'spoiling the true air of the Piece' by crudely accenting the first beat of every bar.[87] Leopold Mozart surprisingly contributes little about accentuation, but his various editions of the treatise largely remain faithful to the downbow rule, even though he admits occasions for modifying it in his musical examples. However, equality of 'accent' in up and down strokes was

---

[83] F. W. Marpurg, *Kritische Briefe 1759–63*, letter 13, 'Von den Verschiedenen Taktarten', 15 September 1759, sect. 2, p. 99; *Anleitung zur Musik überhaupt und zur Singkunst besonders mit Uebungsexampeln erläutert* (Berlin, 1763), §7, p. 70.

[84] J. A. Hiller, *Anweisung zum musikalisch-richtigen Gesange* (Leipzig, 1774), §14, p. 47: 'Dieser Umstand hat seinen Grund in dem natürlichen Gefühle der Menschen, und äußert sich sogar in der Sprache'.

[85] See, for example, L. Mozart, *Versuch* (1756), chap. 4 and chap. 12, §9, p. 257; J. G. Albrechtsberger, *Gründliche Anweisung zur Komposition* (Leipzig, 1790, repr. 1968), p. 46; Türk, *Clavierschule*, 'Anmerkung 3', pp. 91–2; Hummel, *Ausführliche theoretisch-practische Anweisung* (trans.), chap. 2, §§8–9, pp. 59–62.

[86] S. Sadie, ed., *The New Grove Dictionary of Music and Musicians* (London, 1980), vol. 3, 'Bowing'.

[87] Geminiani, *The Art*, p. 4.

suggested as an aim by some of the revisers of his treatise, who, like Geminiani, advise against slavish adherence to the downbow rule.[88]

Although accentuation was hardly ever notated in music, Sulzer, typically, was one eighteenth-century theorist who attempted to prescribe it, indicating emphasis by a 'long' scansion sign, the degree of emphasis by the number of such signs, and unaccented parts of the bar by a 'short' scansion sign (ex. 7a). Türk, on the other hand, uses dynamics to prescribe the appropriate degrees of emphasis, and he warns that any departure from the normal accentuation (ex. 7b) should be expressly indicated (ex. 7c). He widens his survey to take in phrasing and

Example 7

(a) Sulzer, *Allgemeine Theorie* (1771)

(b) Türk, *Clavierschule* (1789)

(c) Türk, *Clavierschule* (1789)

[88] Anon., *Violin-Schule* (1806), p. 21; Quantz and Tartini, among others, had prescribed this practice fifty years or so earlier.

illustrates (by means of +, + +, or + + +) both how the first note of each phrase should be given even greater emphasis than an ordinary 'good note', and how restarts after perfect and imperfect cadences should be distinguished (ex. 8):

As necessary as it is to place an emphasis on the first note of a section or phrase, it is also important to bear in mind the following limitation: only the first note that falls on a strong beat must be so stressed. The A marked with an 0 in the sixth bar should therefore not be struck as loudly as the following B, although that section as a whole should be played more strongly than the preceding one.[89]

Example 8 Türk, *Clavierschule* (1789)

In this connection, performers of Wolfgang's music should be wary of those printed texts (e.g. the old Breitkopf edition) which do not always preserve his original *Alla breve* markings in certain Andante and Larghetto movements. Such irresponsible 'editing' may lead to misunderstandings and false readings regarding accentuation, since the edited version effectively doubles the normal number of 'good' beats per bar originally intended by the composer.

Prolongation also provided a flexible, musicianly solution for the stressing of important notes of a musical sentence other than the first note of a phrase, notably a note that is longer or markedly higher or lower than its predecessors, or the 'peak' of a phrase, which is often the highest note.[90] Alternatively, such an important note in a phrase might be delayed somewhat for optimum expressive emphasis by means of a silence. However, dissonances (prepared or unprepared), whatever their position, should be 'more pronounced than consonances; for it is especially by dissonances that the passions are aroused. If, when following

[89] Türk, *Clavierschule*, chap. 6, §14, p. 336:

So nothwendig jeder erste Ton eines Ab- oder Einschnittes, der erwähnten Regel gemäß, einen Nachdruck erhalten muß; so nöthig ist dabey die Einschränkung, daß man nur die Anfangstöne, welche auf gute Takttheile fallen, merklich zu markiren hat. Das mit 0 bezeichnete A, im sechsten Takte, darf daher doch nicht völlig so stark angeschlagen werden, als das folgende H, obgleich der Gedanke im Ganzen stärker vorzutragen ist, als der vorhergehende.

[90] L. Mozart, *Versuch* (1756), chap. 12, §13, pp. 259–60.

this rule, one pays particular attention to the degree of dissonance, it then follows that the sharper the dissonance or the more dissonances that occur in a chord, the more it should be emphasised.'[91] Good taste and musicianship were normally the arbiters as to the extent of the prolongation, but Türk claims that this depends chiefly on the degree of importance of the note itself, the value of the note and its relation to other notes, and the basic harmony. But as a general guideline he suggests that 'no note should ever be lengthened for more than half of its proper value. Often this prolongation should be hardly noticeable, as when, for example, the note is already distinguished by an accidental or by high pitch or by an unexpected harmony, etc. It goes without saying that the following note should lose as much of its value as has been gained by the accentuated note.'[92]

Performers naturally required a sound appreciation of harmony and timbre in order to implement eighteenth-century theories of accentuation and phrasing. In string playing, uniformity of tone colour within the phrase was widely encouraged, and the higher left-hand positions were increasingly exploited for expressive purposes. Approaches to fingering were influenced to some extent by the various methods of holding the violin and resulted in a system of articulation comparable to the paired fingering system in keyboard playing. Like Leopold, most theorists preferred the smaller upward hand shifts, using adjacent fingers, (e.g. 23–23 or 12–12) to the bolder leaps (e.g. 1234–1234 or 123–123) suggested by, for example, Geminiani; but the larger shifts were occasionally favoured in faster tempos, and they certainly gained preference in descending passages (e.g. 4321–4321), whatever the speed. Few treatises include information about the mechanics of shifting, but Leopold Mozart clearly shows that shifts were generally made on repeated notes (ex. 9a); by the phrase in sequential passages (ex. 9b); after an open string, a rest, or a pause between staccato notes (ex. 9c); or

---

[91] Türk, *Clavierschule*, chap. 6, §32, pp. 350–1; this is in accordance with the view of C. P. E. Bach, amongst many others:

> die Dissonanzen oder dissonirenden Akkorde überhaupt stärker anzuschlagen, als die konsonirenden, und zwar deswegen, weil die Leidenschaften ins besondere durch die Dissonanzen erregt werden sollen. Wenn man bey dieser Regel vorzüglich auf den Grad des Dissonirens Rücksicht nimmt, so folgt, daß je härter eine Dissonanz ist, oder je mehr Dissonanzen in einem Akkorde enthalten sind, je stärker muß man die Harmonie anschlagen.

[92] Ibid. chap. 6, §18, pp. 338–9. Particular prolongation problems associated with dotted rhythms are discussed on p. 153:

> daß man eine Note nicht mehr als höchstens um die Hälfte verlängern könne. Oft darf das Verweilen kaum merklich werden, wenn der Ton schon an und für sich z.B. durch ein zufälliges Versetzungszeichen, durch auszeichende Höhe, durch eine unerwartete Harmonie u. dgl. wichtig genug wird. Daß die folgende Note so viel von ihrem Werthe verliert, als die zu accentuirende davon erhält, versteht sich von selbst.

Example 9 Leopold Mozart, *Versuch* (1756)

after a dotted figure when the bow was generally lifted off the string (ex. 9d). Comfort and economy of shifting thus seem to have been prime considerations in the selection of fingerings, but the higher positions were increasingly used 'in the interests of elegance when *cantabile* notes occur closely together and can be executed easily on one string.'[93] Furthermore, as ex. 9b bears out, sequences were played wherever possible with matching fingerings, bowings and string changes, and open strings were avoided when stopped notes were technically viable – in descending scale passages involving more than one string, especially slurred; in trills (except in double trills where there was no alternative), appoggiaturas and other such ornaments; and in most melodic or expressive contexts. Evidence is conflicting regarding the incidence of portamenti. However, that some theorists rejected them outright suggests that they were employed by some string and vocal performers, especially in solo contexts; even Leopold implies a portamento in a solo cadenza passage of an Adagio.

By far the commonest specific ornaments in Wolfgang's music are single-note appoggiaturas and trills. Mordents and turns are comparatively few. The articulation, in keeping with the speed, the duration and the weight of these ornaments was dependent on numerous factors, not least the character of the music, the precise context of the ornament, the particular instrument and the acoustics of the

[93] L. Mozart, *Versuch* (1756), chap. 8, sect. 1, §2, p. 148: 'Und endlich bedienet man sich der *Applicatur zur Zierlichkeit*, wenn nahe zusammen stehende Noten vorkommen, die *cantabel* sind, und leicht auf einer Seyte können abgespielet werden.'

venue. Leopold's instruction regarding their execution is by no means exhaustive, but he does provide some fundamental advice about the articulation of appoggiaturas, which generally made a melody 'more song-like'. Just as a suspension or other dissonance was always smoothly joined to its resolution, appoggiaturas (whether indicated by a cue-sized note, or in notes of normal size) were always slurred and gently stressed, even if a slur was omitted in the text (almost invariably the case in Wolfgang's autographs) and their notes of resolution slightly shortened. A delayed resolution was the only exception to the general rule that an accented passing-note should be joined to the succeeding note. The durations of 'long' appoggiaturas varied considerably according to context. The ornament might take up to two thirds of the value of a dotted principal note or even three quarters of the value of a principal note of a minim's duration or more,[94] but uniformity of tone colour in their performance was considered essential. The so-called short appoggiatura was also slurred, but it was generally played as rapidly as possible – but presumably with some leeway for melodic expressiveness if appropriate – with the emphasis falling on the principal note.[95] The following paragraph was added in the 1787 edition concerning ex. 10:

Example 10 Leopold Mozart, *Versuch* (1756)

But it must be well observed that the *Anschlag* of two equal notes in examples [a] and [c] is played softly and only the principal note played strongly; while in the dotted *Anschlag* in examples [b] and [d], on the contrary, the dotted note is played louder, sustained longer, and the short note is slurred softly on to the principal note.[96]

Leopold also discusses unaccented passing-note appoggiaturas, which, though not universally accepted, took their value not from the succeeding note but from the previous one, the emphasis falling on the principal note rather than on the appoggiatura itself (ex. 11).

[94] *Ibid.* chap. 12, §§1 and 3. See also, for example, C. P. E. Bach, *Versuch*, vol. 1, chap. 2.
[95] *Ibid.* chap. 9, §9, pp. 199–200: '[Der kurze Vorschlag wird] so geschwind gemacht, als es möglich ist . . .'
[96] *Versuch* (1787, trans.), chap. 9, §12, p. 174.

Example 11 Leopold Mozart, *Versuch* (1756)

(a) written   (b) played

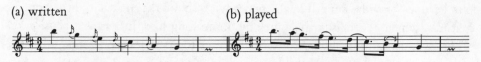

Trills were normally taken in one bow-stroke, 'for it would be just as illogical to change the bow and disconnect it as it would be for a singer to take a breath in the middle of a long note'.[97] Leopold adds (1787) that he thinks little of those who pander to the audience by taking several bows to extend final cadenza trills. Successions of trills were normally taken in the same stroke, if possible; if not, a bow change was implemented at the beginning of a bar, or, in common time, at the third crotchet (i.e. on 'good' notes). The bow never left the string but conveyed 'a scarcely perceptible accent' to articulate the start of each trill.[98] The mordent traditionally gave emphasis to the principal note, 'biting' it quickly and quietly and vanishing rapidly. Leopold gives three types, of which only the first tallies with the mordent of today.[99]

Articulation was naturally an important tool in expressing the various affects intended. As 'the soul of the instrument that it touches'[100] and the string player's primary source of emotional expression, the bow's role was to clarify the meaning of the musical text in the greatest detail possible through subtleties of articulation, phrasing, accentuation, ornamentation and other technical and expressive means. Bowing, according to Leopold, gave 'life to the notes' and proved the means by which the character implicit in tempo directions such as Allegro, Adagio, etc., might be conveyed to the listener.[101] He does not assign pulses per minute to his tempo markings, but he describes a range of terms from Grave to Prestissimo, linking 'a light and somewhat shorter stroke' with Prestissimo/Presto Assai,[102] 'a lighter and livelier, but at the same time somewhat more serious and

[97] *Versuch* (1756), chap. 10, §9, p. 221: 'Denn manchmal muß man eine lange Note aushalten die mit einem Triller bezeichnet ist: und es würde eben so ungereimt lassen dabey abzusetzen, und den Bogen zu ändern, als wenn ein Sänger mitten in einter langen Note Athem holen wollte.'

[98] *Ibid.* chap. 10, §21, pp. 227–8: '. . . einen kaum merklichen Nachdruck . . .'

[99] *Ibid.* chap. 11, §§10–13, pp. 243–4.

[100] L'Abbé le fils, *Principes*, p. 1, among many others: 'l'Ame de 'l'Instrument qu'il touche'.

[101] L. Mozart, *Versuch* (1756), chap. 7, sect. 1, §1, p. 122: '[daß der Bogenstrich] die Noten belebe'. See also Quantz, *Versuch* (trans.), pp. 199–200 and Reichardt, *Ueber die Pflichten*, pp. 25–8.

[102] Several theorists, among them Leopold Mozart, used 'assai' to indicate an intensification (i.e. 'very') rather than a tempering ('quite') (as customary nowadays) of the prevailing tempo. See S. Deas, 'Beethoven's "Allegro Assai"', *Music & Letters* 31 (1950), p. 333.

rather broader bowing' with the various gradations of Allegro, 'long strokes' for Largo, 'long, rather heavy and solemn bowing' with Grave, and so on.[103] Türk, too, distinguishes between 'heavy' (*Schwer*) and 'light' (*leicht*) execution in expressing the character of a piece, these two adjectives referring chiefly to whether the notes should be sustained or separated from each other (i.e. the finger lifted from the key somewhat sooner than the actual duration prescribed), although degrees of volume and emphasis were naturally also implied.[104] 'A Presto', he claims,

must be executed more lightly than an Allegro, an Allegro more lightly than an Andante, and so on. The heaviest performance is generally required by compositions in slow tempo.[105]. . .Yet the manner of playing, whether heavy or light, must be adjusted not only to an entire piece, but also to each single part of it. A piece in a gay mood which ought to be played lightly may nevertheless contain more dignified sections which demand a heavy style. In fugues and contrapuntal compositions, for example, the subject and its imitation must be played with particular emphasis in order that they may stand out.[106]

Clearly the system based on tempo terms was far from infallible as a means of establishing the optimum speed on which the music's proper effect so vitally depended. The relationship of terms to each other varied, and national tastes differed, so much responsibility was placed on the performer to recognise the inherent tempo of a piece. Leopold counts the process of recognition 'among the chiefest perfections in the art of music', for 'every melodious piece has at least one phrase from which one can recognise quite surely what sort of speed the

---

[103] L. Mozart, *Versuch* (1756), chap. 1, sect. 3 ('Musical Technical Terms'), pp. 48–52: [Prestissimo/Presto] 'ein leichter und etwas kurzer Bogenstrich'. [Allegro] 'ein zwar leichter und lebhafter, jedoch schon mehr ernsthafter und nimmer so kurzer Strich'. [Grave] 'einen langen, etwas schweren und ernsthaften Bogenstrich'.

[104] Türk, *Clavierschule*, chap. 6, §§35 and 43, pp. 353 and 358–9. Similarly Quantz (*Versuch* [trans.], chap. 17, sect. 2, §26, pp. 230–2) generally makes distinctions between light and heavy bowstrokes in his discussion of time-words and the passions they might convey.

[105] Türk, *Clavierschule*, chap. 6, §46, p. 360: 'Ein Presto muß leichter vorgetragen werden, als ein Allegro; dieses leichter als ein Andante u.s.w. Den schwersten Vortrag erfordern also, im Ganzen genommen, die Tonstücke von langsamer Bewegung.'

[106] Ibid. chap. 6, §50, pp. 363–4: Der schwere oder leichte Vortrag muß aber nicht nur dem Ganzen, sondern jeder einzelnen Stelle eines Stückes entsprechen. In einem leicht vorzutragenden Tonstücke von munterm Charakter können dessen ungeachtet erhabene Stellen enthalten seyn, welche einen schwerern Vortrag erfordern . . . So muß man z.B. in Fugen oder gearbeiteten Tonstücken vorzüglich das Thema (Subjekt) und die nachahmenden Stellen mit Nachdruck vortragen, damit sie desto hervorstechender werden.

piece demands'.[107] He recommends that in order to comply with the prevalent character, 'merry and playful passages should be played with light, short, and lifted strokes, happily and rapidly; just as in slow, sad pieces one performs them with long strokes of the bow, warmly and tenderly'.[108] Reichardt lays greater emphasis on bow speed:

In Andante, the bowing must have the lightness of an Allegro stroke but without its briskness, and the beginning of the stroke should not be of the speed used in Allegro . . . The same applies to Allegretto, but here the bow should be given some liveliness and at times some briskness as well . . . In Allegro, a brisk bow for staccato and a fast stroke at the beginning of a bow is absolutely essential. Directions intensified by terms such as Allegro di molto, Allegro assai, Presto, Prestissimo, refer to the tempo alone without changing the character of bowing . . . Modified markings such as Allegro ma non troppo, non tanto, moderato etc., do not change the character of bowing but influence only the tempo. If, however, the term cantabile, dolce, or something similar, is added, which specifies the mood of the piece, it refers to the bowing and this must be gentler and smoother . . . If terms like maestoso, affettuoso, mesto, grave are added in slow movements, it means that the longer bows must receive more weight and expression, and that notes preceding rests must not be stopped abruptly but should gradually fade out.[109]

---

[107] L. Mozart, *Versuch* (1756), chap. 1, sect. 2, §7, p. 30: 'Und hieraus erkennet man unfehlbar die wahre Stärke eines Musikverständigen. Jedes melodisches Stück hat wenigstens einen Satz, aus welchem man die Art der Bewegung, die das Stück erheischet, ganz sicher erkennen kann.'

[108] Ibid. chap. 12, §18, p. 262: 'Lustige und tändelnde Passagen müssen mit leichten und kurzen Bogenstrichen erhoben, frölich und geschwind weggespielet werden; gleichwie man langsame und traurige Stücke mit langen Bogenzügen, nahrhaft, und mit Zärtlichkeit vortragen muß.'

[109] Reichardt, *Ueber die Pflichten*, pp. 26–7:

> Bey dem Andante muß der Bogen die Leichtigkeit des Allegrobogens haben, ohne seine Schärfe, und in den Abzügen ohne seine Schnelligkeit . . . Eben so auch beym Allegretto; nur bekommt der Bogen hier schon etwas mehr Lebhaftigkeit und zuweilen auch schon etwas Schärfe . . . Bey dem Allegro aber ist endlich die Schärfe des Bogens in gestoßenen Noten, und die Schnelligkeit in den Abzügen höchst nothwendig. Die verstärkte Ueberschrift wie z.B. Allegro di molto, Allegro assai, Presto, Prestissimo, geht blos auf die Bewegung und verändert im Charakter des Bogenstrichs nichts.
>
> Eben so auch machen die Ueberschriften, die die Geschwindigkeit des Allegros vermindern, wie z.B. Allegro ma non troppo, non tanto, moderato u.s.w. keinen Unterschied in dem Charakter des Bogens, sondern gehen bloß auf die Bewegung. Steht aber cantabile, dolce oder sonst eine Benennung die den Charakter des Stücks näher bestimmt, so bezieht sich das auf den Bogen, und dieser muß sanfter und aneinanderhängender gehen.
>
> Eben so zeigen sich bey den langsamen Sätzen die Ueberschriften maestoso, affettuoso, mesto, grave, an, daß die längeren Bogenstriche einen stärkeren, ausdrückendern Accent erhalten sollen, und dann müssen die Noten vor den Pausen nicht kurz abgezogen werden, sondern sich nur allmählich verlieren.

A flexible approach to rhythm, especially to dotted rhythms, within a regular pulse was a notable characteristic of eighteenth-century style, the value of the dot and its related note(s) on either side depending on the musical context, tempo and the desired effect. The dotted note was often lengthened and its complementary note shortened and played in 'lifted' style, the style of performance thus becoming 'more enlivened'[110] (ex. 12a). When the dotted notes are to be slurred (ex. 12b), 'Not only must the dotted note be prolonged . . . but it must also be attacked somewhat strongly, slurring the second decreasingly and quietly onto it'.[111] Similarly, in ex. 12c, 'The dot must rather be held too long than

Example 12 Leopold Mozart, *Versuch* (1756)

(a) dotted

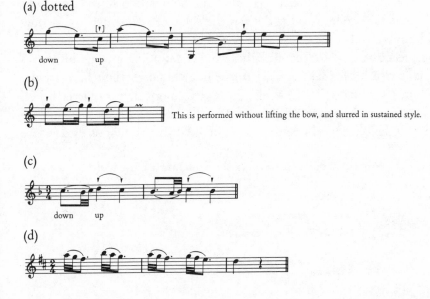

(b)

This is performed without lifting the bow, and slurred in sustained style.

(c)

(d)

too briefly', so that the ensuing notes are played more rapidly than indicated;[112] and in ex. 12d, the demisemiquavers would normally have been performed rather shorter and the dotted quaver rather longer than marked. The practice of prolonging the first of a group of two, three or four, or even more, notes slurred together and hurrying while diminishing the tone of the others has already

110 L. Mozart, *Versuch* (1756), chap. 1, sect. 3, §10, p. 39: '[jede Note von den andern abgesondert und] springend vorgetragen.'
111 Ibid. chap. 7, sect. 2, §2, p. 144: 'Man muß aber die punctirte Note nicht nur allein lange anhalten; sondern selbe etwas stark angreifen, und die zwote verlierend und still daran schleifen.'
112 Ibid. chap. 7, sect. 2, §3, pp. 144–5: 'Man muß allemal den Punct eher zu lang als zu kurz halten.'

been mentioned.[113] Türk endorses most of Leopold's views, claiming that ex. 13a should be performed sustained and with weight as in ex. 13b if the piece is of a serious, solemn or lofty nature; somewhat lighter, as in ex. 13c, if the piece is gay or cheerful; as in ex. 13d for passionate, defiant, etc., pieces or for those

Example 13 Türk, *Clavierschule* (1789)

marked staccato.[114] He adds as a footnote: 'It is impossible to describe all cases of dotted notes but it can be taken as a rule that the duration of the dot is not prolonged if the note following the dot has the value of a time-unit or, in slow tempo, of a time-member.'[115]

Wolfgang seems to have heeded his father's advice regarding making his rhythmic intentions clear,[116] for he normally wrote out dotted rhythms in a manner that approximated as closely as possible his desired interpretation. Nevertheless, instances remain in his œuvre where the dotted rhythm prescribed should be performed as if double dotted (see ex. 14). Leopold does not address directly the

Example 14 W. A. Mozart, Sonata in A for violin K 402, first movement

additional question of altering dotted and other figures in the melodic context of triplets, but he claims that the dot should be lengthened in ex. 15a and therefore, like Quantz, appears to be unsympathetic to the preference of C. P. E. Bach and others for assimilating the dotted-note figure to the triplet (ex. 15b).

[113] See p. 138.

[114] Türk, *Clavierschule*, chap. 6, §48, pp. 361–3.

[115] A time-member denoted a note of half the value of a time-unit. 'Alle mögliche Fälle sind nicht zu bestimmen; indessen kann man hierbey als Regel annehmen, daß als dann die Geltung des Punktes nicht verlängert wird, wenn die darnach folgende Note völlig die Dauer eines Takttheiles oder, in langsamer Bewegung, eines Taktgliedes hat.'

[116] L. Mozart, *Versuch* (1756), chap. 1, sect. 3, §11, pp. 39–40.

Example 15

(a) Leopold Mozart, *Versuch* (1789)

(b) Türk, *Clavierschule* (1802)

Although Leopold, like many of his contemporaries, was concerned principally with strict time-keeping,[117] he does admit tempo rubato within his rules for bowing and slurring. He also mentions it in his discussion of concerto accompaniment, confirming the need for the accompaniment to remain steady if the full expressive effect of the soloist's rubato is to be gained.[118] This involves a type of rubato similar to that described by C. P. E. Bach, Wolfgang Mozart and Türk in respect of keyboard playing, in which the left hand plays in strict time while the right hand plays slightly more freely than prescribed.[119] Türk considers this an exceptional means of enhancing the expression and provides numerous examples, including one based upon syncopation and types incorporating anticipation and retardation, as well as one involving spontaneous decoration of the text.[120] Tempo rubato also extended in certain cases to the modification of dynamics and/or the displacement of natural accents (resulting, for example, in unaccented 'strong' beats of the bar);[121] the expansion of the bar(s) to incorporate more notes than the time-signature theoretically allowed, and a flexible yet rhythmically controlled performance of these passages;[122] and a flexibility of tempo by hesitating (in tender, languishing or sad moments), and introducing arbitrary, unwritten accelerandos (e.g. in passages of passionate, angry or violent emotion) or ritardandos (e.g. in the tender moments of pieces

[117] Ibid. chap. 1, sect. 2, §12, p. 32; chap. 7, sect. 1, §§8, 11, 16 and 17, pp. 125–9; chap. 7, sect. 2, §§2, 3 and 5, pp. 144–5; chap. 12, §20, p. 262–3.

[118] Ibid. chap. 12, §20, p. 263.

[119] Türk, *Clavierschule*, chap. 6, §§63–4, pp. 370–1, and §§66–8, pp. 371–2; C. P. E. Bach, *Versuch* (trans.), chap. 3, §28, p. 161; Wolfgang Mozart, letter to Leopold Mozart dated 23 October 1777, in Anderson, *Letters*, p. 340. See also, for example, Quantz, *Versuch* (trans.), chap. 17, sect. 7, §48, p. 284; L. Mozart, *Versuch* (1756), chap. 7, §2, pp. 144–6 and chap. 12, §20n, p. 263; C. P. E. Bach, *Versuch* (trans.), chap. 3, §8, pp. 150–1.

[120] Türk, *Clavierschule*, chap. 6, §§63–4, pp. 370–1, and §72, pp. 374–5.

[121] Ibid. chap. 6, §72, pp. 374–5.

[122] C. P. E. Bach, *Versuch* (trans.), chap. 3, §28, pp. 160–1.

that suggest two contrasting moods).[123] Significantly, perhaps, the various early nineteenth-century German revisions of Leopold's text recommend 'an appropriate hurrying and delaying' as a useful expressive ploy in suitable solo contexts. Thus, the most important, expressive notes in a melody may be held rather longer than their written value, while passagework may be quickened up in order to inject life and vigour where appropriate. Such variations of the prescribed text naturally required tasteful and sparing introduction if they were to have their full effect.[124]

Leopold acknowledges that his treatise is not comprehensive, but his half-promise of a sequel was never fulfilled.[125] Nevertheless, it is remarkable how his principles of violin playing withstood the test of time during such a crucial period of transition. Of the changes in the three editions he sanctioned, relatively few affect the major issues concerning articulation. Apart from an occasional error or re-ordering of material, even those revised German publications not sanctioned by Leopold in no way distort his articulation 'policy' by making glaring omissions or significant emendations to suit the taste of the time. Most of the revisers of his treatise aimed at greater conciseness, some accusing him of long-windedness, of meddling in the insignificant, of deficiencies of arrangement and of erroneous statements.[126] In the 1804 edition, for example, Leopold's three chapters on ornaments are reduced to two, and the final chapter on good execution is revised and supplemented. But despite these criticisms and modifications, the skeleton and much of the flesh of the original text and musical examples remain unaltered in those publications that emanated from Austria and Germany.

The same may be said for the relevant section of text in the one English source consulted, *Mozart's Violin School on the Art of Bowing* (a mere eighteen pages in length), but less so for two of the three relevant treatises published in France. This is perhaps not surprising, because the ascendant French school was in the vanguard of technical and interpretative developments in string playing in the late eighteenth century. It reached its zenith with the expressive style of Giovanni Battista Viotti (1755–1824), who essentially established the foundations on which the celebrated French school of the nineteenth century, based at the Conservatoire in Paris, was built. Valentin Roeser's French 'translation' of Leopold's treatise appeared in *c.* 1770, but Leopold surprisingly knew nothing about it for some time – about eight years after its publication he was urging Wolfgang to send

[123] See H. Koch, 'Über den technischen Ausdruck: Tempo rubato', *Allgemeine musikalische Zeitung* 10 (1807), cols. 513–19.

[124] Anon., *Violin-Schule* (1806), p. 75: '. . . ein zweckmässiges Eilen und Zögern . . .'

[125] L. Mozart, *Versuch* (1756), chap. 12, §22, p. 264.

[126] Anon., *Leopold Mozart's Violinschule* (1804), 'Vorrede'.

him a copy from Paris, or to bring one home with him.[127] It is a shortened version of the original with some differences in content (e.g. the sections about holding the violin and bow), but the essence of Leopold's material is for the most part faithfully reproduced. The cases of Cartier's *L'art du violon* (1798) and Woldemar's *Méthode* (1801), however, are rather different. Cartier's text is, on his own admission, an amalgamation of extracts from the treatises of Geminiani, Leopold Mozart, Tarade and l'Abbé le fils,[128] but he does include some of Leopold's own 1787 revisions, notably the more advanced left thumb position. *L'art du violon*, dedicated to the new Conservatoire de musique in Paris, thoroughly commended by that institution's staff and adopted initially in its curriculum, confirms the advent of a more uniform and international approach to violin playing at the turn to the nineteenth century.

Woldemar acknowledges the treatises of Geminiani and Leopold Mozart as the most esteemed available but considers them inadequate for nineteenth-century usage, especially in respect of the recommended violin hold and many of the principles for fingering and bowing. His treatise champions the Tourte-like 'Viotti bow', and his numerous musical and textual revisions result in a publication which bears little resemblance to Leopold Mozart's original work in either layout or content. Nevertheless, the common ground between the two authors' theoretical principles (e.g., the bowing rules, duets, divisions, ornaments, examples regarding shifting, etc.) is perhaps sufficient to justify the inclusion of Leopold Mozart's name in the title.

Such was the significance of Leopold Mozart's *Versuch* that it retained its value in Germany even after the appearance of a German translation (Leipzig, [c. 1810]) of Rode's, Baillot's, and Kreutzer's influential *Méthode de violon* (Paris, 1803), which served unchallenged as the standard text of the French violin school at the Paris Conservatoire until well into the 1830s. The preface of the 1817 revision of Leopold's treatise claims that both publications 'belong together, so to speak, and supplement each other'. But the last word on the importance of Leopold's treatise belongs to Carl Friedrich Zelter, who wrote to Goethe in 1829: 'His Violinschule is a work which will be worth using as long as the violin remains a violin'.[129]

---

[127] Letter of 11 June 1778, in Anderson, *Letters*, p. 548. See also p. 544.

[128] Cartier, *L'art du violon*, preface, p. ii.

[129] Letter of 12 March 1829 in M. Hecker, ed., *Goethe-Zelter-Briefwechsel*, vol. 3 (Leipzig, 1918), p. 132: 'Seine Violinschule ist ein Werk, das sich brauchen läßt, so lange die Violine eine Violine bleibt.'

8

MOZART ACCORDING TO MENDELSSOHN: A CONTRIBUTION TO *REZEPTIONSGESCHICHTE*

R. LARRY TODD

'He is the Mozart of the nineteenth century, the most brilliant musician, who looks most clearly through the contradictions of the present, and who for the first time reconciles them.'[1] This was Robert Schumann's assessment of Mendelssohn in an 1840 review of the D minor Piano Trio Op. 49, a work Schumann lauded as an exemplary 'master trio of the present'. Not infrequently, Schumann ascribed such Mozartian, 'classical' traits as balance, poise, grace, and refinement to Mendelssohn's music.[2] Nor was the comparison lost on some of Schumann's contemporaries, who placed the 'noble' Mendelssohn at the forefront of a modern classicist school endeavouring to uphold traditional musical values against the onslaught of philistinism. Thus C. F. Becker filled an 1842 review of Mendelssohn's *95th Psalm* Op. 46 with allusions to classical antiquity. A work of such perfection, he suggested, could not be criticised, but only viewed with detachment, for it had sprung forth from the wellspring of the composer's feelings in 'complete beauty' ('voller Schönheit'), a process Becker likened to Minerva emerging in full armour from the head of Jupiter. For Becker, Mendelssohn stood as a 'Coryphaeus of art'.[3]

This use of Mozartian and classical metaphors to describe Mendelssohn's position in German music during the 1830s and 1840s was but one manifestation of a profound shift in critical thought about the music of the eighteenth-century Viennese classicists and, above all, about Mozart. Earlier in the nineteenth century, Mozart had actually been received as the composer who had opened up new *romantic* realms in German instrumental music. Thus E. T. A. Hoffmann, in the

---

[1] *Neue Zeitschrift für Musik* 13 (1840), 198 (19 December). 'Er ist der Mozart des 19ten Jahrhunderts, der hellste Musiker, der die Widersprüche der Zeit am klarsten durchschaut.'

[2] See Leon Plantinga, 'Schumann's Critical Reaction to Mendelssohn', in *Mendelssohn and Schumann: Essays on Their Music and Its Context*, ed. J. W. Finson and R. L. Todd (Durham, N. C., 1984), pp. 17–18.

[3] 'Felix Mendelssohn-Bartholdy: Der fünfundneunzigste Psalm, für Chor und Orchester', in *Allgemeine musikalische Zeitung* 44 (1842), col. 1 (5 January). Of course, in 1853, Schumann reused the Minerva myth to introduce the young Brahms.

celebrated review from 1810 of Beethoven's Fifth Symphony, detected in Mozart a 'premonition of the infinite',[4] while some found in *Don Giovanni* and other works the sinister and the exultation of the sublime.[5] Beethoven's efforts to augment the domain and purpose of instrumental music were at first understood as an extension of the romanticising *Tendenz* of Haydn's and Mozart's music – for Hoffmann, a bold exploration into the realm of the 'colossal'. But the later music of Beethoven – eventually considered by many as strange, even incomprehensible – forced a critical revaluation. The increasingly abstract, eccentric qualities of Beethoven's work after the Congress of Vienna – qualities that Salieri's pupil Schubert evidently found difficult already in 1816[6] – proved irresistible to the romantics of the 1820s and 1830s – among them, of course, the young Schumann and Mendelssohn. In the resulting critical realignment, Beethoven's music was celebrated for its romantic, liberating qualities, while Mozart's music, as if in opposition, was thought to exhibit elements of 'grace, elegance, and of the plainly beautiful'.[7]

The 1830s and 1840s in fact marked the establishment of the now familiar classic-romantic dichotomy in the periodisation of music history. When Mendelssohn in 1833 assumed the direction of opera in Düsseldorf, he began his tenure by announcing a series of 'classic' productions, including Mozart's *Don Giovanni*.[8] A particularly important centre of the new thought was Leipzig, where Mendelssohn arrived in 1835 as municipal music director. Amadeus Wendt's *Ueber den gegenwärtigen Zustand der Musik, besonders in Deutschland und wie er greworden*, which appeared in Leipzig in 1836, is often cited as one of the first clear formulations of a classic music period centred on Mozart.[9] In the two leading Leipzig music journals the new concept was further developed and refined. Thus, in the pages of Schumann's *Neue Zeitschrift für Musik*, F. A. Gelbcke drew in 1841 a clear line between Mozart and Beethoven:

. . . If Beethoven founded the present school, it can hardly be denied that the artistic principles which Mozart adopted as the basis of his work have been altogether lost. That

[4] *AmZ* 12 (1810), col. 632.

[5] See M. Staehelin, 'Zum Verhältnis von Mozart- und Beethoven-Bild im 19. Jahrhundert', in *Mozart-Jahrbuch 1980–1983*, pp. 17–22.

[6] *Franz Schubert's Letters and Other Writings*, ed. O. E. Deutsch (London, 1928; repr. New York, 1970), p. 29. Of course, within a few years Schubert considerably modified his views of Beethoven.

[7] Staehelin, p. 19.

[8] See the account in W. S. Rockstro, *Mendelssohn* (London, 1890), p. 53, and Mendelssohn's letter of 28 December 1833 to his father (in *Briefe aus den Jahren 1830 bis 1847 von Felix Mendelssohn Bartholdy*, ed. P. Mendelssohn Bartholdy (Leipzig, 1878), vol. 2, p. 11).

[9] See A. Forchert, '"Klassisch" und "romantisch" in der Musikliteratur des frühen 19. Jahrhunderts', *Die Musikforschung* 31 (1978), 412f.

composure, that peace of mind, that serene and generous approach to life, that balance between ideas and the means of expression which is fundamental to the superb masterpieces of that unique man, these were the most blessed and fruitful characteristics of the age in which Mozart lived . . .[10]

Similarly, K. A. T. Kahlert asserted in the *Allgemeine musikalische Zeitung* in 1848 that Mozart

was the most truly classical of all composers; others were classical in only certain specific ways. He was so imaginative, he had such a balanced feeling for musical form, that those who examined his music with a critical eye found it to be as comprehensible as it was inventive. His music possessed lightness and yet the greatest depth and skill. It was universally admired both for its simplicity and for its ineffable profundity. Then along came his great successor, who explored new paths.[11]

Perhaps all too understandable was the temptation to place Mendelssohn – the 'Mozart of the nineteenth century' – into a kind of neoclassic school. Franz Brendel, who succeeded Schumann as editor of the *Neue Zeitschrift* in 1845, and then gradually steered the journal toward the 'progressive' aims of the new *Zukunftsmusik* of Wagner and Liszt, offered this judgment: 'Mendelssohn proceeds from the outside to the inside: from what is generally approved and established to self-recognition and poetry.' And, stating the matter more directly, 'Mendelssohn is a representative of classicism in our time; for that reason he is

---

[10] 'Classisch und Romantisch: Ein Beitrag zur Geschichtsschreibung der Musik unserer Zeit', *NZfM* 14 (1841), 189; trans. in *Music and Aesthetics in the Eighteenth and Early-Nineteenth Centuries*, ed. P. le Huray and J. Day (Cambridge, 1981), p. 527. See also 'Was heisst Klassisch?', *AmZ* 37 (1835), cols. 838, 841.

> . . . und die jetzt laufende mit Beethoven beginnen läßt, so kann man wohl nicht läugnen, daß für uns jener Standpunct der Kunst, von welchem aus Mozart schaffte und wirkte, gänzlich verloren gegangen ist. Diese Sammlung, diese Ruhe des Gemüthes, diese heitere, großartige Weltanschauung, und das Gleichgewicht der Ausdrucksmittel mit den Ideen, woraus die herrlichen Meisterstücke dieses einzigen Mannes hervorgingen, und welche überhaupt die segensreichen und befruchtenden Eigenschaften seiner Zeit waren, haben wir unmerklich, wahrscheinlich ohne unsere Schuld, aber nichts desto weniger gewiß verloren.

[11] 'Ueber den Begriff der klassischen und romantischen Musik', *AmZ* 50 (1848), col. 291; trans. in le Huray and Day, p. 561.

> Von allen Tondichtern vereinigte am Meisten er alle Eigenschaften des Klassikers, während bei anderen nur einzelne davon in's hellste Licht getreten waren. So reich seine Erfindung, so ebenmässig war jede seiner musikalischen Formen, daher seine Verständlichkeit neben dem Reichthume, den er doch jedem kritischen Forscher darbot. Ueberall zeigte sich Licht, und doch die grösste Tiefe der Kombination. Seine Einfachheit bewunderten Alle nicht minder, als seine Unergründlichkeit. Da erhob sich sein grosser Nachfolger, der einen neuen Weg einschlug . . .

not an expression of the present time in its entirety, least of all of future trends.'[12] Two years later, Mendelssohn's early death in 1847 at the age of thirty-eight served only to reinforce this view of him as a Mozart-like classicist. Thus Schumann, who assembled a sketch-like series of anecdotal *Erinnerungen* of his friend, marvelled at the 'perfection' of Mendelssohn's early masterpiece, the Octet Op. 20, and declared that Mendelssohn's brief life had been a consummate work of art (*Sein Leben ein Kunstwerk – vollendet*).[13] And in 1848 Mendelssohn's early biographer W. A. Lampadius initiated a process of idealisation which continued during the century: 'But what has made Mendelssohn's a classic Muse? Foremost of all, the master's pure and lofty aspiration, which set for itself only the highest ideal . . .'[14] 'Consummate', 'pure', 'lofty', 'ideal' – these words are never far removed from those Winckelmannian attributes that Schumann and others had preempted and applied to Mozart.

In our own time, Mendelssohn is usually viewed as a 'classic romantic' whose music shows strong evidence of a stylistic dependence on the work of earlier masters. But if Mendelssohn's efforts on behalf of and stylistic debt to the music of J. S. Bach and Handel are well documented, and if his assimilation of Beethoven's forceful musical language is generally acknowledged,[15] his attitudes toward the high classical style of Haydn and Mozart have not yet been examined in detail. In particular, Mendelssohn's response to Mozart forms a significant chapter in the Mozart *Rezeptionsgeschichte* of the nineteenth century. In brief, Mendelssohn's efforts as a performer of Mozart served to strengthen and confirm Mozart's canonisation in the classical school, a process that gained momentum during the 1830s and 1840s, at the very height of Mendelssohn's career. The present study, relying in part on some little known sources, seeks to explore

[12] 'Robert Schumann mit Rücksicht auf Mendelssohn-Bartholdy und die Entwicklung der modernen Tonkunst überhaupt', *NZfM* 22 (1845), 114, 149; see also J. Thym, 'Schumann in Brendel's *Neue Zeitschrift für Musik* from 1845 to 1856', in *Mendelssohn and Schumann*, pp. 21–38, from which the present translations are extracted. ('M. strebt von außen nach innen, durch das Geltende und allgemein Anerkannte nach Selbsterfassung und Poesie,'. . . 'er ist Repräsentent des Classischen in der Gegenwart, darum aber auch nicht Ausdruck der gesammten Zeit, am wenigsten des Zukunftstrebens derselben.')

[13] Robert Schumann, *Erinnerungen an Felix Mendelssohn Bartholdy*, ed. G. Eismann (Zwickau, 1947), pp. 55, 61. For a revised, slightly corrected redaction of the text see H.-K. Metzger and R. Riehn, 'Aufzeichnungen über Schumann', in *Felix Mendelssohn Bartholdy: Musik-Konzepte 14/15* (Munich, 1980), pp. 97–122.

[14] *Felix Mendelssohn Bartholdy: ein Denkmal für seine Freunde* (Leipzig, 1848); trans. W. L. Gage as *Life of Felix Mendelssohn Bartholdy* (Boston, 1865), pp. 176–177.

[15] See J. Godwin, 'Early Mendelssohn and Late Beethoven', *Music & Letters* 55 (1974), 272; and my 'A Mendelssohn Miscellany', *Music & Letters* 71 (1990), 52–64.

how Mendelssohn viewed and performed Mozart's music, and how, to begin
with, his response to Mozart shaped his own development as a composer.

I

We may probably credit Carl Friedrich Zelter, with whom young Mendelssohn
began to study theory and composition around 1819, for Mendelssohn's earliest
meaningful exposure to Mozart's music. Of course, Zelter is best remembered
for inculcating his prize pupil with a deep respect for the music of J. S. Bach;
indeed, Zelter's plan of tuition was evidently modelled on a similar methodology
in the treatise of Bach's pupil J. P. Kirnberger, *Die Kunst des reinen Satzes* (1771–9),
the stated aim of which was to transmit the pedagogical approach of Bach. Not
surprisingly, Mendelssohn's early student workbooks were filled with exercises
in figured bass, chorale (note against note and embellished), canon, and fugue,[16]
and thus set apart from the method of instruction Mozart employed during the
mid 1780s with Thomas Attwood, which featured Fuxian species counterpoint.[17]
Nevertheless, when Zelter in 1824 declared that Mendelssohn had completed
his apprenticeship as a composer, he placed him 'in the company of Mozart,
Haydn, and of old Bach', with Mozart's name conspicuously listed first.[18] What is
more, in Zelter's letters to Goethe, Mozart's name figures prominently;[19] and
there is little doubt that for Zelter, Mozart served with Bach as a master whose
music, worthy of emulation, could provide didactic models.

Thus, among the severe, learned fugues of Mendelssohn's early student work-
book (1819–21) we find an ingratiating classical melody with Alberti-type accompaniment; its general contours and chromatic appoggiatura in bar 4 resemble
strikingly the Andante of Mozart's Sonata in C major K 545 (ex. 1). Admittedly
this classical allusion is short-lived: the theme is followed by a minor-key variation
which unfolds as a strict canon at the octave, yet another purely contrapuntal
display by the student. On the other hand, Mendelssohn's Bachian attraction
to learned counterpoint was more than challenged by his encounter with the

---

[16] See my *Mendelssohn's Musical Education: A Study and Edition of His Exercises in Composition*
(Cambridge, 1983).

[17] Edited by Erich Hertzmann and C. B. Oldman in the *Neue Mozart Ausgabe*, X/30, 1 (Kassel,
1965). During his first visit to England in 1829 Mendelssohn met Attwood; in 1833 he
inscribed a Kyrie for him and in 1837 dedicated his Three Preludes and Fugues for Organ,
Op. 37, to him.

[18] The occasion was Mendelssohn's fifteenth birthday, on which his fourth Singspiel, *Die beiden
Neffen*, was rehearsed. See S. Hensel, ed., *Die Familie Mendelssohn 1729 bis 1847*, 14th edn
(Berlin, 1911), vol. 1, p. 139.

[19] See K. F. Zelter, J. W. Goethe, *Briefwechsel: eine Auswahl* (Leipzig, 1987), *passim*.

Example 1

(a) Mendelssohn, piano piece in G amjor (Bodleian Library, M. Deneke
     Mendelssohn C. 43)

(b) Mozart, Sonata in C major for piano K 545, Andante

'Jupiter' Symphony, which he heard performed in the Leipzig Gewandhaus in
October 1821. Writing a few days later from Weimar, where, during his celebrated visit to Goethe he played for Mozart's pupil J. N. Hummel, Mendelssohn inscribed a stretto-like study of the 'Jupiter' motive, which he sent to his
friend Eduard Rietz as a demonstration of the motive's contrapuntal potential
(Fig. 8.1).[20] At some point Rietz copied out the symphony for Mendelssohn;
this copy remained a prized possession in the composer's library.[21]

The 'Jupiter' Symphony indeed cast its influence on a variety of Mendelssohn's
compositions from the 1820s. The finale of the Singspiel *Die beiden Pädagogen*,[22]
completed in March 1821, already alludes in its closing bars to a passage from
the closing of the first movement of the symphony (exx. 2a, 2b), with a conspicuously similar scoring: a tremolando figure in parallel tenths in the strings supported by a pedal point in the brass, almost as if Mendelssohn were attempting
to recreate that special, luminescent sound world of the symphony. (No less
compelling a Mozartian gesture occurs somewhat earlier in the finale, where
Mendelssohn experiments with a polymetrical passage that points unmistakably
to the first finale of *Don Giovanni*. Here he sets a rustic *Tanz* in 6/8 time against
a chorus in 2/4; the dance melody is given to a solo violin that, as in the opera,

---

[20] Letter of 4 November 1821 (New York Public Library).
[21] In a list Mendelssohn prepared in 1844 of Mozart's works in his library we find the entry
'Symph. c dur geschr. v. Ritz.' Oxford, Bodleian Library, M. Deneke Mendelssohn C. 49,
fol. 29 (see Fig. 8.2).
[22] Available in an edition by K. H. Köhler for the *Leipziger Ausgabe der Werke Felix Mendelssohn
Bartholdys*, series 5, vol. 1 (Leipzig, 1966).

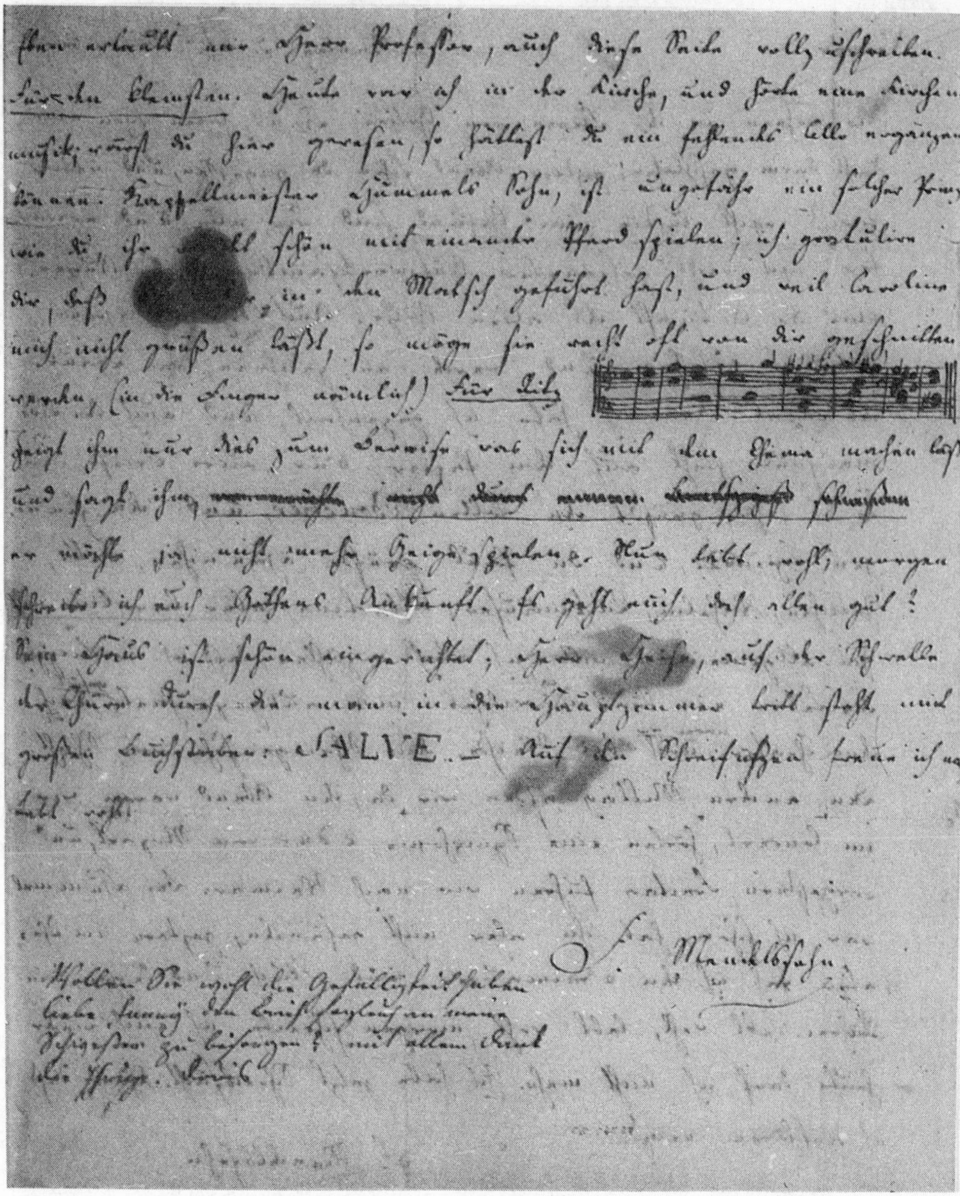

Figure 8.1 Mendelssohn, letter of 4 November 1821 [New York Public Library]

Example 2

(a) Mendelssohn, *Die beiden Pädagogen*, finale

(b) Mozart, 'Jupiter' Symphony K 551, first movement

(c) Mendelssohn, subjects used in *Sinfonia VIII*, finale

(d) Mozart, subjects used in 'Jupiter' Symphony, finale

(e) Mendelssohn, *Sinfonia VIII*, finale

Ex. 2 (*cont.*)

(f) Mozart, 'Jupiter' Symphony, finale

(g) Mendelssohn, *Sinfonia VIII*, finale (wind version)

(h) Mendelssohn, Fugue in E♭ Op. 81 No. 4

(i) Mendelssohn, *Reformation* Symphony Op. 107, first movement

is first allowed to tune itself. What is more, the melody itself is clearly reminiscent of the slow movement from Mozart's Violin Sonata K 301. All in all, the naive charm of this homage to Mozart falls considerably short of the complex poly-metrical combinations in the finale of Mozart's opera, where, of course, three dances in as many metres are introduced and contraposed.)

A considerably more sophisticated response to the 'Jupiter' Symphony appears in Mendelssohn's *Sinfonia VIII* of 1822, one of thirteen string *sinfonie* rapidly written between 1821 and 1823; the finale of this work, marked Allegro molto, is closely modelled on the Allegro molto fugal finale of the 'Jupiter', and calls for extended discussion here. This *sinfonia* represented a special achievement for the thirteen-year-old Mendelssohn, who took the trouble to produce a second version for full orchestra – his very first symphony, in fact, for full orchestra.[23] Perhaps in deciding to add woodwinds and brass, Mendelssohn was again at-tempting, consciously or unconsciously, to bring the finale closer to its model by adopting a distinctly classical type of orchestration.[24]

As in the 'Jupiter' Symphony, Mendelssohn's finale is based on four contrapun-tal subjects (exx. 2c, 2d) which are introduced, juxtaposed, and contraposed, all in the context of a ternary sonata-form movement. The first subject, a graceful, Mozartian, ten-bar period, is heard first *piano* in the strings with tremolo accom-paniment, and then repeated *forte* by the full orchestra, more or less in accordance with Mozart's procedure. In the bridge, the second subject appears; introduced by an upbeat of three repeated notes, it describes a rapid descending scale, and is clearly taken from Mozart's second subject. After combining the two subjects Mendelssohn presents the third, a turn-like figure which also springs from an upbeat of repeated notes. The approach to the dominant and second thematic group – via a secondary dominant seventh and a rest – is again borrowed from the Mozart ('Jupiter', bar 73). But here Mendelssohn departs somewhat from his model: instead of devising a fourth subject as his second theme, he reuses the first subject, which is now stated three times, in the flute, bass, and flute. In the closing passage of the exposition, all three subjects are reviewed: in one striking passage (bars 125ff), subjects 1 and 2 are combined in a rising sequence that again vividly brings to mind the 'Jupiter' (bars 135ff); like Mozart, Mendels-sohn here gives his second subject in both its prime and mirror inverted forms (exx. 2e, 2f).

---

[23] Both versions are available in an edition by H. C. Wolff for the *Leipziger Ausgabe*, series 1, vol. 2 (Leipzig, 1965).

[24] In comparison, several of Mendelssohn's other string symphonies are stylistically closer to the eighteenth-century North German string symphony tradition of Emanuel Bach, Christoph Nichelmann, and other Berlin composers, or are clearly indebted to Johann Sebastian Bach.

The first part of the development is devoted to the fourth subject, which appears in a five-part fugato (in comparison, Mozart employs a five-part fugato for a statement of his *first* subject, in bars 36ff of the exposition). Mendelssohn's choice of a five-part texture is especially meaningful: it enabled him, as it did Mozart, to enrich the counterpoint of the four-part string ensemble; and it required him, as it did Mozart, to divide the bass line into two parts for the celli and contrabass. Further on in the development, Mendelssohn combines the fourth subject with the first, and eventually experiments with various juxtapositions of all four. But all of this pales in comparison with the impressive erudition exhibited in the coda of the movement (bars 449ff), which, following the more or less straightforward recapitulation, takes as its point of departure the celebrated concluding stretto of the 'Jupiter'. In a kind of contrapuntal summary, Mendelssohn here systematically combines all four subjects, to which he adds a 'fifth' subject drawn from a diminished version of the fourth – a technique similar to that employed by Mozart. Ex. 2g provides a brief idea of Mendelssohn's method; the accompanying tables 1 and 2 compare Mendelssohn's and Mozart's display of quintuple counterpoint. Of special note is Mendelssohn's orchestration of the passage: starting in bar 457, winds are employed to double individual statements of the subjects in the strings; and, as the coda gains in complexity, trumpets and drums appear to give lustre to the sound – all in all, a carefully calculated rehearing of Mozart's pellucid scoring.[25]

Of course, in no way does the finale of the fourteen-year-old Mendelssohn attain the refined mastery of Mozart's score. For one thing, Mozart's orchestration is brilliantly co-ordinated with the display of quintuple counterpoint, so that the five woodwinds (one flute, two oboes, and two bassoons) exactly double the five string parts; Mendelssohn's eight-part woodwind choir is not conducive to a similar arrangement. For another, Mozart's permutations of the contrapuntal subjects are worked out according to a symmetrical scheme of rotations, in which each subject systematically appears in ascending order (shown by the diagonals in Table 1); again, Mendelssohn's studied counterpoint does not match what may only be described as Mozart's flawless artistry.

Nevertheless, in 1823, Mendelssohn's *sinfonia* finale marked an impressive summary of his contrapuntal mastery, an achievement facilitated, as we have seen, by his discovery of Mozart's 'Jupiter' Symphony. Scarcely two years later, Mendelssohn attained a new contrapuntal summit in the finale of the Octet, where he amassed an eight-part fugato and combinations of multiple subjects in a stunning

[25] On Mozart's use of texture as a structural device, see further my 'Orchestral Texture and the Art of Orchestration', in *The Orchestra: Origins and Transformations*, ed. J. Peyser (New York, 1986), pp. 207–8.

Table 1. *Mozart, 'Jupiter' Symphony, finale, stretto, order of subjects*

	b. 372	376	380	384	388	392	396	399
fl., vn 1	—	—	4	1	3	(4 dim., 3)	2	1
ob. 1, vn 2	—	4	1	3	(4 dim., 3)	2	4	3
ob. 2, vla	4	1	3	(4 dim., 3)	2	4	1	4
bn 1, cello	1	3	(4 dim., 3)	2	4	1	3	(4 dim., 3)
bn 2, bass	—	—	—	4	1	3	(4 dim., 3)	2

Table 2. *Mendelssohn, Sinfonia VIII, finale (wind version), stretto, order of subjects*

	b. 449	453	457 (winds added)	461	465
violin 1	1	4	3	2 (fl.)–3	4
violin 2	2–3	4	1 (ob.)	4 dim. (ob.)	3–1 inv. (cl.)
viola	1	2	2	1 (cl.)	4 dim. (tr., cl.)
cello	—	1	4 (hn)	4 (bn)	2
bass	—	—	—	—	1 (hn)

contrapuntal *tour de force* – all with a remarkable grace, clarity of texture, and classically balanced phrase structure. In at least two other works, Mendelssohn responded directly to the 'Jupiter' motive itself. The posthumously published Fugue in E♭ major for string quartet Op. 81 No. 4 (1827) incorporates the motive into its opening subject (ex. 2h); subsequently, a second, more flowing subject is introduced, and the two are combined, so that the composition comprises, in fact, a double fugue. As Friedhelm Krummacher has noticed, the tempo indication, *A tempo ordinario*, suggests the invocation of the *stile antico*,[26] and it may well be that Mendelssohn was responding in his fugue more to the distinguished fugal traditions behind the 'Jupiter' motive (e.g. J. S. Bach's Fugue in E major from the second volume of the *Well-Tempered Clavier*, Froberger's Fantasia in the phrygian mode, etc.) than to Mozart's particular use of it.[27] Finally, in the opening of the 'Reformation' Symphony Op. 107 (1830), a work which Mendelssohn eventually withdrew, he cited the motive in an imitative passage (ex. 2i). Here, the carefully regulated treatment of dissonance and the ascending imitative entries at the interval of a fifth (i.e. non-fugal) suggest again an invocation of the *stile antico*, in particular, as Judith Silber Ballan has recently proposed,[28] the Palestrinian tradition of Catholic church polyphony that had interested other Leipzigers, chiefly J. S. Bach in *Clavierübung III*.

Still, in all likelihood it was the Leipzig performance of the 'Jupiter' Symphony Mendelssohn heard in 1821 that served as the primary inspiration for his own experiments with the motive, which continued to fascinate him during his student period of the 1820s. In later years, he would have several additional encounters with the 'Jupiter' Symphony, which he frequently performed in Leipzig at the Gewandhaus (see Table 3). On 4 February 1841 he concluded a concert in the Gewandhaus devoted to Mozart with the symphony, prompting Robert Schumann to report that all Germany should have been present to marvel at the resplendence of the music.[29] An earlier performance of 9 March 1837 prompted one reviewer to describe the symphony as 'the immortal model and ideal of all symphonies' ('das unsterbliche Vorbild und Muster aller Symphonien').[30] And, finally, in 1845, Mendelssohn received for perusal from the publisher Johann Anton André – who in 1799 had purchased the Mozart *Nachlass* from

---

[26] *Mendelssohn – der Komponist: Studien zur Kammermusik für Streicher* (Munich, 1978), p. 187.

[27] See A. H. King, *Mozart in Retrospect* (Oxford, 1955), pp. 262–3; and S. Wollenberg, 'The Jupiter Theme: New Light on its Creation', *Musical Times* 116 (1975), 781–3.

[28] See J. K. Silber, 'Mendelssohn and the *Reformation* Symphony: A Critical and Historical Study' (Ph.D. diss., Yale University, 1987), pp. 110ff.

[29] *NZfM* 14 (1841), p. 89.

[30] *AmZ* 39 (1837), col. 242.

the composer's widow, Constanze – the autograph of the symphony. To his delight, Mendelssohn discovered a revision in the closing bars of the Adagio, where Mozart decided as an afterthought to reintroduce the opening theme. Writing to Ignaz Moscheles on 7 March, Mendelssohn mused, 'Isn't that a fortuitous revision?' ('Ist das nicht eine glückliche Änderung?')[31]

II

In the finale of *Sinfonia VIII* we find, perhaps, the clearest example of Mendelssohn's response as a composer to Mozart's music; there the young musician undertook a concerted effort to assimilate Mozart's approach to counterpoint into his own developing style. Other student works occasionally show again Mendelssohn's turn to Mozart for inspiration. We shall examine briefly the little known Kyrie in D minor for five-part chorus and orchestra from 1825. In this case, Mendelssohn's procedure was more to allude to Mozart stylistically than to base the work closely on a Mozartian model. Here, the relevant work is the opening movement of the Requiem, again, a work with which Mendelssohn was intimately familiar through performance.

As early as February 1822 Mendelssohn had heard the Requiem,[32] which was highly esteemed by Zelter, who performed it frequently at the Singakademie in Berlin during the 1820s, defended it when its authenticity was questioned in a series of articles by the theorist Gottfried Weber beginning in 1825, and referred to it affectionately as 'unser Requiem'. Then, on 5 December 1824, at a concert organised by the Geheimrath Crelle on the anniversary of Mozart's death, Mendelssohn himself presided over a performance of the work from the piano, which took the place of the orchestra.[33] A few months later, Mendelssohn arrived with his father in Paris. There, on 31 March, he participated in another performance of the Requiem, this one with orchestra, in which he presumably played either

[31] *Briefe aus den Jahren 1830 bis 1847 von Felix Mendelssohn Bartholdy*, vol. 2, pp. 288–9. The revision occurs on fols. 25 and 26 of the autograph. A facsimile is available in *Documenta musicologica*, 2. Reihe, vol. 8 (Kassel, 1978). Mendelssohn had in his possession at least two other Mozart autographs. From a letter of 10 February 1830 we learn that he received a Mozart sketchbook from Heinrich Beer (see *Felix Mendelssohn-Bartholdys Briefwechsel mit Legationsrat Karl Klingemann*, ed. K. Klingemann, Essen, 1909, p. 75). And in 1836 Mendelssohn obtained from Aloys Fuchs an autograph of K 312 which he included in the autograph album he prepared as a Christmas present for his wife Cécile. The album is in the M. Deneke Mendelssohn Collection at Oxford (C. 21, fols. 8–9).

[32] See S. Grossmann-Vendrey, *Felix Mendelssohn Bartholdy und die Musik der Vergangenheit* (Regensburg, 1969), p. 17.

[33] See I. Moscheles, *Recent Music and Musicians* (New York, 1873; repr. 1970), p. 67.

violin or viola.[34] In October 1834, Mendelssohn performed the work in Düsseldorf, and, finally, in September 1840, part of it in Birmingham (see Table 3).

The highpoint of Mendelssohn's 1825 Parisian sojourn was his introduction to the indomitable *directeur* of the Conservatoire, Luigi Cherubini, to whom Abraham Mendelssohn Bartholdy brought his son for advice about his future prospects as a composer. Cherubini was more than suitably impressed[35] and, evidently, encouraged young Mendelssohn to try his hand at a sacred work. The result, the Kyrie in D minor, was completed on 6 May, and brought to Cherubini for criticism a few days later. We do not know what Cherubini's verdict was; but Zelter, writing to Goethe on 28 May 1825, reported:

He prepared there for Cherubini a Kyrie, which was allowed to be heard and seen; all the more, as the brave youth, according to his versatile nature, fashioned the piece in a spirit almost ironic, which, if not the proper one, nevertheless is one such as Cherubini has always sought, and, if I am not much mistaken, has not much found.[36]

'Fast ironisch' – could Zelter have been referring to the striking similarities between his prize pupil's Kyrie and the opening movement of Mozart's Requiem? Indeed, Cherubini's own *Missa solemnis* in D minor (1811) recalls in several details the musical gestures and contrapuntal language of Mozart's Requiem, as if Cherubini were seeking to emulate Mozart. What is more, Cherubini's Kyrie culminates in a learned fugue on a subject especially similar to a subject employed by Mendelssohn in his Kyrie (exx. 3a, 3b), suggesting that Mendelssohn knew

Example 3

(a) Cherubini, *Missa solemnis* in D, Kyrie fugue subject

(b) Mendelssohn, Kyrie in D minor (1825), fugue subject

---

[34] Reported in Mendelssohn's letter of 1 April 1825 to Berlin (New York Public Library).

[35] In his letter of 6 April 1825 to Berlin, Mendelssohn reported Cherubini's remark, 'Ce garçon est riche, il fera bien.'

[36] L. Geiger, ed., *Briefwechsel zwischen Goethe und Zelter in den Jahren 1799 bis 1832* (Leipzig, n.d.), vol. 2, pp. 322–34.

> Er hat dem Cherubini ein Kyrie dort angefertigt, das sich hören und sehen lässt, um so mehr, als der brave Junge, nach seinem gewandten Naturell, das Stück fast ironisch in einem Geiste verfasst hat, der, wenn auch nicht der rechte, doch ein solcher ist, den Cherubini stets gesucht und, wenn ich nicht sehr irre, nicht gefunden hat.

Cherubini's Mass intimately.[37] The stylistic evidence points to the tentative conclusion that Mendelssohn, aware of Cherubini's debt to Mozart, had in mind to compose a sacred work in a style and tonality similar to Cherubini's effort, but one nevertheless clearly and primarily inspired by Mozart. Mendelssohn's letters to his family in Berlin teem with negative comments about musical life in Paris (with a certain relish he reported Pierre Rode's pronouncement, 'C'est ici une dégringolade musicale'),[38] and as a German musician Mendelssohn felt a strong need to defend German music. He was shocked at the ignorance of Bach's music and, indeed, of Beethoven's *Fidelio*; no doubt, he readily seized the opportunity to present to Cherubini a work reminiscent of Mozart's final masterpiece.

Mendelssohn's Kyrie alludes to the opening movement of the Requiem in a conspicuous, if limited, way. External similarities include the D minor tonality, Adagio tempo, common time, and piano opening. Several internal details betray how Mendelssohn sought to recreate the texture of Mozart's opening (exx. 4a, 4b). An imitative figure, introduced in the winds, is set against a detached, staccato quaver line in the strings. In the Mozart, the wind figure, D–C#–D–E–F, is heard in the first bassoon; in the Mendelssohn, the same figure is heard, rhythmically altered, in the second bassoon. In Mozart's string accompaniment, a rising bass line is answered a third above by the violas off the beat; in Mendelssohn's accompaniment, the two parts play together in parallel thirds.

Example 4

(a) Mendelssohn, Kyrie in D minor (1825)

(b) Mozart, Requiem K 626

[37] See the Preface to my edition of the Kyrie in the Mendelssohn series, *Ausgewählte Werke vokaler Kirchenmusik* (Stuttgart, 1986), p. 5.

[38] See Mendelssohn's letter of 9 May 1825 to Berlin (New York Public Library).

Ex. 4 (*cont.*)

(c) Mozart, Concerto in D minor for piano K 466, first movement

(d) Mozart, Requiem, 'Te decet'

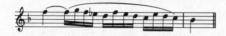

In the fourth measure of the Kyrie, Mendelssohn seems to depart from the allusion to the Requiem by abruptly changing the texture: we now hear a rising, slurred chromatic line in the strings and woodwinds accompanied at the sixth below and supported by the brass and timpani. If not reminiscent of the Requiem, this new gesture is nevertheless in all likelihood Mozartean; it seems to recall a similar passage from the first movement of the D minor Piano Concerto K 466, a work Mendelssohn frequently performed himself (ex. 4c; see Table 3). Other details in the Kyrie, too, quite possibly revive the style of the concerto: the use of the Neapolitan as a chromatic colouring, for instance, and, especially, the characteristically Mozartean mixture of the major and minor modes (a device used to fullest advantage, of course, in the finale of the concerto).

Further on in the Kyrie, Mendelssohn again alludes to the Requiem – at least by way of Cherubini. The fresh, flowing semiquaver subject so similar to Cherubini's fugal subject (see exx. 3a, 3b) is not unlike the new figure Mozart introduces in the 'Te decet' (ex. 4d). And, what is more, Mendelssohn, like Mozart (and Cherubini), treats the subject in mirror inversion. But here, admittedly, the resemblance ends, for, despite these tantalising thematic and textural comparisons, Mendelssohn's Kyrie observes its own formal plan: following the section devoted to the second subject, Mendelssohn brings back the opening measures, then tests the second subject in mirror inversion before combining it with its prime form. Mozart's movement, which of course culminates in a double fugue on 'Kyrie eleison' and 'Christe eleison', divides earlier into several discrete sections according to the textual divisions of the Introit. Mendelssohn, in contrast, sets only the text 'Kyrie eleison', a limitation that enables him to pursue his love of artful counterpoint, which, in the end, prevails over the homage to Mozart.

Sinfonia VIII and the Kyrie thus present two different compositional responses of Mendelssohn to Mozart. In the one, the didactic role of Mozart is preeminent:

the 'Jupiter' finale serves unquestionably as a model, and Mendelssohn's symphonic movement is permeated with specific references to Mozart that affect its thematicism, scoring, and formal design. In the Kyrie, the references to Mozart, while conspicuous enough, are fewer in number, and are assimilated more thoroughly than before into Mendelssohn's own emerging style. We now turn to Mendelssohn's second response to Mozart's music, that is, to his role as a performer.

III

Mozart figured prominently in Mendelssohn's concert activities throughout his career as pianist and conductor. To give some idea of his efforts in this regard we have assembled in Table 3 a preliminary listing of Mendelssohn's Mozart performances which may be documented through concert reviews in the *Allgemeine musikalische Zeitung (AmZ)* and *Neue Zeitschrift für Musik (NZfM)*, Mendelssohn's letters, and other primary sources. An invaluable secondary source for Mendelssohn's Leipzig period remains Alfred Dörffel's work on the Gewandhaus concerts, which first appeared in 1884;[39] in addition, in 1969 Susanna Grossmann-Vendrey presented a wealth of documents relating to Mendelssohn's activities in music festivals in Germany and England.[40] For the most part the table includes performances of major works, or of works in which Mendelssohn appeared as a soloist; not included are the numerous performances of individual arias from operas, offered by a series of celebrated singers (Clara Novello, Sophie Schloss, and Jenny Lind among them) who frequently appeared at the Gewandhaus and at the several music festivals in Germany and England which Mendelssohn directed.

Table 3 should not be read as a comprehensive compilation. For one thing, Mendelssohn travelled frequently and occasionally delegated the directorship of individual concerts at the Gewandhaus to his deputies, including, during the 1840s, Ferdinand Hiller and Niels Gade; regrettably the *AmZ* and *NZfM* do not always clearly state who presided over a particular concert. Similarly, in 1844, when Mendelssohn undertook the directorship of the *Symphoniesoirée der Königl. Capelle* in Berlin, he alternated conducting duties with Wilhelm Taubert; again, the periodicals do not always provide precise information on the directorship of individual concerts. A different issue concerns the Mozart repertoire itself; individual works, in particular the symphonies, are not always clearly identified (usually, the 'Jupiter' Symphony is labelled 'mit der Schlußfuge', and the 'Prague', the symphony 'ohne Menuett'; presumably, the unlabelled C-major symphony

---

[39] *Geschichte der Gewandhausconcerte zu Leipzig* (Leipzig, 1884; repr. 1972).
[40] *Felix Mendelssohn Bartholdy und die Musik der Vergangenheit* (Regensburg, 1969).

Table 3. *Mendelssohn's performances of Mozart: a preliminary list*

Date	Location	Work(s) performed	Source(s)
Early 1822	Berlin	Improvisation on the subject of the Fugue in C minor K 426 for Prince A. H. Radziwill	GV 17
14 November 1824	Berlin	Piano Concerto in C minor K 491	Lampadius, 23
5 December 1824 (memorial concert)	Berlin	Requiem K 626, directed from the piano without orchestra	Moscheles, 67
16 October 1825	Berlin	Fantasia in F minor [K 608?] as piano duet with Sir George Smart	Smart, 179
17 October 1831	Munich	Improvisation on 'Non più andrai', *Le nozze di Figaro*	*Reisebriefe*, 221
Winter 1831–2	Paris	Piano concertos with string quartet accompaniment (Pierre Baillot)	Hiller, 18
1 June 1832	London	Double Piano Concerto in Eb major K 365 with Ignaz Moscheles; cadenzas by Mendelssohn	*Harmonicon* 10 (1832), 154
24 October 1832	Berlin	Piano Concerto in D minor K 466 with cadenzas by Mendelssohn	*AmZ* 34 (1832), col. 802
26 January 1833 (memorial concert)	Berlin	Piano Concerto in C minor K 491	*AmZ* 35 (1833), col. 126
13 May 1833	London	Piano Concerto in D minor K 466 played from memory, with cadenzas by Mendelssohn	*Harmonicon* 11 (1833), 134–5
28 December 1833	Düsseldorf	*Don Giovanni*	*Reisebriefe* II, 11
3 May 1834	Düsseldorf	Overture to *Die Zauberflöte*	GV 64
October 1834	Düsseldorf	Requiem K 626	GV 61
11 October 1835	Leipzig	Symphony in Eb major [No. 39, K 543?]; *Don Giovanni*, second finale	*AmZ* 37 (1835), col. 706; *NZfM* 3 (1835), 128

Table 3. (cont.)

Date	Location	Work(s) performed	Source(s)
12 November 1835	Leipzig	La clemenza di Tito, chorus and first finale	AmZ 37 (1835), col. 836; NZfM 3 (1835), 168
10 December 1835	Leipzig	Symphony No. 40 in G minor K 550	AmZ 38 (1836), col. 87; NZfM 3 (1835), 199
21 January 1836	Leipzig	Symphony No. 38 in D major ('Prague') K 504	AmZ 38 (1836), col. 104
28 January 1836	Leipzig	Piano Concerto in D minor K 466, cadenzas by Mendelssohn	NZfM 4 (1836), 62; Reisebriefe II, 72–73; AmZ 38 (1836), col. 105
4 February 1836	Leipzig	'Schlußscene', Handel's Acis and Galatea, arranged by Mozart	NZfM 4 (1836), 70; AmZ 38 (1836), cols. 105–6
18 February 1836	Leipzig	Così fan tutte, first finale	NZfM 4 (1836), 74
17 March 1836	Leipzig	Symphony No. 41 in C ('Jupiter') K 551	NZfM 4 (1836), 120
23 May 1836	Düsseldorf	Davidde penitente K 469	NZfM 4 (1836), 188
November 1836	Leipzig	Overture to Die Zauberflöte	AmZ 39 (1837), col. 10
3 November 1836	Leipzig	Symphony in Eb major [No. 39, K 543?]	Sterndale Bennett, 50; AmZ 39 (1837), col. 10
8 December 1836	Leipzig	Symphony in G minor [No. 40, K 550?]	NZfM 5 (1836), 194; AmZ 39 (1837), col. 12
1 January 1837	Leipzig	Hymn, Gottheit, Dir sei Preis und Ehre K 336a	NZfM 6 (1837), 4; AmZ 39 (1837), col. 46
2 February 1837	Leipzig	La clemenza di Tito, first finale	NZfM 6 (1837), 38
9 March 1837	Leipzig	Symphony No. 41 in C ('Jupiter') K 551; La clemenza di Tito, finale	NZfM 6 (1837), 82; AmZ 39 (1837), col. 242

Table 3. (cont.)

Date	Location	Work(s) performed	Source(s)
19–22 September 1837	Birmingham	Symphony No. 38 in D major ('Prague') K 504; organ fugue improvised on a theme from the symphony	*NZfM* 7 (1837), 118–9
16 October 1837	Leipzig	Handel's *Messiah*, arr. by Mozart	*NZfM* 7 (1837), 167–8
19 October 1837	Leipzig	Symphony in D major ['Haffner', K 385?]	*NZfM* 7 (1837), 136
30 November 1837	Leipzig	*La clemenza di Tito*, finale	*NZfM* 7 (1837), 180
7 December 1837	Leipzig	Overture to and selections from *Don Giovanni*	*NZfM* 7 (1837), 188
1 January 1838	Leipzig	Symphony No. 40 in C ('Jupiter', K 551)	*NZfM* 8 (1838), 4; *AmZ* 40 (1838), col. 32
1 March 1838 (historical concert)	Leipzig	Overture to *Die Zauberflöte*; *Non più tutto ascoltai* K 490; Quartet from *Zaide*; Piano Concerto in C minor K 491	*AmZ* 40 (1838), col. 168; GV 161; *NZfM* 8 (1838), 80
4[?] June 1838	Cologne	Symphony in D major [K 504 or 385?]	*AmZ* 40 (1838), col. 439
25 October 1838	Leipzig	Overture to *Die Zauberflöte*	*AmZ* 40 (1838), col. 755; *NZfM* 9 (1838), 142
21 January 1839	Leipzig	Symphony in Eb major [No. 39, K 543?]	*NZfM* 10 (1839), 40
June 1839	Düsseldorf	Overture to *Die Zauberflöte*; Handel's *Messiah*, arr. by Mozart	*AmZ* 41 (1839), col. 464
13 October 1839	Leipzig	Symphony in Eb major [No. 39, K 543?]	*NZfM* 11 (1839), 128
5 December 1839	Leipzig	Symphony in C ['Linz', No. 36, K 425?]	*NZfM* 11 (1839), 192
23 January 1840	Leipzig	Symphony No. 40 in G minor K 550	*NZfM* 12 (1840), 40; *AmZ* 42 (1840), col. 94
25 January 1840	Leipzig	Violin Sonata in A major K 454, 526(?) with Ferdinand David	*AmZ* 42 (1840), col. 117; *Reisebriefe*, II, 140

Table 3. (cont.)

Date	Location	Work(s) performed	Source(s)
30 January 1840	Leipzig	Double Piano Concerto in Eb major K 365 with Ferdinand Hiller; cadenzas by Mendelssohn	NZfM 12 (1840), 152; Hiller, 161; AmZ 42 (1840), col. 117–18
13 February 1840	Leipzig	La clemenza di Tito, finale	NZfM 12 (1840), 64; AmZ 42 (1840), cols. 163–4
7 March 1840	Leipzig	Theme and Variations in G major K 501; Fantasia in F minor [K 608] with Ferdinand Hiller	Dörffel, 122; Hiller, 161; AmZ 42 (1840), col. 241
23 September 1840	Birmingham	Requiem K 626 (part)	Deneke, No. 109
22 October 1840	Leipzig	Symphony No. 39 in Eb major K 543	AmZ 42 (1840), col. 909
14 November 1840	Leipzig	Piano Quartet in G minor K 478 with Ferdinand David, C. Eckert, and C. Wittmann	AmZ 42 (1840), col. 990
1 January 1841	Leipzig	Overture to Die Zauberflöte	AmZ 43 (1841), col. 61; NZfM 14 (1841), 16
4 February 1841 (historical concert)	Leipzig	Overture to La clemenza di Tito; Non più tutto ascoltai K 490; Piano Concerto in D minor K 466; Das Veilchen K 476; An Chloe K 524; Symphony No. 41 in C ('Jupiter' K 551)	NZfM 14 (1841), 89; AmZ 43 (1841), col. 195
18 March 1841	Leipzig	La clemenza di Tito, finale	NZfM 14 (1841), 117
c.22 March 1841	Leipzig	Violin sonata with Ferdinand David	NZfM 14 (1841), 98
2 October 1842	Leipzig	Non più tutto ascoltai K 490	AmZ 44 (1842), col. 804; NZfM 17 (1842), 145
24 November 1842	Leipzig	Così fan tutte, first finale	AmZ 45 (1843), col. 24; NZfM 17 (1842), 202

Table 3. *(cont.)*

Date	Location	Work(s) performed	Source(s)
15 December 1842	Leipzig	*La clemenza di Tito*, first finale	*NZfM* 18 (1843), 24
15 January 1843	Leipzig	*Don Giovanni*, second finale	*NZfM* 18 (1843), 48
19 January 1843	Leipzig	*Idomeneo*, chorus, trio, and finale	*NZfM* 18 (1843), 50
30 March 1843	Leipzig	Symphony in E♭ major [K 543?]	*NZfM* 18 (1843), 146
December 1843(?)	Berlin	Symphony in E♭ major [K 543?]	*AmZ* 46 (1844), col. 76
10 January 1844	Berlin	Symphony in C major ['Jupiter', K 551?] (possibly directed by W. Taubert)	*AmZ* 46 (1844), col. 172
28 February 1844	Berlin	Symphony in D major [K 504?] (possibly directed by W. Taubert)	*AmZ* 46 (1844), col. 243
March 1844	Berlin	Symphony No. 40 in G minor K 550; Symphony in D major [K 504?]: directed by Mendelssohn and Taubert	*AmZ* 46 (1844), col. 319
13 May 1844	London	Symphony in E♭ major [K 543?]	Foster, 185
24 June 1844	London	Symphony in C ['Linz', K 425?]	Foster, 187
16 January 1845	Leipzig	*Idomeneo*, second finale	*AmZ* 47 (1845), col. 60
4 December 1845	Leipzig	Symphony No. 38 in D major ('Prague') K 504	*AmZ* 47 (1845), col. 891
17 December 1845	Leipzig	*Così fan tutte*: 'Sento o Dio', 'Bella vita militar', 'Di scrivermi ogni giorno'	*AmZ* 47 (1845), col. 932
1 January 1846	Leipzig	Overture to *Die Zauberflöte*	*AmZ* 48 (1846), col. 11
8 January 1846	Leipzig	*Idomeneo*, second finale	*AmZ* 48 (1846), col. 29
15 January 1846	Leipzig	*Don Giovanni*, sextet	*AmZ* 48 (1846), col. 66
5 February 1846	Leipzig	*Die Zauberflöte*, second finale	*AmZ* 48 (1846), col. 105
14 February 1846	Leipzig	*Non più tutto ascoltai* K 490	*AmZ* 48 (1846), col. 121

Table 3. (*cont.*)

Date	Location	Work(s) performed	Source(s)
26 February 1846	Leipzig	Overture to *Die Entführung aus dem Serail*; Symphony in Eb major [K 543?]	*AmZ* 48 (1846), col. 166
5 March 1846	Leipzig	*La clemenza di Tito*, finale	*AmZ* 48 (1846), col. 176
31 May 1846	Aachen	Handel, *Alexanderfest*, arr. by Mozart; Symphony in D major [K 504?]	*AmZ* 48 (1846), col. 405; GV 117
2 June 1846	Aachen	Overture to *Die Zauberflöte*; Hymn *Gottheit, Dir sei Preis* K 336a	*AmZ* 48 (1846), col. 405
29 October 1846	Leipzig	Symphony No. 41 in C major ('Jupiter') K 551	*AmZ* 48 (1846), col. 733; *NZfM* 25 (1846), 181
3 December 1846	Leipzig	Overture to *Idomeneo*; *Ave verum corpus* K 618	*AmZ* 48 (1846), col. 821
28 January 1847	Leipzig	Symphony No. 40 in G minor K 550	*NZfM* 26 (1847), 42; *AmZ* 49 (1847), col. 70
25 February 1847 (historical concert)	Leipzig	Overture to *Die Zauberflöte*; *Das Veilchen* K 476	*NZfM* 26 (1847), 148; *AmZ* 49 (1847), col. 145

Sources:

AmZ	*Allgemeine musikalische Zeitung* (Leipzig, 1798–1848)
Deneke	Bodleian Library, Oxford, M. Deneke Mendelssohn Collection D 53 (Greenbooks XXVII)
Dörffel	Dörffel, A., *Geschichte der Gewandhausconcerte zu Leipzig* (Leipzig, 1884; repr. 1972)
Foster	Foster, M. B., *History of the Philharmonic Society of London, 1813–1912* (London, 1912)
GV	Grossmann-Vendrey, S., *Felix Mendelssohn Bartholdy und die Musik der Vergangenheit* (Munich, 1969)
Harmonicon	*Harmonicon, A Journal of Music* (London, 1823–33)
Hiller	Hiller, F., *Mendelssohn: Letters and Recollections*, trans. M. E. von Glehn (London, 1874; repr. 1972)
Lampadius	Lampadius, W. A., *Felix Mendelssohn-Bartholdy*, trans. W. L. Gage (New York, 1865; repr. 1978)
Moscheles	Moscheles, I., *Recent Music and Musicians* (New York, 1873; repr. 1970)
NZfM	*Neue Zeitschrift für Musik*
Reisebriefe	*Briefe aus den Jahren 1830 bis 1847 von Felix Mendelssohn Bartholdy*, ed P. Mendelssohn Bartholdy (Leipzig, 1878), vol. 1
Smart	*Leaves from the Journals of Sir George Smart*, ed. H. B. and C. L. E. Cox (London, 1907)
Sterndale Bennett	Sterndale Bennett, J. R., *The Life of William Sterndale Bennett* (Cambridge, 1907)

performed on 5 December 1839 was the 'Linz', and the symphonies in E♭ major and G minor were Nos. 39 and 40, K 543 and 550).

Relatively few performances may be documented during Mendelssohn's student period of the 1820s. But from 1831 on performances may be traced during every year of his life – eight each in 1837 and 1840, nine in 1836, and eleven in 1846. The centre of activity was the Gewandhaus in Leipzig, where, between 1835 and 1847, the majority of the Mozart performances took place. The culmination of Mendelssohn's efforts on behalf of Mozart occurred in a series of three historical concerts given in 1838, 1841, and 1847: in the first and third, Mendelssohn assigned portions of concerts to Mozart; in the second, he devoted an entire concert to him.[41] Mendelssohn's series offered the music-loving middle-class Leipzig audiences a kind of synoptic historical progression beginning with Bach, and including Handel, Haydn, Mozart, and Beethoven, as well as works of lesser composers. In keeping with the design of the series, the Mozart programme presented a mixture of the familiar (an overture, symphony, or concerto) and the unfamiliar (the quartet from *Zaide* K 344, or the aria with obbligato violin solo, 'Non più, tutto ascoltai' K 490, for example).

The effect of these historical concerts, and of Mendelssohn's numerous other Mozart performances, was to reinforce Mozart's place as a classical master in the continuum of German instrumental music, and to recognize Mozart's music as belonging to a distinctly earlier, classical period that preceded the innovations of Beethoven and of contemporary romantic composers. In part Mendelssohn's work reflected the new musical historiography of the time. Earlier, we cited the work of Amadeus Wendt and others during the 1830s and 1840s in establishing a classical period centred on Mozart; around this time, other composers too took an interest in the classification of musical periods. Thus in 1840 Ludwig Spohr composed as his Sixth Symphony a historical symphony 'in the style and manner of four different periods' ('im Styl und Geschmack vier verschiedener Zeitabschnitte'): Bach and Handel (1720), Haydn and Mozart (1780), Beethoven (1810), and the most modern (1840).[42] We might justifiably view Spohr's compositional efforts as a parallel to Mendelssohn's work as a performer, but whereas Spohr's symphony enjoyed only a mixed reception (apparently not all understood the satiric intent of the finale – a deliberately melodramatic work with clangorous percussion[43]), Mendelssohn's work in Leipzig over a twelve-year period as a per-

---

[41] Full details of the historical series are in Grossmann-Vendrey, pp. 159–169. See also *AmZ* 43 (1841), col. 175, and Klingemann, p. 256 (letter of 24 January 1841).

[42] Available in a modern reprint in the Garland Symphony Series, ed. Joshua Berrett (New York, 1980), series C, vol. 9.

[43] Mendelssohn performed the symphony in Leipzig early in January 1841 and set down his reaction to it in a letter dated 8 January (Oxford, Bodleian, M. Deneke Mendelssohn C. 42,

former no doubt contributed significantly, and in a consistent manner, to the canonisation of historical periods in music, and to Mozart's particular place as a classical composer.

Table 3 shows that Mendelssohn appeared in three different capacities as a performer of Mozart: as a conductor, solo pianist, and performer of chamber music. (A special category is represented by his improvisations on themes of Mozart, of which at least three may be documented: in 1822, he extemporised on the subject of the Fugue in C minor K 426 for Prince Radziwill, one of Beethoven's patrons; in 1831, he improvised on 'Non più andrai' from *The Marriage of Figaro* for the Saxon king in Munich; and in 1837, he took a theme from the 'Prague' Symphony as the subject for an organ fugue at the Birmingham Music Festival.) As a conductor Mendelssohn's repertory centred on the final four symphonies, and sizable portions, including overtures and finales, of the late operas (the full production of *Don Giovanni* in Düsseldorf in 1834 appears to have been his only complete performance of a Mozart opera). Among other works performed were the Requiem, *Davidde penitente*, and *Ave verum corpus*. Of special note were the concert aria with violin solo, *Non più tutto ascoltai* K 490, which Mendelssohn conducted at least four times, and Mozart's arrangements of Handel's *Messiah*, *Alexander's Feast*, and *Acis and Galatea*, to which Mozart had added parts for winds. Mendelssohn's discovery of Mozart's Handel would have been especially meaningful: during his 1829 visit to England, Mendelssohn carefully studied Handel's autographs preserved in Buckingham Palace (eventually transferred to the British Museum); later, of course, Mendelssohn himself would be involved with the Handel edition.[44]

As a solo pianist Mendelssohn performed at least three concertos, including two solo concertos, K 466 and 491, and the Double Concerto K 365. According to Ferdinand Hiller, Mendelssohn performed Mozart concertos in Paris during the winter of 1831–2 with the accompaniment of a string quartet led by the violinist Pierre Baillot. Regrettably, Hiller did not specify which works were performed, but corroborating evidence for at least this singular manner of performance is at hand: Frédéric Chopin, making his Parisian debut at this time, evidently performed his E minor Piano Concerto Op. 11 on 26 February 1832 with a string ensemble accompaniment led by Baillot.[45]

fols. 25–26). He, too, took exception to the light, 'picant' manner of the finale, having preferred instead a more serious and profound ('recht ernsthaft und vielsagend') movement in Spohr's own style to form a more effective close to the symphony. See also C. Brown, *Louis Spohr* (Cambridge, 1984), p. 244.

[44] See H. C. Wolff, 'Mendelssohn and Handel', *Musical Quarterly* 45 (1959), 175–90.

[45] See Jean-Jacques Eigeldinger, 'Les premiers concerts de Chopin à Paris (1832–1838)', in *Music in Paris in the Eighteen-Thirties*, ed. Peter Bloom (Stuyvesant, New York, 1987), pp. 263f. For a

During the 1840s Mendelssohn took part in a series of chamber music concerts held to supplement the regular subscription orchestral season at the Gewandhaus. Designated 'musikalische Abendunterhaltungen', these concerts were designed to replace an older series of 'Quartettsoiréen', directed by Ferdinand David (the concertmaster of the orchestra), so that in addition to string quartets, other types of chamber scorings such as violin sonatas and piano trios could be heard.[46] Of Mendelssohn's Mozart performances in this series, we may document at least two violin sonatas, performed with David in 1840 and 1841,[47] two piano duets, performed with Hiller in 1840 (Theme and Variations in G major K 501 and the Fantasia in F minor, likely K 608, the two described as 'two truly classical pieces' ('zwei wahrhaft klassische Stücke'[48])), and, finally, the G minor Piano Quartet K 478, performed with David, C. Eckert, and C. Wittmann in 1840.

Not surprisingly, a substantial portion of Mendelssohn's personal library was devoted to Mozart's works. In a list of *Musikalien* drawn up by Mendelssohn probably during the fall of 1844, as he prepared to pack up his belongings and effects before he left Berlin,[49] Mozart occupies a prominent position along with Handel and Bach (see Fig. 8.2). The list shows that by 1844 Mendelssohn owned at least the full scores of the final six operas, concert arias, symphonies, string quartets, the cantata *Heiliger sieh* (K Anh. 124), parts for the Double Piano Concerto K 365, and several volumes of the Breitkopf & Härtel *Œuvres complettes*, originally published between 1798 and 1806, and then expanded with later issues up to 1842.[50] In all likelihood these materials were used by Mendelssohn in many of the Mozart performances listed in Table 3; no doubt, they could yield valuable information about nineteenth-century performance practice and Mendelssohn's own approach to Mozart. But the library has long since been dispersed, so that the provenance after Mendelssohn's death of only a few of the volumes can be

facsimile of the programme for Chopin's concert, in which Mendelssohn participated, see *The New Grove Dictionary of Music and Musicians* (London, 1979), vol. 4, p. 295.

[46] See *AmZ* 42 (1840), col. 116.

[47] The second sonata, performed on 31 March 1841, remains unidentified. According to Mendelssohn (letter of 7 February, 1840; *Reisebriefe*, vol. 2, p. 140) the first, given on 25 January 1840, was a sonata in A major. According to the *AmZ*, the work was 'Sonate II, H dur', from 'Cahier IX' of the Mozart *Œuvres complettes* published by Breitkopf & Härtel. The second sonata of Cahier IX is, in fact, K 526, in A major, and it is likely that this was the work performed.

[48] *AmZ* 42 (1840), col. 241.

[49] See Peter Ward Jones, 'The Library of Felix Mendelssohn Bartholdy', in *Festschrift Rudolf Elvers zum 60. Geburtstag*, ed. E. Hertrich and H. Schneider (Tutzing, 1985), p. 289.

[50] A detailed account of the 1844 list has appeared in the third volume of the *Catalogue of the Mendelssohn Papers in the Bodleian Library, Oxford*, edited by Peter Ward Jones (Tutzing, 1989). I am indebted to the editor for sharing with me pages from the catalogue before its publication.

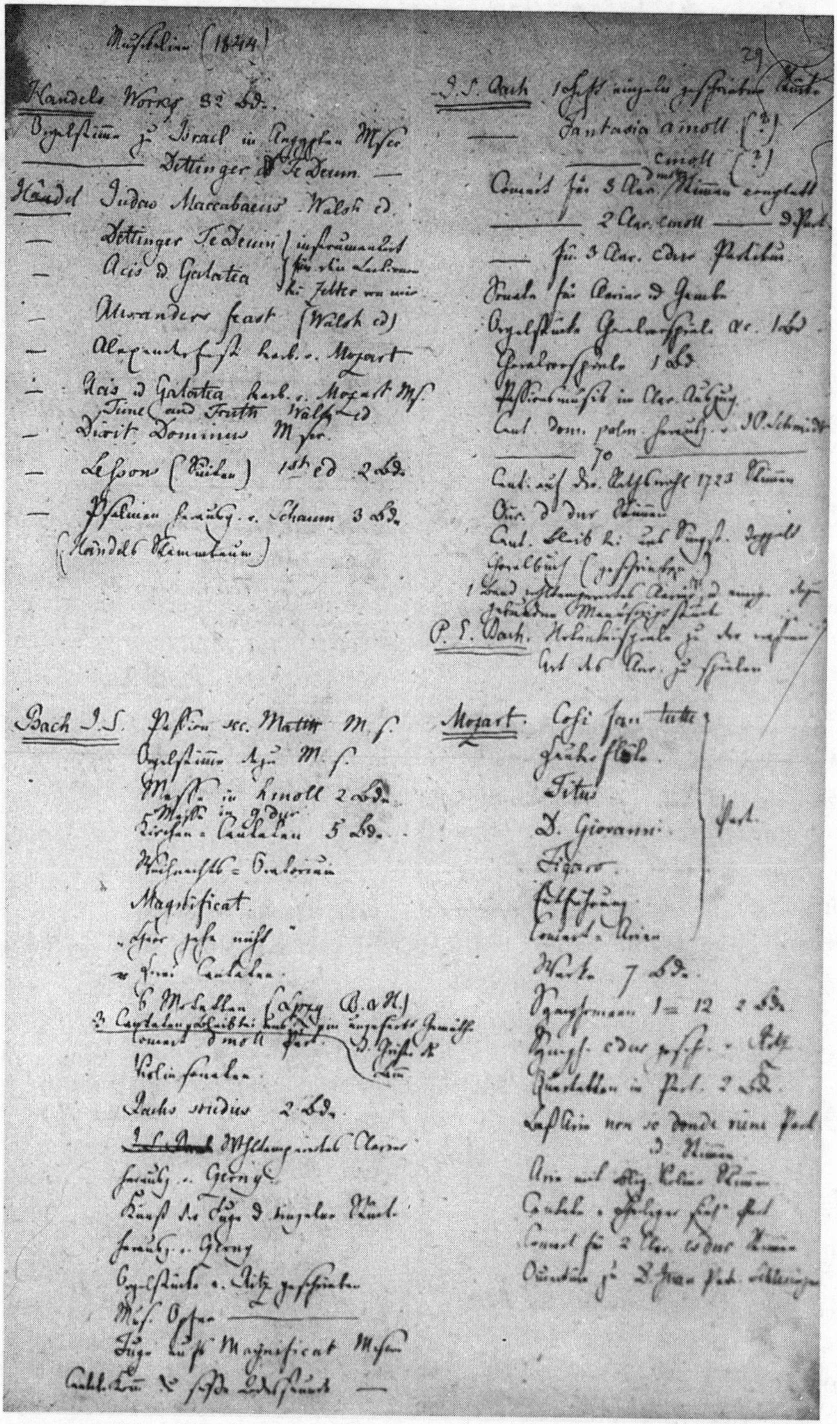

Figure 8.2 Mendelssohn, 'Musikalien' (1844) [Oxford: Bodleian Library, M. Deneke Mendelssohn C. 49, fol. 29]

traced. Nevertheless, at least one important item from the library, the multi-volume copy of the *Œuvres complettes*, has survived, and calls for further consideration here.

This source, preserved in the Firestone Library of Princeton University, consists of seventeen *Hefte* of Mozart's piano music and chamber music with piano, all gathered into six bound volumes, and a seventh volume of concert arias (not originally part of the *Œuvres complettes* though issued by Breitkopf & Härtel).[51] Each volume bears Mendelssohn's signature, though none offers any evidence as to when he acquired the collection. In 1972 Lewis Lockwood hypothesised that Mendelssohn received the volumes as a unit from the publisher perhaps during the 1840s; the plate numbers present in several volumes indicate that the majority were issued during the years 1824–9 and 1837–40; the seventh, a volume of sonatas for piano duet, appeared in 1842.

Of special interest are numerous markings in pencil, which chiefly comprise fingerings but also include some dynamic markings and corrections of printing errors. Understandably, one is tempted to assume that these markings are by Mendelssohn, though, however intriguing this possibility, prudence favours caution. For one thing, not all markings appear to be in a consistent hand; indeed, some could have been added after Mendelssohn's death by subsequent owners. On the other hand, given that Mendelssohn owned these volumes, we are on safe ground in supposing that at least some of the markings are authentic comments by Mendelssohn, which might yield clues about his individual manner of performing Mozart at the keyboard.

Lockwood's tabulation of the markings reveals that eleven of the seventeen *Hefte*, including solo and duo piano works, violin sonatas, and other chamber works, contain markings. Now if we compare these annotated works with Mendelssohn's documented performances of Mozart's chamber music, we find at least two common works. The Variations in G for piano duet K 501 and the Piano Quartet in G minor K 478, which Mendelssohn performed in 1840, not only appear in the Princeton collection but contain performance markings.[52] Arguably, then, the Princeton copies of K 501 and 478 may be the copies Mendelssohn actually used during his performances. At the least, the case for these particular markings being in Mendelssohn's hand seems to be an especially compelling one.

Only a few markings occur in the *Andante con variationi* (K 501), and there only in the *primo* part. But in the G minor Piano Quartet pencilled fingerings and dynamic markings are scattered throughout the three movements. And in the

[51] See Lewis Lockwood, 'Mendelssohn's Mozart: a New Acquisition', in *Princeton University Library Chronicle* 34/1 (1972), 62–68.

[52] The Violin Sonata in A major K 526, which Mendelssohn may have performed on 25 January 1840, appears in Cahier IX but has no markings. Cf. n. 47.

extended piano trill that prefigures the final return of the refrain in the Rondo (bars 311–21), the bars are numbered from 1 to 11 – in a hand resembling Mendelssohn's – suggesting, indeed, that the Princeton copy was used in rehearsal or performance (Fig. 8.3). The majority of the fingerings occur in extended passages

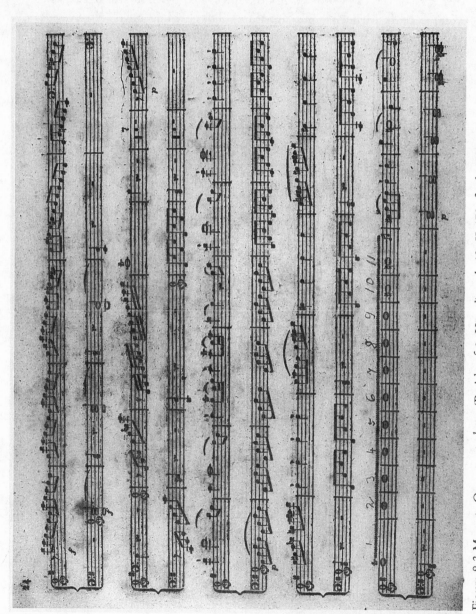

Figure 8.3 Mozart, *Œuvres complettes* (Breitkopf & Härtel), vol. 13, K 478, finale [Princeton University: Firestone Library]

of rapid runs; in nearly every case the selection of fingerings seems designed to guarantee a smooth legato style of performance. Thus in bars 30–1 of the first movement (ex. 5a), the use of thumb crossings effectively creates a slur over the two bars. To twentieth-century ears, there is, of course, nothing extraordinary here; in fact, in the later nineteenth-century edition of K 478 for the *Mozart Werke* overseen by Köchel for Breitkopf & Härtel and issued between 1877 and 1883,[53] an editorial slur does appear over these two bars. But in Mendelssohn's copy of the *Œuvres complettes*, an edition originally released in 1802, there is no slur. Indeed, the contours of the passage, consisting of a turn figure on strong beats followed by stepwise motion on weak beats, might well have been performed by Mozart with four slurs (each for two beats), instead of one continuous slur.

Example 5 Mozart, Quartet in G minor for piano and strings K 478, *Œuvres complettes* (Firestone Library, Princeton)

(a) first movement

(b) first movement

(c) second movement

[53] *W. A. Mozarts Werke* (Leipzig, 1877–83), series 17, vol. 2.

Similarly, in ex. 5b, the closing theme from the exposition of the first movement, the fingerings for the left hand ensure an unbroken quaver accompaniment (note the use of the thumb after the fifth finger in the first bar), even though in the *Œuvres complettes* no slur appears (again, in Köchel's *Werke*, the passage is slurred). And, finally, in the Andante, the use of a thumb crossing mitigates the disruptive effect of an octave leap in bar 19 (indeed, here the thumb appears on a black note: ex. 5c). In short, Mendelssohn evidently had in mind a smooth, legato style of performance, even though the passage in the *Œuvres complettes* has no slur (in the *Werke* we find one slur extending for more than four bars).

Some evidence suggests that Mendelssohn did not always opt for a seamless manner of performing passagework. The dramatic conclusion of the first movement (bars 239–51) is one case in point. In the *Œuvres complettes* the final thirteen bars are simply marked *forte*: there is no attempt to differentiate through dynamics or phrasings the explosive, eight-bar Alberti-bass passage of semiquavers (bars 239–46) from the final statement of the opening theme in the closing five bars (247–51). In the *Werke*, the dynamic marking is intensified to *fortissimo*, to which, in lieu of an extended slur, is added *legato*. Mendelssohn's markings in the *Œuvres complettes* show a strikingly original approach to the conclusion. The first four bars, which divide into two-bar groupings, are performed *forte*. Then, for the fifth bar, Mendelssohn prescribes a sudden drop to *piano* followed immediately by a bar of *forte*, and a *piano* crescendoing to *forte*. The final five bars are marked *fortissimo*. The result is a division of the concluding thirteen bars into four portions: *f*; *p–f*; *p* crescendoing to *f*; and *ff*. The passage is thus forcefully articulated, and the final statement of the opening theme made even more emphatic by the preparatory crescendo.

I V

The two sides of Mendelssohn's *Mozartbild* we have discussed – his responses as a composer and performer – intersected in the arena of the piano concerto. As a rule, Mendelssohn prepared his own cadenzas for the Mozart concertos he performed (a matter of practical necessity for at least two works in his repertoire, K 466 and 467, for which authentic cadenzas by Mozart did not survive). Contemporary concert reviews indicate unanimously that Mendelssohn's performances met with unqualified success. What is more, the reviews indicate that his cadenzas differed sharply from the fanciful cadenzas then being disseminated by the fashionable virtuoso pianists, which bore little relation to the concertos to which they were appended. On the contrary, Mendelssohn's cadenzas were carefully constructed, tasteful creations appropriate to or stylistically related to Mozart. Here again, we see Mendelssohn's historicist sympathies; here again, his role as an upholder of 'traditional' musical standards emerges. Thus, his performance of the C minor Concerto K 467 in 1833 was received as 'complete and expressive in the spirit of the splendid composition' ('fertig und ausdrucksvoll im Geiste der grossartigen Composition').[54]

The D minor Concerto K 466 occupied a special place in Mendelssohn's repertory; more significant for our purpose, several concert reviews, and, indeed, a letter from Mendelssohn himself, offer some clues about the type of cadenzas he prepared. His 1832 performance of the work in Berlin elicited this response from the *AmZ*, which bewailed the prejudice of the then prevalent 'Finger-Virtuosen', for whom Mozart's concertos had long been out of fashion: 'Herr Felix Mendelssohn Bart[h]oldy performed the exquisite concerto with much taste and thorough skill, the melodic Andante with uncommon tenderness, simplicity, and lovely tone production. The cadenza, added at the end of the first movement and the performer's own creation, was founded on some motives of the movement totally in the spirit and style of this masterful composition.'[55] An English reviewer reacted similarly to Mendelssohn's performance in London at a Philharmonic Concert on 13 May 1833:

The performance of Mozart's Concerto by M. Mendelssohn was perfect. The scrupulous exactness with which he gave the author's text, without a single addition or *new reading* of his own, the precision in his time, together with the extraordinary accuracy of his execution, excited the admiration of all present; and this was increased, almost to rapture, by his two extemporaneous cadences, in which he *adverted* with great address to the subjects of the concerto, and wrought up his audience almost to the same pitch of enthusiasm which he himself had arrived at. The whole of this concerto he played from memory.[56]

The reviewer's emphases make clear just how unusual for the time Mendelssohn's performance style was: evidently, pianists usually took the liberty to introduce their own readings into concertos, and further, typically offered cadenzas which had little to do with the thematic material of the work at hand.

Early in 1836 Mendelssohn performed K 466 again, this time in Leipzig, when he took the occasion to jot down in a letter to his sister Fanny a musical summary of the conclusion of the cadenza:

---

[54] *AmZ* 35 (1833), col. 126.
[55] *AmZ* 34 (1832), col. 802.
     Das treffliche Concert . . . trug Hr. Felix Mendelssohn Bartoldy [*sic*] mit vielem Geschmacke und solider Fertigkeit, das melodische Andante ungemein zart, einfach und mit schönem Tone vor. Die am Schlusse des ersten Satzes hinzugefügte Cadenz, von eigener Erfindung, war auf einige Motive desselben ganz im Geiste und Style der meisterhaften Composition gegründet.
[56] *Harmonicon* 11 (1833), 135.

In the first movement I made a cadenza, which succeeded wonderfully and caused a tremendous sensation among the Leipzigers. I must write down the end for you. You remember the theme, of course? Towards the close of the cadence, arpeggios come in pianissimo in D minor, thus:

etc., to the close in D minor. Our second violin player, an old musician, said to me afterwards, when he met me in the passage, that he had heard it played in the same hall by Mozart himself, but since that day he had heard no one introduce such good cadenzas as I did yesterday – which gave me very great pleasure.[57]

---

[57] *Reisebriefe* vol. 2, pp. 72–3; trans. from Felix Mendelssohn, *Letters*, ed. G. Selden-Goth (New York., 1945), pp. 255–7.

From this sketch we may indeed discern just how intimately Mendelssohn's cadenza was related to Mozart's concerto. Mendelssohn concluded the cadenza by drawing upon the very opening piano solo of the first movement, and extracting from it the descending two-note 'sigh' (*Seufzer*) figure. Turning to the subdominant G minor, this sigh figure was rhythmically altered to appear in augmented minims; then, at the subtle change to a ii⁶ harmony, contracted to a dotted note figure; and shortly thereafter diminished to a repeated, more insistent figure in quavers. In the final step, Mendelssohn allowed the sigh to dissolve into the *forte* trill, subsequently reinforced as a double trill with a broken octave accompaniment in the bass. The conclusion of the cadence thus inextricably grew out of the original piano entrance, tying the ending of the movement to its beginning. For all the spontaneity of Mendelssohn's performance, the cadenza must have impressed as a carefully crafted, well thought-out creation – as it were, a miniature study in composition, in which he indeed 'adverted with great address to the subjects of the concerto'.[58]

In devoting such care to his cadenzas Mendelssohn was actually following a procedure already developed by Mozart. Christoph Wolff has recently examined the progression in Mozart's cadenzas from 'spontaneous improvisation' during the Salzburg years toward a compositionally sophisticated type of cadenza thematically and harmonically linked to the movement, a shift in preference which Mozart came to observe more and more as a 'fixed principle' during the Viennese period.[59] The structural integration of the cadenza into the concerto posed, in short, a special compositional challenge for Mozart as it did for Mendelssohn when he performed Mozart, and, indeed, when he produced his own concerti. All of Mendelssohn's cadenzas in his mature concertos are meticulously notated; the most celebrated, that in the first movement of the E minor Violin Concerto Op. 64 (1844), required a special effort, as his correspondence with David, who premiered the work in 1845, testifies.[60] The unusual placement of this cadenza – at the end of the development, where it establishes a prolonged dominant pedal to prepare the recapitulation – was, too, a carefully calculated compositional decision. Since the concerto is 'through-composed', with transitions linking the three movements, Mendelssohn placed the cadenza early in the first movement,

---

[58] Mendelssohn's cadenzas for an 1841 Leipzig performance of K 466 prompted this reaction in the *AmZ*: '. . . die von ihm darin frei ausgeführten Kadenzen waren Meisterleistungen, die man nur geniessen, nicht aber beschreiben kann' (*AmZ* 43 [1841], col. 195).

[59] 'Zur Chronologie der Klavierkonzert-Kadenzen Mozarts', *Mozart-Jahrbuch 1978/79*, pp. 235–46; see also Professor Wolff's study in the present volume.

[60] See his letter of 27 December 1844 in Mendelssohn, *Briefe aus Leipziger Archiven*, ed. H.-J. Rothe and R. Szeskus (Leipzig, 1972), pp. 205ff.

in order to avoid the disruptive effect its traditional placement near the end of the first movement would have had on the continuity of the entire work.

Op. 64 notwithstanding, the most striking evidence of Mendelssohn's approach to cadenza writing survives in two little-known cadenzas he composed for the Mozart Double Concerto in Eb major K 365, which he performed first with Moscheles in London on 1 June 1832 and then, eight years later, with Hiller in Leipzig on 30 January 1840. These two documents provide a unique opportunity to examine in detail Mendelssohn's artistry in fashioning a cadenza: if the first was executed in relative haste, and includes elements of free improvisation, the second shows signs of painstaking revision and stands as a tautly unified compositional structure in its own right. Undoubtedly K 365 offered a special attraction to Mendelssohn. In 1823 and 1824, he himself had composed two double concertos, in E major and Ab major, which he performed at the Mendelssohn household in Berlin with his sister Fanny. Conceivably, Mendelssohn may have known K 365 at that time; his E major Double Concerto, in particular, with its gracefully turned phrases, brings Mozart readily to mind. On the other hand, no documented performance of K 365 with Fanny survives, and, further, Mendelssohn's Ab major Double Concerto displays signs of the influence not so much of Mozart as of Beethoven and John Field.[61] But at least by 1826, Mendelssohn probably knew K 365 well, for in the central portion of an Andante in D major for piano solo written likely early in that year, he incorporated a strict canon that suspiciously resembles a canonic passage in the finale of K 365 (exx. 6a–b).[62] Each

Example 6

(a) Mendelssohn, Andante in D

(b) Mozart, Concerto in Eb for two pianos K 365, finale

---

[61] Especially Beethoven's 'Emperor' Concerto and Field's Second Concerto, in Ab major.
[62] An edition is available in Mendelssohn, *Early Works for Piano* (Cambridge, 1985), pp. 43–5.

Ex. 6 (*cont.*)

canon (at the octave) consists of a descending treble line, decorated by a turn figure and supported by a dominant pedal point (in the Mozart, a pendulating pedal point ornamented by an upper neighbour). For Mendelssohn to recall in his piano miniature a markedly contrapuntal passage from Mozart would be consistent with his irrepressible fascination for the learned forms of part writing.

From a letter written to his father the day he performed K 365 with Moscheles (1 June 1832) we learn that Mendelssohn prepared 'two long cadenzas', namely, for the first and third movements.[63] After the performance the autographs were evidently given by Mendelssohn to Moscheles; though the cadenza for the third movement is not traceable, that for the first movement passed through various owners until 1977, when it came to the auction block. Its present whereabouts is unknown, though a facsimile of the first page (the first piano part) appears in the auction catalogue[64]; this page bears the title 'Cadenz zu Mozarts Doppel Concert', and, in the upper right corner in Moscheles' handwriting, '1ten Juny 1832/ mein Part. I Moscheles', establishing conclusively its use in the 1832 performance.

Mendelssohn to the contrary, the cadenza for the first piano part does not impress as an especially extended passage, nor in fact is it especially elaborate in its design or thematic treatment. It suggests essentially a prolonged flourish around the tonic $^6_4$ harmony. After a pause on the $^6_4$ the cadenza was launched by an ascending scale leading to the flourish with which Mozart actually opens the concerto, a simple trill in octaves on the tonic E♭. Next, Mendelssohn indicated a series of ascending arpeggiations, exchanged between the two instruments, but then, remarkably enough, abruptly interrupted the musical notation to resort to a prose instruction: 'hereby an improvisation which concludes right on the $^6_4$ of E♭ minor' (hierbei eine Improvisation, die eben in $^6_4$ von es moll schliesst). Presumably, this improvisation was intended to be shared by the two soloists, though whether Mendelssohn and Moscheles worked out further details

[63] *Reisebriefe*, vol. 1, p. 269.
[64] *Fine Musical Instruments and Important Musical Manuscripts*, Christie, Manson & Woods Ltd., London, May 10, 1977. In the auction catalogue the manuscript is described on p. 16.

in advance is not clear. In the following passage, with musical notation restored, the second piano part (Mendelssohn's) approached the $^6_4$ on B♭ via a rising bass line (G–A♭–A♮–B♭); this led to a more complete quotation of the opening bars of the concerto in the tonic, followed by yet another reaffirmation of the $^6_4$. In the closing section the soloists executed portions of ascending scales and concluded with brisk E♭-major scales in contrary motion, arpeggiations, and the requisite trill over the dominant harmony.

From all appearances Mendelssohn probably jotted down this first cadenza in short order. The clearest sign of this, of course, is the prose instruction, and its unleashing of the unstructured improvisatory skills of the performers. Second, the manuscript betrays (for Mendelssohn) remarkably few signs of corrections or revisions, perhaps underscoring the haste with which he drafted the cadenza. And, finally, of particular note is the static, focussed harmonic structure: the cadenza essentially prolongs the second-inversion harmony; the notated portion never quite breaks free from the tonic or dominant, and avoids altogether complex harmonic excursions and thematic development. With its fairly routine piano figurations, the cadenza in fact recalls the eighteenth-century tradition of the *Eingang* ('lead-in'), a relatively short, usually improvised passage made up of various figurations (scales, arpeggiations, and the like) which generally decorated a sustained chord and thus were harmonically static. Mozart notated several *Eingänge* in his concerti (typically, in rondo finales, where they introduce successive restatements of the refrain) and solo piano works; numerous others, of course, were improvised during performances. Despite its relatively modest proportions, Mendelssohn's cadenza of 1832 was well received: the *Harmonicon* went so far as to state that in the cadenza 'musical skill and powers of execution were exhibited that certainly none in the present day could surpass, and very few would dream of rivalling'.[65]

If Mendelssohn's 1832 cadenza for K 365 relies heavily on improvisation and is harmonically limited in scope, his second surviving cadenza, almost certainly that intended for the 1840 performance of K 365 with Ferdinand Hiller, reveals just the opposite – a meticulously crafted miniature composition with a carefully unified thematic, harmonic, and tonal structure. Whereas the 1832 cadenza fills less than one page, the second cadenza, now in the Brotherton Collection of the University of Leeds, occupies more than two pages (see Fig. 8.4). In addition, it comes down to us with an equally complex cadenza for the third movement, also fully two pages in length. Here we shall consider the cadenza to the first movement; examination of the cadenza for the finale must await another occasion.

---

[65] *Harmonicon* 10 (1832), 154.

Two primary documents – a review of the 1840 concert and a brief description by Hiller of the cadenza for the first movement – furnish significant clues that corroborate the proposed identification of the Leeds autograph as the 1840 cadenza. In the *AmZ* we find an especially lavish description of the two cadenzas:

Both cadenzas, up to their conclusions and transitional lead-ins, were performed by the esteemed artists in a totally free manner; one heard, so to speak, a free double fantasy. The one lay in wait for the other, in order to follow him, direct him, or procure for him terrain for some freely independent excursion. Each found and took the opportunity to perform various motives of the concerto plainly and to develop them. Interesting in the highest degree was how in the first cadenza Herr Hiller performed for some time several themes and reworked them in excellent fashion, and how directly Mendelssohn in a masterly way caused those themes to be taken up, pursued further, and rewoven with new motives, thereby producing, so to speak, a veritable contest that in itself formed a unified whole, yet that was performed independently by two different artists. One cannot describe the entrancing artistic pleasure that resulted; one had to listen to comprehend and perceive the high quality [of the performance]. The applause of the public was immense; both artists celebrated a true triumph this evening.[66]

From the performer's point of view, Hiller left a shorter description in his memoirs which offers further details:

Mendelssohn and I were to play Mozart's E-flat Concerto for 2 Pianos, and had prepared the Cadenza for the first movement thus. I was to begin extemporizing and make a pause on some chord of the 7th. Mendelssohn was then to continue and pause on another chord which we had fixed upon, and for the finish Mendelssohn had written a few pages for both instruments, now separately, now together, till the return of the Tutti. The

---

[66] *AmZ* 42 (1840), cols. 117–18.

Beide Kadenzen wurden von der geehrten Künstlern bis auf den Schluss einer jeden und den leitenden Uebergang in das Stück ganz frei ausgeführt; es war so zu sagen eine freie Doppel-Fantasie. Einer lauschte dem Andern, um ihm zu folgen, ihn zu leiten oder ihm Terrain zu einer freien selbständigen Bewegung abzugewinnen. Jeder nahm sich und erhielt Gelegenheit, verschiedene Motive des Konzerts rein aus und durchzuführen, und es war im höchsten Grade interessant, als in der ersten Kadenz Herr Hiller mehrere Themen lang ausgeführt und auf ausgezeichnete Weise verarbeitet hatte, nun unmittelbar Mendelssohn mit seiner Meisterschaft eingreifen, diese Themen weiter fortführen mit neuen Motiven verweben und so gewissermaassen einen Wettkampf herbeigeführt zu sehen, der in sich eine zusammenhängendes Ganze bilden musste und doch von zwei verschiedenen Künstlern selbständig geführt wurde. Der hierdurch hervorgezauberte Kunstgenuss lässt sich nicht beschreiben, so Etwas muss man selbst mit anhören, um den hohen Werth desselben begreifen und empfinden zu können. Der Beifall des Publikums war unermesslich und beide Künstler feierten wahrhaften Triumf an diesem Abende.

Figure 8.4 Mendelssohn, cadenza for Mozart's Concerto for two pianos K 365, first movement (1840) [University of Leeds: Brotherton Collection]

Figure 8.4 (*cont.*)

thing succeeded perfectly and the audience, few of whom could make out how we had managed it, applauded enthusiastically.[67]

On the whole the cadenza at the University of Leeds agrees well with these two accounts, at least to the extent we are able to judge, for the Leeds manuscript comprises just the *primo* part, with occasional cues for the *secondo*, and thus transmits, strictly speaking, only half of the cadenza. Nevertheless, a great leap of the imagination is not required to confirm the two accounts. The overall effect is indeed that of a 'double fantasy' in which the soloists engage in a kind of contest of themes and motives woven together to form a coherent, unified whole ('zusammenhängendes Ganze'). And, what is more, the cadenza does begin with a series of flourishes on seventh (ninth) chords exchanged between the two instruments, more or less according to Hiller's account. In one respect, however, the manu-

[67] Ferdinand Hiller, *Mendelssohn: Letters and Recollections*, trans. M. E. von Glehn (London, 1874; repr. New York, 1972), p. 161.

script would seem to depart from Hiller's version. Whereas Hiller claimed to have begun the cadenza by extemporising, Mendelssohn's autograph shows that the entire cadenza was written down and worked out in detail. There are no prose indications for a free extemporisation, as in the 1832 cadenza. Indeed, the very opening bars, which commence with a brief treatment of part of the first theme over a dominant pedal, reveal several corrections and revisions – clear signs of Mendelssohn's deliberate hand as a composer. Perhaps these opening bars were intended as a general guide, and perhaps Hiller did indeed extemporise on them before reaching his seventh chord. Be that as it may, Mendelssohn seems to have left little to chance in producing his second cadenza; indeed, as we shall now attempt to show, he succeeded in treating this cadenza as a unified compositional whole, a procedure, appropriately enough, reminiscent of Mozart's approach in the elaborate cadenzas of his Viennese period.

Analysis of the cadenza reveals that it divides into four sections, each carefully articulated either by fermatas, which mark the end of the first and second sections, or by a bar of rest, which separates the third from the fourth section. As noted above, the first section (Fig. 8.4, system 1 to system 3, bar 1), is built upon a B♭ pedal. It reworks the second phrase of the first theme (see ex. 7a) before pausing on a seventh chord (Hiller's chord?) and yielding to a series of flourishes between the two pianos. The last of these concludes with a deceptive turn to a diminished-seventh chord – Mendelssohn's chord? – and a fermata. Notwithstanding the shifting harmonies in the treble, the B♭ is retained in the bass throughout this opening passage.

Example 7 Mozart, Concerto K 365, first movement

(a) first tutti and solo

Ex. 7 (*cont.*)

(b) bridge theme

Pfte I

Pfte II

(c) Mendelsohn, first-movement cadenza (1840), analytical reduction

In the second section (Fig. 8.4, system 3, bar 2 and the remainder of the page), the bass line begins, beneath *pianissimo* arpeggiations, to describe a stepwise descent that eventually reaches G – the third below B♭ – as its goal. At this point, Mendelssohn recalls the motive from the first theme heard at the outset of the cadenza. This is now developed in sturdy bass octaves beneath a brilliant passage of semiquaver figuration in the treble. The thrust of the passage is to exploit G as dominant to C minor; but then, unexpectedly via an augmented sixth chord on E♭, D is introduced as dominant to G minor. Now the dynamic level drops to *piano*, and, against an insistent staccato pedal in the treble, we hear a diminished portion of the first-theme motive in G minor in quavers. The compacted figure is repeated, then extended, and within a few bars, inverted to the treble through a swell in the dynamics. With a Beethovenian insistence Mendelssohn reiterates the figure, finally reaching a series of three held chords, with arpeggiated flourishes, that bring the section to a German sixth chord on A♭ and a fermata. In sum, the second section engages in the first serious modulations of the cadenza, secures G minor as a short-term tonal goal, and develops the first theme through fragmentation, diminution, and invertible counterpoint.

The first movement of K 365 offered Mendelssohn an especially fertile field of themes for treatment, and in the third section of his cadenza he turned to a contrasting theme which appears first *dolce* and in G major with a simple chordal accompaniment (see the second page of Fig. 8.4, first system). His choice for the new theme was a short motive from the bridge of the exposition (ex. 7b). In the cadenza, the theme is introduced by a few measures of semiquaver arpeggiations in the treble (exactly what Mendelssohn meant by the diagonal strokes and "x" in the very first bar of the second page is unclear; perhaps the notation indicated some transitional passage to be performed by the other pianist). A cancelled passage after the *dolce* G-major statement of the new theme shows that Mendelssohn at first intended to repeat it in the dominant B♭; instead, he turned to a repetition in C minor and here introduced the turning semiquaver accompaniment used by Mozart (ex. 7b). Reaching A♭ major, the third below C minor, Mendelssohn devised a rising sequential passage which, traversing the fifth A♭ to E♭, effectively regained the tonic. Just as sudden as the reappearance of the tonic was the insertion of a bar of rest, dramatically marking the end of the third section (second page of Fig. 8.4, system 3, bar 4). Once again, to summarise: in the third section Mendelssohn drew upon a fresh theme for development, and, after affirming G major as his point of departure, regained the tonic E♭ major.

The fourth section presents an especially brilliant, crowning conclusion to the whole. Shifting to a triplet accompaniment in the treble, Mendelssohn brings back the motive of the first theme in *fortissimo* octaves in the bass. After touching on the subdominant A♭, he employs a rising bass line (G–A♭–A♮–B♭) to reach B♭, thereby bringing us full circle, and returning to the $^6_4$ harmony with which the cadenza began; the entire passage thus suggests a strong bass motion (E♭–A♭–B♭) in preparation of the final cadence. Our expectations seem confirmed by what follows: an extended, ascending scale-like line in parallel sixths leading to a double trill and announcing the dominant. But here Mendelssohn executes one final delaying tactic – a master stroke. Sustaining the trill in the treble, he now introduces in the bass a descending triadic figure from the beginning of the first theme (Fig. 8.4, second page, last system; see also ex. 7a). This new figure is led through a chromatic sequence that progressively ascends, step by step, to B♭ an octave above. A broken double-octave arpeggiation in E♭ major then leads to the concluding trill on the dominant.

The reduction of ex. 7c offers a convenient summary of the large-scale plan of the cadenza. In brief, it shows an especially taut design in which the principal tonal motion, from the B♭ of the opening through the mediants G minor and G major, and through the tonic E♭ to, finally, the returning B♭, unfolds a middleground arpeggiation of the $^6_4$ chord itself. The closing, rising sequence essentially summarizes, now in ascending order, the underlying bass motion. And the closing bars, with the cascading arpeggiations in double octaves, serve as one final reminder of the unifying role of the arpeggiation, and, of course, as a final reference to the opening theme.

As a pianist Mendelssohn was no doubt keenly aware of the rapidly accelerating evolution of keyboard technique in his own time, yet his piano music, and by extension, his performance practice, in no way approached the new technical limits so often tested and surpassed by Liszt and countless other virtuosi in the 1830s and 1840s.[68] Rather, in many ways Mendelssohn's pianism looked back on an earlier, golden age; and so his 1840 cadenza for K 365, with its balanced structure, clear tonal plan, rich thematicism and extensive thematic development, was appropriately redolent of Mozart. Throughout his short, brilliant career Mendelssohn took quite seriously his role as a proselytiser for German music, and in the pantheon of German composers – Bach, Handel, Haydn, Mozart and Beethoven among them – Mozart occupied a special place. In performing Mozart's music Mendelssohn worked effectively to establish the view of Mozart as an enduring classicist. And if today that view is a commonplace, in Mendelssohn's time it was a novelty, as we learn in a letter from his Italian sojourn of 1830: 'the best pianists there, male and female, have not played a single note of Beethoven, and when I maintained that there was something to him and Mozart, they said: "So are you an admirer of classical music?" Yes, I replied.'[69]

---

[68] A relatively unusual exception to this feature of Mendelssohn's piano music was his embrace of and experimentation with the so-called 'three-hand' technique of Thalberg and Liszt, a device which figures frequently in the solo piano music and in the first movement of the D minor Piano Concerto Op. 40. Concerning Mendelssohn's own views of his piano music, see my study, 'Piano Music Reformed: the Case of Felix Mendelssohn-Bartholdy', in *19th-Century Piano Music* (New York, 1990) p. 179.

[69] *Reisebriefe*, vol. 1, p. 32. ('die besten Clavierspieler und Clavierspielerinnen dort nicht eine Note von Beethoven gespielt, und als ich meinte, es sei doch an ihm und Mozart etwas, so sagten sie: "Also sind Sie ein Liebhaber der klassischen Musik?" – Ja, sagte ich.')

9

SOME THOUGHTS ON MOZART'S USE OF THE CHROMATIC FOURTH

PETER WILLIAMS

If performance practice studies include (as I think they usefully could) questions not only of how music was performed but also of how it was *heard*, its elements perceived by the composer and other listeners of the time, then such studies have every reason to look at those elements and assess their purpose and effect. Such a look would not be aiming at analysis as such, nor would the question of how those elements were performed necessarily be a chief focus. Of course, in asking what such-and-such a motif or musical idea signified to composers or listeners, one would very often assume that it would be something by no means hidden or lost in performance. On the contrary, it might well be marked in some way, even conspicuously so, for example by a sudden change in texture or dynamic, or by slurs over the notes. Nevertheless, the main interest is that it is there, not how it was played: the *quidditas* not the *quomodo*.

An example of such a motif that springs to mind in the work of several (all?) major composers between the late sixteenth and the mid-nineteenth century is the stepwise six-note motif called the chromatic tetrachord or the chromatic fourth. The acceptable terminology for this motif may change according to the period under discussion. One cannot quite imagine the same term serving both Dowland and Beethoven, though they both used the motif for telling *Affekt*. For present purposes, 'chromatic fourth' is a useful term, since it serves as a reminder that we are almost always talking of the chromatic notes as they ascend from dominant to tonic or descend from tonic to dominant in a diatonic idiom, e.g. A up to D or D down to A in the key of D minor or major. Mozart is not the least interesting user of this motif, and one can often see that he had in mind a particular way of playing it, not allowing it to be lost in the total tapestry of the movement concerned.

In his Sonata in F major for keyboard, flute/violin and cello K 13, the eight-year-old Mozart naturally began his chromatic Menuetto I in the Sonata's key of F, but in the sequence that occurs immediately the chromatic melody passes to D minor (see ex. 1).

Example 1 Mozart, Sonata in F for flute or violin and cello K 13, Menuetto

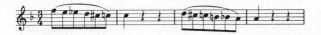

That descending sequence produces – by chance, or was it aiming towards it from the first? – one of the seventeenth and eighteenth centuries' most common thematic allusions. Whether the allusion is witting or unwitting is hard to say, for young composers are often enthusiastic about melodic chromaticism.[1] But there can be little doubt about a still youthful but somewhat later example, used less *en passant* (see ex. 2).

Example 2 Mozart, Mass in D minor K 65, Kyrie eleison

[Elei -] son.   Ky - ri - e - e - lei - son.

Since the Mass in D minor K 65 is not characterised by chromatics generally, the fourth used for the Kyrie eleison can be seen as a reference to the old tradition of descending tetrachords in laments. Syllabic setting of the chromatic fourth, such as also appears in the Benedictus of the same Mass (now in G minor), need not suggest a *marcato* or *détaché* or *non legato* effect, but rather reflects the commonsense view that for most purposes it is more convenient to sing a chromatic phrase not to one syllable (which is rather taxing) but to several.

In the D minor Quartet K 173 a different set of associations is operating. The fugal finale uses the theme in a forthright, unlamenting manner: it is not slurred; it is not a dance, has no words (with an *Affekt* to convey directly) and is neither a melody-above-accompaniment nor a bass-line-below-harmonies (all situations in which the chromatic fourth is found in Mozart's work of the 1760s and 1770s). As an 'objective' fugue subject, the chromatic fourth has another, quite specific, pedigree,[2] one that we can be sure was familiar to the Salzburgers. Mozart's answer to the subject deserves special attention (see ex. 3).

[1] Another example: the ten-year old Wilhelm Friedemann Bach includes no fewer than three regular chromatic fourths within the five bars he adds to his father's Allemande incipit (BWV 836) in the *Clavier-Büchlein vor Wilhelm Friedemann Bach*. None of those phrases moves the music to the cadence that one assumes his teacher intended for the second half of a binary movement. (See *Neue Bach Ausgabe* V/5 *Kritischer Bericht*, pp. 77–8.)

[2] Thomas Morley already quoted it in A minor (ascending) as a 'point' used by 'our organists', i.e. during the period when madrigalists used it with affective or graphic purpose in mind. See *A plaine and easie Introduction to practicall Musicke* (London, 1597), 'Annotations'.

Example 3 Mozart, Quartet in D minor for strings K 173, finale

(a) subject

(b) answer

This fugal answer, logical enough in its own terms, is exactly what Fux had ruled against:

Versum in genus Cromaticum, responsum sic se habebit:

Example 4

Joseph. Non potuisset subjectum responso integrum servari, retentis omnibus Semitoniis? e.g.

Example 5

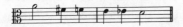

Aloys. Nequaquam. Quia E. molle nimis alienum est, & minimeè conveniens Modo D.

(For a phrase in the chromatic genre, the answer will be as follows: (ex. 4)
Joseph. Is it not possible for the subject in fact to serve as answer, keeping all the semitones like this: (ex. 5)
Aloysius. Absolutely not. Because E♭ is too foreign and not at all conformable to the key of D minor.)

Some other details in Fux's following remarks seem also to have a bearing on K 173, in particular the *stretto* use to which this subject can be put (as indeed it is in K 173).[3] Whether one should see Mozart's fugal answer as a lively boy's disagreement with an influential teacher and theorist or simply as an imaginative

[3] J. J. Fux, *Gradus ad Parnassum* (Vienna, 1725), pp. 235–6.

response to show how it might be made to work in so 'unacademic' a context as string quartets, can only be guessed. It was probably the latter, judging by his avowed respect for the late Kapellmeister.[4] Fux's objection to the fully chromatic answer – that the Eb was too far from *tonus primus* – must have meant little to most professional composers of the time, at least when they were composing quartet finales. The Fuxian rules *de variis Fugarum subjectis* were something for Haydn to play cat-and-mouse with in Op. 20, and anyone intimately acquainted with the *Gradus* would have realised that the chromatic fourth was in the first place an exception to old harmonic rules, indeed something rather difficult to explain in Zarlinian terms.

A second book of great influence on the young Mozart may also be behind this interest in the chromatic fourth and how to deal with it. In its opening sections, Leopold Mozart's *Versuch einer grundlichen Violinschule* explains rudiments and gives the passage in ex. 6 below to demonstrate the use of natural signs.

Example 6 Leopold Mozart, *Versuch*, chap. 1, III §13

The latter excerpt is not presented as the incipit of a fugal answer – it has a different key signature and is serving only to demonstrate notational rudiments – but it could certainly be taken to be one, as far as it goes. Who knows what seed it may have planted? For one thing, the D minor/major framework is clear, such keys being especially appropriate for a violin tutor. Yet for such composers as Bach and Handel – in any case, for their generation – the second and third tones (G minor and A minor) were almost as often associated with the chromatic fourth as D minor, and increasingly popular keys such as C minor and even F minor also had their share. It rather looks as if Fux and Leopold Mozart maintained a pedagogic association with D minor/major that was by then less relevant for composers, except perhaps in the most traditionally minded Augsburg-Vienna area, in the period before 1760. If so, the Austrians kept this association under the influence of older German theorists and Catholic organists rather than the Italian composers whom one might suppose to have been influential in Salzburg or Vienna in the second quarter of the eighteenth century. The German theorists

<hr />

[4] For Mozart's relationship to the *Gradus ad Parnassum*, see Alfred Mann, preface to facsimile edition (*J. J. Fux Sämtliche Werke* VII/1 (Kassel, 1967), pp. xviiff). Leopold Mozart's copy of Fux's treatise was dated by him 1746 ('copy still at Salzburg', ibid., p. xviii).

go back to Bernhard for the D minor chromatic fourth and its uses,[5] while by Leopold Mozart's time Italian composers had long had wider horizons. Corelli himself had no difficulty in introducing the chromatic fourth in C♯ minor when the tonic was E major. Biber, importing Italian interests to Salzburg, seems to have had no marked interest in the D minor/major chromatic formula, though he does use it occasionally in C minor or G minor forms (e.g. ascending in No. 6 of the *Sonatae* of 1681), where it remains *en passant*. It is always possible, of course, that virtuosos like Biber improvised above an ostinato chromatic fourth: his published passacaglia (like Bach's Chaconne) suggests a D minor 'full-dress version' of what might be prompted by such *figurae* in the hands of an able player. Presumably on the basis of what many composers across Europe were doing in the decades around 1600, the D minor association for the chromatic fourth was one natural for a German theorist picking up what he could of more southerly practice. But Italian composers went much farther afield with it, gradually dropping its formula-like recognisability.

By the time of G. B. Martini's voluminous textbook, there is really no such thing as 'the chromatic 4th in D minor', only more convoluted chromatics, generally no more than transitional sliding semitones. Minor composers or minor repertories might keep the old formula alive in Italy, but the major did not. Longer chromatic lines would incorporate the chromatic fourth but only by disguising it with strings of diminished sevenths or by decorating it with extraneous notes.[6] Characteristically, Martini's illustrations centre on Neapolitan-like chromatics, and his formulae are of this kind rather than the straightforward chromatic fourth (see ex. 7).

Example 7 G. B. Martini, *Esemplare o sia Saggio fondamentale pratico*, book 2

[5] For Fux's indirect, possibly direct, knowledge of Bernhard, see A. Mann, *Gradus*, p. xv, and on the general Italianate influences in Austrian theory, see Helmut Federhofer, 'Zur handschriftlichen Überlieferung der Musiktheorie in Oesterreich in der zweiten Hälfte des 17. Jahrhunderts', *Die Musikforschung* 11 (1958), pp. 264–79, especially p. 277 (re *figurae*), and 'Mozart und die Musiktheorie seiner Zeit', *Mozart-Jahrbuch 1978/79*, pp. 172–5.

[6] E.g. Martini's *Esemplare o sia Saggio fondamentale pratico*, book 2 (Bologna, 1775), pp. 36 (fugal, decorated) and 150 (Example 7). Examples of 'minor Italian repertories' in which conventional chromatic fourths appear (e.g. in a Requiem mass) can be found in Umberto Pineschi, ed., *Musiche pistoiesi per organo* (Brescia, 1978).

This passage is so typical of Italian idioms as they were in the 1770s that one can only assume such composers as Michael Haydn to have been deliberately reverting to earlier tradition when they used clearly defined chromatic fourths for functional vocal music well into the 1780s, passing them on to Schubert and composers of his generation. Typical examples in Michael Haydn are:

G minor, once, for 'alleluja' near end of gradual *Pro Dom. II Ex Sion*
B minor, once, for opening phrase 'angelis suis', *Pro Dom. I Angelis*
A minor, G minor and C minor in the graduals *Tribulationes* and *Eripe me*

These examples could be multiplied dozens of times from the church music of Hapsburg Europe. In Michael Haydn, such appearances consist of a single statement of the chromatic fourth, i.e. not as part of an extended chromatic passage but with a striking text of some kind, set syllabically and placed on the strong beats. They may be conspicuous and part of the rhetoric – the last example, in C minor, is to the text 'a viro iniquo' and is sung crescendo – but they are not developed much or intricately paraphrased, glossed, extended or varied. In short, they are formulaic, and their performance will generally be forceful in one way or the other.

Viewed against this backdrop, W. A. Mozart's chromatic fourths are recognisable both here and there as simple formulas but also as well-developed *ideas* that may control longer paragraphs. Furthermore, they are generally associated with particular kinds of phrasing (slurred, usually) that make them stand out from their surroundings. A taste for chromatics and for slurring them is already clear from ex. 1. Quite where he will have learnt such elements is not always possible to pin down exactly, of course, but theory books must have played a part.[7] Leopold Mozart has several things to say on the subject of chromatic motifs and their playing styles. Writing in 'the well-known phraseology of painters', as he calls it, he refers to 'light and shade' as put into practice by violinists by means of a *forte* and a *piano* that was natural to certain chromatic lines:

Eben so muss man eine durch (♭) und (♮) angebrachte schnelle Erniedrigung durch die Stärke unterscheiden.

(Similarly, one must distinguish a sudden lowering (of notes) by a flat or natural with the *forte*.)

---

[7] Another allusion to consider is the opening of the next sonata in the set dedicated to the Queen of England: K 14 is a typically galant trio from bar 3, but before the movement settles down there is an introductory flourish like some of those in Handel's early preludes, which are themselves the kind of thing recommended by Niedt for beginning improvised *praeludia*. See Handel suites HWV 443, 450 and 563; and J. Mattheson, ed., *Friederich Erhard Niedtens musicalische Handleitung anderer Theil* (Hamburg, 1721), p. 122.

Example 8

(a) Leopold Mozart, *Versuch*

(b) W. A. Mozart, Quartet in G for strings K 387, Menuetto

Note that the first key signature suggests G major, so the chromatics are outside the key and thus the more striking.[8] The tenor of such remarks is that both the slurs and the dynamics are part of the performer's understanding of the musical context, to be played thus without necessarily having been notated by the composer himself:

Man muss das Schwache mit dem Starken, ohne Vorschrift, auch meistens selbst abzu-wechseln und jedes am rechten Orte anzubringen wissen.

(One must know how to exchange *piano* and *forte* without written-in directions, doing it mostly oneself and bringing in each at the right place.)

Am rechten Orte is a phrase full of constructs, suggesting not a theorist so much as a responsive, experienced composer/player fully aware of what is happening in contemporary music. The exchanging of *piano* and *forte* could colour many a comparable chromatic passage in W. A. Mozart's string music, especially that of the earlier years, though it could well be that when the D minor chromatic fourth came to him in his maturity, the *galant* contrasts of loud/soft had gone and he was more likely to want either the one or the other. Thus one might find a vigorously troped version of the motif played *forte* by violins, and a softer or smoother version played slurred and *piano* by the basses, as in ex. 9.

---

[8] L. Mozart, *Versuch einer gründlichen Violinschule* (Augsburg, 1756). chap. 12, §8: *nach dem bekannten Malersprache, Licht und Schatten.* In the example, the final cue is on the b′ (flat?), but a′ seems more likely. That the chromatics are 'outside the key' may link L. Mozart with older pedagogic traditions: Joachim Burmeister, in *Musica poetica* (Rostock, 1606), had noted the *pathopoeic* effect as Lassus introduces notes foreign to the mode (*apta ad affectus creandos*).

Example 9

(a) Mozart, Mass in C minor K 427, Gloria

(b) Mozart, Requiem K 626, first movement

Basses, too, could be *forte* and *détaché*, of course: see 'qui tollis' from K 427, now in G minor. Or the notes could be paired for syllables as they sometimes are in string music: see 'et incarnatus est' from K 427 and ex. 13c below. Variety of articulation or of dynamic was clearly possible, since what was at stake with the motif was what one might call the principle of marked *Affekt*, one way or the other.

It seems to be generally true that some of the earliest motifs to receive slurs in keyboard music were scales, usually diatonic. (The other prime example was the so-called *dragging motif*: paired quavers or semiquavers descending or ascending by step after the beat.) Sometimes the slur marking scales appears to be simply a visual device – not a playing indication as such but something to make it easy for the eye to grasp quickly which notes are to be grouped together as a unit, usually one beat or two. Printed examples of such slurs are found in Suite No. 2 of Mattheson's *Pièces de clavecin* (1714). At other times, the slur might indicate something more specific, such as a single-finger *glissando,* which, too, is a kind of unit: examples are found in the Sonate of A. della Ciaja (*c.* 1727). In Leopold Mozart's chromatic phrasing, the slur is more specific still, indicating the bowing and not, as it does here and there in keyboard music, that the passage is played *un poco sostenuto*, with the notes held down. Many a passage in later quartets illustrates such bowing (see ex. 10).

Example 10

(a) Leopold Mozart, *Versuch*, chap. 11, §27

Ex. 10 (*cont.*)

(b) W. A. Mozart, Quartet in G for strings K 387, first movement

(c) W. A. Mozart, Quartet in D minor for strings K 421, second movement
(d) W. A. Mozart, K 421, finale

As one of Leopold's examples of the quick *tirata* – a decorative device linking the main notes – this chromatic phrase is typical of chromatic motifs generally in his treatise. Within the notational habits broadly characteristic of the earlier eighteenth century, it suggests that a visual device originating as a curved line (a kind of horizontal bracket) came to take an expressive role, as a slur or a phrase-mark. Whether or to what extent it fulfilled such a role originally is an interesting question,[9] though its change of function is not difficult to understand. Bowing was certainly one element of the expressiveness conveyed by Leopold Mozart's third reference to the chromatic fourth in D minor, which was an exercise in continually trilling first and second fingers (see ex. 11).

Example 11 Leopold Mozart, *Versuch*, chap. 10 §24

The bowing or slurring of the chromatic fourth became customary for W. A. Mozart in certain contexts, in a way that we can be sure it did not for most older composers. But while he could have learnt this *figura* from his father, he

[9] Another example is the triplet: whether this is marked 3 or 3 could well be more significant than modern editors sometimes assume. The 'slur' over the 3 was partly a visual device to make triplet grouping more conspicuous to the eye, but it was not the only such device: another was to write the triplets twice too fast (quavers instead of crotchets, for instance), either with a slur, as in the sources for Scarlatti's Sonata Kk 6, or without, as in the autograph copy of the Bach chorale BWV 608.

would also have found it in the repertories represented at their best by Joseph Haydn's early piano sonatas, where (at least in some editions) this figure may well present the only slur, or the longest slur, within a whole melodic paragraph or even a whole movement (see ex. 12).

Example 12 Haydn, Sonata for piano Hob. XVI/23 (1774 edn)

There are many such examples in these sonatas. While the slurs remind one of the bowed chromatics of string music like that in ex. 10, they may well have had a quite different source in the field of keyboard music generally. For the slurred chromatic phrases in the fortepiano sonata of the Haydn generation rather confirm the suspicion that indeed there had long been a tradition of slurring chromatic lines. For example, in long chorale-fantasias of the Weckmann-Bruhns generation, the chromatic section (generally the penultimate or thereabouts) could well have brought with it a conventional *manière* of performance without the composers so directing (or even being able to do so) in their tablatures: slurred, *piano e dolce e affettuoso*, perhaps with the organ *Tremulant*. In Mozart's textures, and as a point of imitation, the *figura's* chromaticism is not so very different, and it is further emphasised in practice by a slur in an otherwise very bright movement. This is an *Affekt* particularly clear in mature works (e.g. ex. 13a); although there it is frequently marked in some other way – with *détaché/staccato* dots (as in ex. 13b) or slurs connecting, not the whole phrase, but pairs of notes (as in ex. 13c):

Example 13
(a) Mozart, K 387, finale

Ex. 13 *(cont.)*

(b) Mozart, K 421, first movement

(c) Mozart, K 421, finale

On the other hand, although earlier on he was less careful with slurs, Mozart seems to distinguish in the Quartet K 173 between a non-slurred and no doubt forceful subject (ex. 2 above) and a slurred *stretto* derived from the subject, a *stretto* that could be either *forte* or *piano* (ex. 14).

Example 14 Mozart, Quartet in D minor for strings K 173

The slurred, serpentine chromatics of ex. 13 lead to serpentine woodwind lines in all four movements of the G minor Symphony K 550, as they do to slurred or melismatic chromatic fourths in *Don Giovanni* (when the Commendatore has been killed) or *Die Zauberflöte* (Queen of the Night's aria in Act II). A particularly clear context for the slurred chromatic fourth occurs in the final bars of the D major Sonata *a due cembali* K 448, where the exuberant finale is given a touch of extra finality by this means. Indeed, the Symphony K 550 and the Sonata K 448 realise fully two particular uses Mozart found for the motif: serpentine lines, melodic and essentially decorative; and bass lines, harmonic and coda-like (see ex. 15).

Example 15

(a) Mozart, Symphony in G minor K 550, first movement

(b) Mozart, K 550, finale

(c) Mozart, Sonata in D for two pianos K 448, finale

(stated twice)

To achieve finality by means of the chromatic fourth may well be a convention that was particularly appropriate to choral music, as in the first Michael Haydn example cited above, but the slur in K 448 is equally striking in a movement otherwise virtually without written-in slurs.[10] Such inner or incidental chromatic motifs (almost always the chromatic fourth) become a general hallmark for Mozart, more I think than for any contemporary composer, and slurring is part of the motif's signification.

While certain peaks of chromatic activity might be discerned from time to time in the Mozart œuvre, it is also the case that particular occasions were especially propitious. For instance, D minor in any genre might bring with it the chromatic fourth; both a minuet and a kyrie might, whatever their key; and

[10] The longest slur in the whole Sonata is for this chromatic line in the coda, at least in the autograph: the 1795 print either omits slurs or shortens them (see *Neue Mozart Ausgabe* IX/24/1 KB, p. 31).

instrumental pieces otherwise marked by bright, open *Affekt* might avail themselves of momentary chromatics with this particular motif. Such categories do seem clear, but several conditions can be present on a single occasion, as in the minuet to the G major Quartet K 387 (see ex. 8b). In fact, the whole Quartet K 387 alludes surprisingly often to chromatic fourths – surprising in view of one's overall impression of the work – and their *Affekt* becomes virtually subliminal. Then there is the question of atmospherics: the chromatic fourth can bring with it a sense of expectancy, even anxiety. A good example is the introduction to the symphony as it was becoming established, i.e. the prelude to the first Allegro. So, for example, in the introduction to the 'Prague' Symphony, there are several appearances of the chromatic fourth in one guise or another, but I think the final 'expectant' figure in the woodwind (bar 34, plus the trumpets and drums characteristic of solemn D minor evocations) leave a far stronger impression on the listener than the others:

bar 10   B down to F♯, violins, slurred quavers
bars 29, 31   C♯ up to A (a sixth), woodwind, slurred semiquavers
bar 34   D down to A, woodwind and violins, slurred sextuplets.

The thirty-six-bar introduction has three quite different uses for the chromatic fourth, the differences being of the same order of conscious variety as J. S. Bach's use of, say, one and the same *figura suspirans* in the *Orgelbüchlein* (e.g. BWV 627, 628, 629, 630). One might guess that the *Affekt* of its appearance in b. 34 of the 'Prague' Symphony is due not only to the trumpets-and-drums and to the slithering woodwind but also to the fact that it is the tonic–dominant fourth being invoked, with an ambiguity between major and minor.

The 'expectant' character of the motif is made good use of elsewhere in the Austrian symphonic canon. Certainly in his most mature symphonies, Haydn has passed beyond the easy formula stage with it, introducing it within broader chromatic lines and minor tonalities such as are typical of his symphonic introduction, hiding it and even (if one can speak in such terms) disguising it. The chromatic fourth appears in several of these introductions, but I am not sure we would usually hear it as such:

Symphony No. 80 in D minor (a longer line, like bar 29 of the Prague Symphony),
Symphony No. 94 (over the interval of a fifth, not fourth),
Symphony No. 97 (E to A),
Symphony No. 99 (chromatic line),
Symphony No. 100 (E to B),
Symphony No. 101 (D to A),
Symphony No. 102 (F to B-flat).

In all of these, there is a general chromatic element in the music, and Haydn has integrated the fourth within the overall *Affekt*. Beethoven, too, picks up the idea of the chromatic fourth at transitional moments, producing such examples as the transitional passage into the recapitulation in the first movement of the Violin Concerto and the coda of the first movement of the Ninth Symphony. Both involve the D-to-A chromatic fourth, and both are 'anxious': trumpets and drums in the first, *tremolo* in the second, both a veritable *passus duriusculus ex tono primo*. We can surmise that the element of expectancy which the *figura* can bring with it comes from old associations in Italian string music, in particular those links between sections that were made with the Phrygian cadence. Both the descending chromatic fourth and the Phrygian cadence involve a falling bass semitone, eventually onto a note that functions as the dominant, thus Bb to A when the fourth is in D minor. A simple example of this Phrygian cadence Bb to A (i.e. without other chromatic notes) can be seen in the introduction to Haydn's Symphony No. 93, while an extenuated version of both the Phrygian cadence and the chromatic fourth is found to inform the whole of the opening introduction to Beethoven's Seventh Symphony. This introduction can be viewed as one long descending chromatic fourth followed by a final Phrygian cadence – literally this time, for the final semitone is F to E. The comparison in ex. 16 suggests that Mozart is being the most conventional or formulaic in his use of the *figura*.

But such a conclusion could be misleading. Rather, the point would be that, unlike the other two composers, Mozart makes frequent use of the chromatic fourth, both as an easy formula and as something infinitely less 'easy'.

Example 16

(a) Mozart, 'Prague' Symphony K 504

(b) Haydn, Symphony No. 101

Ex. 16 *(cont.)*

(c) Beethoven, Symphony No. 7

In the case of the Overture to *Don Giovanni*, we meet several of the salient features in question, and yet it is difficult to be quite sure what the composer is meaning to *Signify* with it. Thus the introduction has the utterly traditional air of expectancy of the descending chromatic fourth, complete with Phrygian semitone; it appears immediately after the opening chords (bars 5–11); it is in D minor; the descending harmonies and their scoring clearly contribute to an intended *Affekt*; and the prevailing rhythm, like the change of dynamic when it begins (*piano*), ensures that it does not slip our attention as it might in a Haydn introduction. So what is being signified? That the chromatic fourth is part of the opera's constant dialectic between humour and terror? It would be difficult to think of a more appropriate *figura*. Whether Mozart under pressure relied more on convention, or whether the conventionality of the *figura* is itself an ironic sign – awesome fate portrayed in set formulas, like the doggerel verse in *Faust* – I do not know, nor are these possibilities mutually exclusive. But when such a formula is used conventionally by a composer able elsewhere to develop its very *unconventional* possibilities, it is easy to believe that some ironic shade is intended here, even if 'irony' is too broad a category to take us very far. Note that when this music returns for the Stone Guest in Act II, it is no longer chromatic. This cannot be because the newly added trombones are ill-suited to chromatics (they play a longer chromatic phrase at the subsequent section 'Tu m'invitasti a cena'); nor can it be because the composer was unable to work new effects from an old formula. Rather it is that dechromaticised, the descending chromatic fourth becomes even more of a musical archetype: D C B♭ A is the Phrygian bass line of universal memory, and the Statue-Chronos-Death figure could not enter to a more basic *figura*.

In Mozart's case, something very conventional can challenge our ability to grasp his finer meanings. Conversely, something less formulaic may well turn out to be less puzzling, since one can assume that any fresh or unique treatment of a formula is the result of alert, fresh deliberation. If D minor itself triggered a reminiscence of the chromatic fourth, and if in a mature quartet he was aiming at a new, genre-specific expressiveness, the result could be a very subtle allusion (ex. 17).

Example 17 Mozart, K 421, Menuetto

Here in K 421, it is the cliché-like tonic cadence that is ironic, not the chromatics: it is the kind of cadence any composer of the day might have written, though he is less likely to write it after a chromatic fourth that has been transformed into a line whose phraseology (*accidents*) counters its usual character (*substance*). The substance is referential: it is a minuet, the key is D minor, and the line is a counter-subject to a Ländler-type minuet with upbeat[11]. But less referential are the phraseology, the witty imitation of the melody's dotted motif, and the distractingly long note with which the cello's chromatic fourth begins. One need think only of the conventional use to which the chromatic fourth is put by Schubert to see that while a formula can be straightforwardly stated in many varied ways by an imaginative composer, variety in itself does not necessarily lead to the kind

---

[11] The chromatic fourth had frequently been a countersubject to other themes, for instance in old permutation fugues of which that in Bach's Cantata 131 is a late example. In the third fugue of his *IX Toccate e Fughe* (Augsburg, 1747), Johann Ernst Eberlin – one of Leopold's teachers and *Domorganist* in Salzburg from 1729 – had rung many, though not very new, changes with the chromatic fourth as the returning codetta of a fugue subject. Wolfgang was still examining Eberlin's *Toccaten und Fugen* in 1782: see letters to his father and to his sister, 10 April 1782.

of transformation seen in ex. 17. Schubert's chromatic fourths remain formulaic despite their variety, brought in as they are for early Kyrie settings (D 31, D 79 – cf. *Stabat mater* D 175), for imitative counterpoint (Quartet in C major D 46 of 1813 – cf. also the opening of the Development section, in D minor), or for such words in song texts as 'Walhallas Ruh' in the early ballade *Eine Leichenphantasie* 'Grab' and 'Tod' in *Der Liedler* (bars 142ff) and 'Harfe' at the beginning of the same song. These opportunities for the chromatic fourth are as conventional as the form it takes on these occasions, as the young composer was quite aware: in the Goethe setting *Wer sich der Einsamkeit ergibt*, not only does it appear for 'Grab' and 'Harfe' again but its simple form at the end has topical significance, for the old harper is lamenting. The piano part signifies both 'old' and 'lament'.

That Mozart had a penchant for chromatics in minuets, from K 13 to the 'Jupiter' Symphony and beyond, is clear also from his instruction of Thomas Attwood, where, in one example, such a chromatic fourth is incorporated into the total bass line, not picked out as a discrete, slurred phrase as it might be in other cases (see ex. 18).

Example 18 Mozart-Attwood Exercises

The chromatic fourth from D to A takes on new spelling and syntax here: the same notes are there, but it is D-flat not C-sharp because the fall is not from tonic to dominant in D minor. It is either a kind of musical pun or a simple accident. However, in ex. 19 (see below), it is again a form of countersubject, as if the composer had this chromatic phrase in the blood when it came to creating interesting countersubjects in their own *genus*. According to the samples in the *NMA* volume, Attwood's own minuets have caught the same chromatic taste, and it is likely that his upbringing in England had conditioned him to older temperaments in which chromatics had special meaning. Any resistance to equal temperament that he can be conjectured to have come across in Mozart himself – and thus any tendency to think of the chromatic fourth as associated with the first, second and third modes – would have met with his approval, so one might think.[12] One can also conjecture that Attwood's teacher's exercises naturally

---

[12] Examples of Attwood's chromatic elements for minuets in *NMA* X/30/1, pp. 195, 196, 217. On Mozart and temperament, see John Hind Chesnut, 'Mozart's Teaching of Intonation', *Journal of the American Musicological Society* 30 (1977), pp. 258–71; on English temperaments of the period, see P. Williams, 'Temperament and the English Organ', *Acta Musicologica* 40 (1968), pp. 53ff.

included various chromatic bass lines. A chromatic bass line is particularly valuable when more complex chords are being discussed and need ample demonstration, such as the $\frac{6}{2}$ found in the Attwood exercises (*NMA*, p. 37). This, too, is part of tradition, for the chromatic fourth as a bass line *exemplum* for harmonic demonstration had long been familiar to writers of figured-bass instructions.[13]

As a regular fugue subject, however, the chromatic fourth was rather too familiar, too common a property, for most purposes in 1775. It seems to have been so already for J. S. Bach a quarter of a century earlier, for considering its key of D minor, The Art of Fugue is very restrained in its use of it, and it appears only from time to time as a countersubject to one or other version of the basic theme. It could have appeared very much more often than it does. Similarly, the Musical Offering only seldom uses the chromatic fourth (now in the modish C minor), doing so chiefly in the second half of the *Ricercar à 3*, though there with much variety and new invention. Is it possible that Mozart, too, consciously held back from using it much in what one might have thought as the most likely of contexts – for example, the C minor *Fuga a due cembali* K 426? This fugue has only one incontrovertible chromatic fourth in nearly two hundred bars of an intensely chromatic idiom, built on slurred semitone *appoggiature* and on diminished intervals.[14] To speak of Mozart's 'avoiding' the chromatic fourth in the fugue K 426 would be an unwarrantable biographical conjecture, and yet its absence is as striking as it is in the case of The Art of Fugue, the more so in view of the myriad uses to which it is put in, say, *Figaro*. The variety with which the chromatic fourth is treated in this opera – contrapuntally, harmonically, melodically, even heterophonically – is an object lesson. In such passages as that shown in ex. 19, it seems to be second nature in precisely those contexts to which fugal counterpoint is totally *in*appropriate – the Overture, or Cherubino's arias (see also 'Non so più', bar 20, etc.).

These events raise two particular questions about such *figurae*. Firstly, in a given verbal context, what are the levels of allusion for chromatics – what are they *signifying* – when they are voluntarily explored by the composer? (By 'voluntarily', I mean to suggest that no composer was obliged to work with such-and-

[13] E.g. Saint-Lambert, *Nouveau traité de l'accompagnement* (Paris, 1707), §6 (a copy with MS Italian translation in Bib. Mus. G. B. Martini, Bologna) and Francesco Gasparini, *L'armonico pratico al cimbalo* (Venice, 1708), p. 67 (in G minor and D minor).

[14] Bars 80–2, a fifth rather than a fourth. (Slurs or bowings in the string version, likewise autograph, are longer.) Bach's *Ricercar* BWV 1079 and Mozart's Fugue K 426 have chromatic *appoggiature* and diminished sevenths in common, and K 426 has some Bach-like motifs (bars 16ff, 98ff), but there is no certain relationship between them. If one were ever found in the documentation, we could speculate that the very *stretti* of K 426 are a kind of reply to BWV 1079, whose royal theme admits of virtually no *stretto* (itself a striking circumstance).

Example 19 Mozart, *Le nozze di Figaro*

(a) No. 11

(b) No. 11

(c) Overture

such a motif for such-and-such an *Affekt*.) In ex. 19, the chromatics must be saying something about Cherubino, though quite what, it might not even be right and proper to try to define; perhaps this is exactly the threshold at which words about music and what it 'says' become otiose. More suitable for discussion is the second question raised by ex. 19 and others in this essay: when is a chromatic line over the melodic interval of a fourth a true 'chromatic fourth'? When is it foreground and/or background, when is it ornamental and/or essential, and so on? Strict distinctions may well not be very plausible in Mozart if one is thinking about how the *figurae* were performed and heard. In ex. 16, the Mozart sample is the most 'ornamental' or 'accidental', and yet its *Affekt*, even its character as a chromatic fourth, is far more striking to the ear than the Haydn or Beethoven examples. Its performance (slurred woodwind lines above trumpets) and its context (the anxious expectancy of a D minor half close in an introduction) ensure this. From the excerpts in this essay, and probably from any other set of twenty such excerpts, one might distinguish foreground from other uses, but I am not convinced that this would be anything more than superimposing theoretical constructs on a living practice. If a type of chromatic *Linie* is discerned in the opening harmonies of the C minor Fantasia for Piano K 475 over its opening bars – C B Bb A Ab Ah Bb Bh A# Ah Ab G Gb F# Gh – and if this *Linie* is a long, paraphrased or troped chromatic fourth down from tonic to dominant – C B Bb A Ab G – then clearly a useful comparison could be made with ex. 16a, where the fourth is so much simpler. Or comparison can be made with ex. 21, where a chromatic fourth is treated to another trope. But it is in performance that the chromatic gesture of K 475 is best understood, since it gives the impression of a great improviser taking a standard descending fourth, going beyond it (i.e. to Gb) and alerting those who speak this language to the tonal implications of Gb itself (i.e. the ambivalence it brings between C and D flat major). This is and would remain a hugely fertile ground for the improviser to explore, manipulating the listener's perception and as it were theorising about the chromatic fourth in very practical, actual terms.

It is not difficult to imagine that any composer conscious of the conventions he manipulates and aware of the games he might play with rhetoric's devices would be open to the potential of using inventively a *figura* invented long ago. Mozart is of course not the first to trope or paraphrase the chromatic fourth. Purcell does it in *The Fairy Queen*, as does Bach in The Art of Fugue (ex. 20).

Example 20

(a) Purcell, The plaint ('O let me weep') from *The Fairy Queen*, Act V

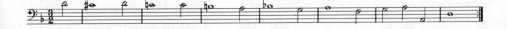

Ex. 20 *(cont.)*

(b) J. S. Bach, *Canon per augmentationem in contrario motu*, from The Art of Fugue

bar 28

As in Mozart, the conventions in Purcell are established by key *(tonus primus)*, *Affekt* (plaintive) and genre *(ostinato)*, and paradoxically it might be claimed that the conception's originality is due not least to a further convention: such a chaconne type requires an eight-bar theme, and the short chromatic fourth *figura* has to be paraphrased to produce it. As for the Bach example, one might compare it with ex. 9a, taking note of the autograph slur.

It may be possible to discern, through these and comparable examples, certain patterns, if not of systematic theory, at least of consistent practice. This practice was multi-layered and could suggest that Mozart had a broad view of the chromatic motif and one that we could divide into various categories. (By the way, the prominence of the chromatic fourth as a discrete *figura* would also suggest that when Mozart does pass beyond it – when a chromatic line is more than a fourth, perhaps a sixth or octave – the gesture signified more than it would for a later composer.) Of the categories, the chronological is plausible: Mozart may have had peaks of activity in which the chromatic fourth appears regularly as a set formula, or as one quite regularly applied in certain genres. One might also speak of shades of significance: thus a discrete slurred chromatic phrase could be part of the background *Affekt* (irony, perhaps, or expectancy) or traditional association (the words of prayer for the 'kyrie' or 'requiem aeternam' in a mass). One would distinguish between its use as melody (ex. 1), as theme (ex. 3), as countersubject (ex. 17) or bass line (exx. 17 or 15), as a kind of gloss or paraphrase (ex. 19) and so on. The categories would combine: thus one could speak of a melodic preponderance in the minuets of a certain period, or of the consciously planned variety of genre or degree of significance when it is used as a bass line. One would certainly have no difficulty in showing that Mozart's use of the chromatic fourth was exceptionally varied – more varied than it was in the hands of anyone else – and that more often than not there was associated with it some manner of performance (dynamic, articulation) that marked it out from its surroundings or contributed to the character of those surroundings.

Nevertheless, such topics as the present one are essentially illustration: they present *exempla* rather than produce a *teoria*, except insofar as writing is necessarily theoretical. Recent work on comparable *exempla*, such as the use made by earlier composers of the *figura circulationis* or by later composers of the augmented triad,[15] may well adopt similar methods. Theorists' references from the period concerned appear to establish a theoretical background to any such use or usage of a musical motif, but whether they really do so is an open question, and whether they should be expected to an even more open question. The creation of systematic theory for the musical phenomena in hand is the aim of a great deal of literate activity since the Greeks, yet it must be doubted whether in certain areas – such as the present, in which an inventive composer responds to a convention – system does any more than give apparent order to very different *exempla*. In other words, there is no real system or theory to be constructed, merely a versatile practice to be observed, illustrated and contemplated. Another author seems to have come to a similar conclusion when he wrote about Mozart's use of the augmented triad in the Minuet K 355 (576b):

Mozart simply wanted those sounds. [They produce a] remarkable fusion of aurally and intellectually motivated procedures characteristic of the greatest composers.[16]

The chromatic fourth may give us a better foothold for the understanding of a composer's thought processes, since as a *figura* it is so much more versatile than the augmented triad, and since it has such a clear history and tradition. For modern scholars, any word association it may have, or any simple label given to it by previous writers, is particularly tempting because it seems to offer an even better foothold: the chromatic fourth signifies certain words or ideas, and the more consistently it can be shown to do so, the better established the 'theory' of rhetoric appears to be and the more 'systematic' musical composition looks. But I am not convinced it is and does.

Take as a last example the opening Adagio of the Quartet K 465. Here there are no less than four chromatic fourths, so different in nature and purpose as, if not to defy categorisation, to reduce it to a preliminary stage after which one studies the music in earnest (see ex. 21).

---

[15] Warren Kirkendale, 'Circulatio-Tradition, *Maria lactans*, and Josquin as Musical Orator', *Acta musicologica* 56 (1984), pp. 69–92. R. Larry Todd, 'The Unwelcome Guest Regaled: Franz Liszt and the Augmented Triad', *19th Century Music* 12 (1988), pp. 93–115.

[16] H. Boatwright, in 'Analysis Symposium', *Journal of Music Theory* 10 (1966), section 3, pp. 27–30.

Example 21 Mozart, 'Dissonance' Quartet K 465, first movement

First comes the descending chromatic fourth over ten bars, long-breathed and troped;[17] then ascending (plain) in bars 13–14, then imitated in bar 15; but then descending (somewhat plain) over bars 14–16. The whole makes an introductory paragraph signifying and serving as a classic example of the dominant preparation for an allegro tonic to follow. The dominant itself is reached with a Phrygian bass (bars 15–16), a consequence of the descending chromatic fourth. When it appears as a simple phrase, the fourth is slurred (bars 13, 14–16 and 15), as are other phrases of the Adagio that are very like, but not quite the same as, chromatic fourths. One could say, therefore, that both in strategy (overall tonic-dominant plan for an introduction) and in tactics (slurred semitone motifs characterising the whole passage), convention is closely observed, astonishingly so for a moment of unique *Affekt* and one whose very opening key is ambiguous[18]. Furthermore, the famous effect of dissonance is created not by the chromatics but by other means: the dissonances and the chromatic fourths exist almost independently, neither responsible for the other.

But if all such remarks as these are preliminary to a grasp of this passage, quite what are they preliminary to in the way of a fuller theory? The difficulty one might have in studying such music is perhaps not a matter of theory at all but of

[17] Curiously, not unlike the paraphrased Royal Theme that appears in the bass at the beginning of the *Sonata à 3* in the Musical Offering, which superficially too the opening of K 465 resembles.

[18] The first three voices suggest a Neapolitan sixth in G – putatively G minor until the A natural of bar 2 and the subsequent G major of bar 3. Clearly, the first three voices could suggest other keys too, but the context of a Viennese quartet would suggest either Neapolitan or German sixth.

practice and perception: one is likely to miss the practical, perceptual significances and allusions, not spotting this or that usage, this or that original touch on the composer's part. These remarks on one particular *figura* surely do no more than scratch the surface of an intense, practical, varied, exploratory musical language as practised by one of its most gifted speakers.

10

CADENZAS AND STYLES OF IMPROVISATION IN MOZART'S PIANO CONCERTOS

CHRISTOPH WOLFF

Performers of Mozart's piano concertos almost invariably turn to the composer's original cadenzas and 'lead-ins' (*Eingänge*) – if such are available. Where they do not exist, as is unfortunately the case with some of the most frequently played works (i.e. the late concertos K 466, 467, 482, 491, 503, and 537), Mozart's cadenzas written for the other concertos are accepted as important and welcome models for a stylistically correct, or at least a musically appropriate re-creation of this essential improvisatory element of concerto performance.[1]

However, what do we actually know about what is stylistically correct and musically appropriate in Mozartean keyboard improvisation? Several questions and problems come to mind. (1) The function of Mozart's cadenzas: Why did he write them out in the first place? Were they for use by his students or actually for himself? (2) In a number of instances we possess more than one original cadenza for one and the same concerto movement. Modern performers ordinarily use the alternative versions rather indiscriminately, mostly opting for the longer versions. But why and for what purpose did Mozart write the alternative versions? (3) Mozart's concerto repertoire originates over a period of eighteen years, from 1773 to 1791, with frequent re-performances of individual works. How do the cadenzas fit into, or reflect the early performance history of Mozart's piano concertos? (4) Between the first and last concertos, K 175 and K 595, the genre of piano concerto undergoes – under Mozart's direction – an extraordinary metamorphosis in which virtually every single work represents a highly individualised compositional solution. In which ways do the cadenzas as improvisatory elements correspond and harmonise with this overall development?

Before turning to the discussion of these questions and in order to be able to meet the challenges of the pertinent problems, one needs to establish a source-critical basis for a chronology of the cadenza material;[2] this, in turn, provides the

---

[1] See especially the discussion in Badura-Skoda, *Interpreting Mozart on the Keyboard* (London, 1962), pp. 214ff.

[2] See Christoph Wolff, 'Zur Chronologie der Klavierkonzert-Kadenzen Mozarts', *Mozart-Jahrbuch 1978–79*, pp. 235–46.

point of departure for a determination and evaluation of any inherent stylistic trends. Table 1 presents a concise survey of the extant original cadenza material, with general references to the sources,[3] their provenance, and their dates:

Table 1: The dates and sources of Mozart's piano concerto cadenzas

Concerto (key, Köchel no.)		Cadenzas (K⁶: 626a, part I)		
D	175/i–iii	a	February 1783	V	*
	175/i–ii, 382	b	1783ff	V	
Bb	238/i–iii		1777/8	S	*
F	242/i–iii (3 clav.)	a	February 1776 (in score)	S	
	(2 clav.)	b	1779 (in score)	S	
C	246/i–ii	a	1777/8	S	*
		b	1777/8	S	*
		c	April 1782ff	V	
Eb	271/i–iii	a	1777	S	*
		b	?March 1783	V	
		c	February 1783	V	
Eb	365/i, iii (2 clav.)	a	November 1781	V	*
		b	before November 1781	V	
A	414/i–iii	a	?1782/3	V	
		b	1785/6	V	
F	413/i–ii		?1783	V	*
C	415/i–iii		?1783	V	(*)
Eb	449/i		?1784	V	(*)
Bb	450/i, iii		?1784	V	
D	451/i, iii		(June–July 1784)	V	(*)
G	453/i–ii	a	?	V	
		b	?	V	
Bb	456/i, iii	a	?1784	V	
		b	?1784ff	V	
		c	?1785/9	V	
F	459/i, iii		?1784/90	V	
d	466		[1785	V	*]
C	467		[1785	V	*]
Eb	482		—	—	

³ Location: see K⁶; *Neue Mozart Ausgabe* (NMA) V/15, Critical Reports; and Wolfgang Rehm, 'Der Eingang zum 3. Satz des B-Dur-Klavierkonzerts KV 595 ist authentisch! Mozarts Kadenzen-Autograph bringt Klarheit', *Mitteilungen der Internationalen Stiftung Mozarteum* 34 (1986), 35–40.

Table 1 (*cont.*)

Concerto (key, Köchel no.)		Cadenzas (K[6]: 626a, part I)	
A	488/i	March 1786 (in score)	V
c	491	—	—
C	503	—	—
D	537	—	—
B♭	595/i, iii	January–March 1791	V

Legend:

S   written in Salzburg
V   written in Vienna
[ ]   lost, documentation extant
—   lost, no documentation extant
*   from the estates of Leopold Mozart and Nannerl Mozart
a–c   alternative versions of cadenzas

The often expressed view that Mozart's piano concerto cadenzas were primarily written for students incapable of improvising cannot be supported by evidence. For instance, the transmission of the cadenza autographs indicates very clearly that the composer intended to reserve these materials primarily for his own use. In two instances, K 271 (set a, movement 3: *Eingänge*) and K 488, the cadenzas were notated directly in the score from which the composer generally read his solo part for his own performances. In all other instances the cadenzas were notated on separate folios, mostly in small format. With quite few exceptions, Mozart kept the cadenza manuscripts in his own possession. By habit he jealously guarded his personal performance materials in order to ensure, in particular, that his concerto scores were not copied without his authorisation.[4] Regarding the cadenzas he seems to have taken a similarly protective stand because, outside the inner family circle, there exist virtually no copies.

The transmission of the cadenza manuscripts reveals a curious pattern. For the concertos K 175 to K 459 the cadenza materials have virtually survived intact. In all likelihood, the autographs were kept in a separate portfolio which was acquired

---

[4] Mozart wrote to his father on 23 March 1782: 'I am sending you at the same time the last rondo [K 382] which I composed for my concerto in D major and which is making such a furore in Vienna. But I beg you to guard it like a jewel – and not to give it to a soul to play . . . I composed it for myself and no one else but my dear sister must play it.' Emily Anderson, ed. and trans., *The Letters of Mozart and His Family*, 3rd edn (3 vols., London, 1985), vol. 3, no. 445.

along with the greater part of the Mozart estate by Johann Anton André in 1800.[5] However, for the remainder of the repertoire, except for K 488[6] and K 595, no cadenzas have survived. From letters we know that Mozart actually wrote cadenzas for at least two of those concertos, K 466 and K 467,[7] even though no sources have been preserved. Nevertheless, the fact that a whole group of apparently contiguous materials (from K 459 to K 537) disappeared suggests the loss of a second more or less complete portfolio of cadenzas.

While the transmission of the sources indicates that the bulk of the cadenza material was clearly written for Mozart's own use, we are able to identify those pieces that he wrote for other performers, most notably for his sister Nannerl.[8] It seems, however, that the cadenzas from Nannerl's library basically represent cadenzas for the composer's own use as well; in most instances he himself or his father, Leopold Mozart, copied them directly from his 'hand-exemplars'. Virtually the only cadenzas specifically written for the use of a student or a dilettant musician are those entered by Mozart into the solo part of the C major Concerto K 246 (set a). This part, which also contains a written-out basso continuo realisation, was used by Mozart for teaching purposes during his Mannheim-Paris trip of 1777–8.[9]

The cadenza manuscripts demonstrate that it was apparently important for Mozart to write the cadenzas down rather than to play them completely *ex tempore*. He may have altered minor details or even major portions in the act of performance. The sources suggest, however, that he generally followed his elaborate and carefully planned improvisatory designs. The cadenzas are by no means just

---

[5] He published most of the cadenzas (*Cadences ou points d'orgue pour pianoforte*, Offenbach, 1804) after Artaria had printed virtually the same material only a few years earlier (*Cadences originales*, Vienna, 1801).

[6] The cadenza for the first movement of this concerto is notated in Mozart's autograph score.

[7] See Mozart's letter to his sister of 8 April 1785 in Wilhelm A. Bauer and Otto Erich Deutsch, eds., *Mozart: Briefe und Aufzeichnungen*, Internationale Stiftung Mozarteum (Kassel, 1962–75). This letter is not in Anderson.

[8] For the cadenzas originating from Nannerl's music library see Table 1. The following family letters document Mozart's supplying his sister with cadenzas:

15 February 1783 (to Leopold Mozart): 'Herewith I send my sister the three cadenzas for the concerto in D and the two short cadenzas (*Eingänge*) for the one in Eb [K 175/382, set a; K 271, *Eingang* c].' Anderson, vol. 3, no. 481.

12 June 1784 (to Leopold): 'She [Nannerl] is quite right in saying that there is something missing in the solo passage in the Andante of the concerto in D [K 451]. I shall supply the deficiency as soon as possible and send it with the cadenzas.' Anderson, vol. 3, no. 515.

21 July 1784: 'I would gladly have sent you the cadenzas for the other concertos, but you have no idea how much I have to do.' Anderson, vol. 3, no. 516.

[9] *NMA* V/15: vol. 2, preface, p. viii.

sketched but most carefully notated. On 22 January 1783, Mozart wrote to his father in Salzburg:[10] 'I shall send the cadenzas and introductions [*Eingänge*] to my dear sister at the first opportunity. I have not yet altered the introductions in the rondo, for whenever I play this concerto [K 271], I always play whatever occurs to me at the moment.' This concluding remark clearly refers to spontaneous improvisation, but there are two aspects worth considering: (1) Mozart specifically mentions the fact that he had not yet 'altered the *Eingänge*' in the K 271 finale, i.e. that he had not made the apparently necessary stylistic adjustments in the cadenzas of this Salzburg concerto from the 1770s; (2) improvisation on the spur of the moment may indeed be an essential element of the earlier Salzburg cadenza style, but less so in regard to the new Viennese style. The majority of the extant cadenzas actually originate from the Vienna years after 1783. The curious absence of written-out Salzburg cadenzas[11] may well reflect an earlier improvisatory practice that from the outset and in principle was not recorded in written-out versions.

The styles of Mozart's piano concerto cadenzas cover an extremely broad spectrum of improvisatory approaches. Trying to establish narrower categories of cadenza manners neither seems possible nor makes sense, especially in light of the increasingly individualised language of the post-Salzburg concertos; nevertheless we need at least to differentiate between two particularly distinct modes of improvisation. First, the extended *non mesuré* mode in the tradition of the mid-eighteenth-century free fantasia: ordinarily notated without barlines and requiring frequent and often abrupt tempo changes, generally extremely free declamation with contrasting textures (from figurative passage work to chordal sections). Second, the *en mesure* mode, basically in strict time (barline notation) with only brief unmeasured passages inserted, emphasising clearly shaped musical phrases and incorporating developmental elements, including elaborate thematic/motivic work. Naturally, both modes are predominantly virtuosic in nature, but they represent two fundamentally different improvisatory conventions and highlight quite different musical aspects.

In the oldest extant piano concerto cadenzas the *non mesuré* mode predominates. The most characteristic examples represent the *Eingänge* (set a) in the finale movement of K 271 from the time of the concerto's origin, 1777 (ex. 1). Incidentally, the very same style can be found in Mozart's modulatory preludes for Nannerl[12]

---

[10] Anderson, vol. 3, no. 479.

[11] The early cadenzas (set a) of K 271 were in part notated in the autograph score. The cadenzas for the double and triple concertos, K 365 and K 242, respectively, had to be written out since they could not have been improvised to begin with. There is no evidence that substantial Salzburg cadenza materials might have been lost.

[12] See Christoph Wolff, 'Mozarts Präludien für Nannerl: Zwei Rätsel und ihre Lösung,' *Festschrift Wolfgang Rehm zum 60. Geburtstag* (Kassel, 1989), pp. 106–18.

Example 1 Concerto in E♭ major K 271, finale; *erster Eingang*

(e.g. K 395/300g; K deest and Anh. C 15.11) from the same period (ex. 2). This kind of whimsical improvisation, with quickly changing figurative passages and textures, and with unpredictable harmonic and tempo changes, no longer occurs in Mozart's Viennese cadenzas. Of course, individual *non mesuré* phrases can still be found, but they are limited to occasional passages, mainly with short runs

Example 2 Praludium in C major K 284a (K395/300g)

(e.g. K 595: first movement cadenza, bars (30) and (36); third movement *Eingang*, bar (8)). In the Viennese period Mozart seemed to prefer more clearly structured, motivically directed cadenzas. A related case in point is provided by the cadenza from the first movement of the B♭ Piano Sonata K 333. This sonata has only recently been redated to 1784.[13] The style of its first-movement cadenza *en mesure* clearly fits this new date; it would have been inappropriate for the old-established much earlier date of 1778.

The chronology of Mozart's cadenza style reflects a move from the motivically free-wheeling fantasia manner to motivically and metrically tightly controlled

[13] See Alan Tyson, *Mozart: Studies of the Autograph Scores* (Cambridge, Mass., 1987), pp. 87–91

improvisational gestures which are gradually more and more removed from genuine improvisation and, instead, come much closer to compositional elaboration. Developmental aspects also play an increasingly significant role in that the principal thematic material undergoes further transformations in the cadenza (see ex. 3). In many instances he also revises the cadenzas by further refining certain key passages. The fact that he more often than not preserves the principal ideas of his cadenzas manifests his increasingly 'anti-improvisatory' approach

Example 3 Concerto in Bb major K 456, first movement cadenza

(a) version a

Ex. 3. (*cont.*)

(b) version b

(c) version c

(see ex. 4). The cadenzas furnished Mozart, the composer/performer, with an important vehicle permitting him to make adjustments to a work that received its basically fixed *Gestalt* after the completion of the score and the copying of the performing parts. Further compositional development, further elaboration of

Example 4 Concerto in F major K 459, finale, cadenza

[a] based on fugal theme, bars 32ff.
[b] based on rondo theme, bars 1ff.

ideas were not possible beyond this point – except in the execution of the solo part. There, however, the improvisational elements are limited to the ornamental profile of the solo part, on the one hand, and especially to the cadenzas and *Eingänge* on the other. Earlier works could be 'updated' in re-performances, and Mozart made deliberate use of this possibility. Thus, in Viennese re-performances of his first piano concerto, K 175, he not only replaced the original finale movement with the new rondo K 382, but he also provided a completely new set of cadenzas from 1783 or later. Consequently, the modern performer must realise that we do not possess any original cadenzas for this concerto in its original Salzburg version; they should be recreated in the proper *non mesuré* manner.

It seems necessary to develop a consciousness of the various stylistic layers that occur in Mozart's piano concerto cadenzas and that permitted the composer/performer to change, modernise, and individualise a finished work through later re-performances. Mozart's piano concerto cadenzas provide us therefore with the welcome documentation of an important facet of the performance history of the works during the composer's lifetime. Nevertheless, our glimpse through the cadenzas into this history can only be fairly narrow. First of all, we need to consider that a relatively small portion of the cadenza material has actually survived. Moreover, the original cadenzas also imply elements that cannot be, and never were, notated: spontaneous improvisation beyond composed improvisation.[14]

---

[14] An important article by Robert D. Levin, 'Instrumental Ornamentation, Improvisation and Cadenzas' (in *Performance Practice: Music after 1660*, ed. Howard Mayer Brown and Stanley Sadie, New York, 1990, pp. 267–91), published after the present essay was written, explores a broader range of pertinent issues.

INDEX OF MOZART'S WORKS

Entries follow numbering of Köchel 1862 or its revisions (2/1905, 3/1937); K⁶ nos., if different, appear to right of main entry.

INDEX OF NAMES